Georgia

Georgia

A Brief History

Christopher C. Meyers

David Williams

MERCER UNIVERSITY PRESS

MACON, GEORGIA

MUP/P446
© 2012 Mercer University Press
1400 Coleman Avenue
Macon, Georgia 31207
All rights reserved

First Edition

Books published by Mercer University Press are printed on acid-free paper that meets the requirements of American National Standard for Information Sciences—Permanence of Paper for Printed Library Materials.

Mercer University Press is a member of Green Press Initiative (greenpressinitiative.org), a nonprofit organization working to help publishers and printers increase their use of recycled paper and decrease their use of fiber derived from endangered forests. This book is printed on recycled paper.

Cataloging-in-Publication Data

Williams, David, 1959-
Georgia : a brief history / David Williams, Christopher C. Meyers.
-- 1st ed.
    p. cm.
Includes bibliographical references and index.
ISBN-13: 978-0-88146-279-1 (pbk. : acid-free paper)
ISBN-10: 0-88146-279-9 (pbk. : acid-free paper)
ISBN-13: 978-0-88146-372-9 (e-book)
ISBN-10: 0-88146-372-8 (e-book)
1. Georgia--History. I. Meyers, Christopher C. II. Title.
F286.W63 2012
975.8--dc23
                    2011050844

Contents

Dedicated to our brothers and sisters:

Carl Meyers

Caren Meyers Rom

Nancy Meyers

Julie Meyers

Scott Williams

Introduction

Based on the most recent research, *Georgia: A Brief History* surveys the people and events that shaped our state's past and present. Beginning with the earliest Indian settlements, the story tells of first contacts between area natives and Spanish from Florida, British from Carolina, and James Oglethorpe leading the effort to found a colony called Georgia. That colony passed out of the British Empire during the American Revolution, a conflict that was as much a civil war as a war for independence. In the following decades, Creek and Cherokee Indians were driven out as Georgia was transformed into a cotton kingdom dominated by a minority of slaveholders, who finally sought to make slavery perpetual in a war that not only pitted Georgians against the Union but also against each other.

In the aftermath of the Civil War, Georgia struggled with the consequences of the conflict—political, social, and economic. The postwar years were highlighted by economic stagnation, questions over the meaning of freedom, and one-party politics. Race relations pervaded the state's history after the Civil War until well into the twentieth century, and those struggles are traced from Reconstruction to Jim Crow to the civil rights era. Economic changes are also traced as Georgia moved from agricultural dominance to a more diversified economy in the wake of the Great Depression and World War II. In the latter half of the twentieth century, and carrying into the twenty-first, Georgia drifted away from the provincialism that characterized its history and moved toward modernity.

Perhaps the foremost challenge in preparing a work of this kind, surveying a history spanning hundreds of years, is that of brevity. Condensing such a time frame into a relatively short book means that not all the detail that we might have wished to include will be present. Certainly anyone already familiar with Georgia history will likely find a favorite story or personality missing, but based on our combined half-century experience in studying, teaching, and researching Georgia history, we have tried to tell a story that makes clear in a concise way how our state came to be and how it became what it is today.

For the many ways in which they have all contributed to making this book possible we owe a debt of gratitude to Valdosta State University, especially to Paul Riggs, Chair of the History Department, Connie Richards, Dean of the College of Arts and Sciences, and Provost Phil Gunter. We also wish to thank Marc Jolley and the staff of Mercer University Press for taking on this project. We would be remiss if we didn't acknowledge the many fine historians of Georgia history upon whose work we have relied. Lastly we owe many thanks to our families for their loving support, Tracy Meyers, Jacob Meyers, and Teresa Williams.

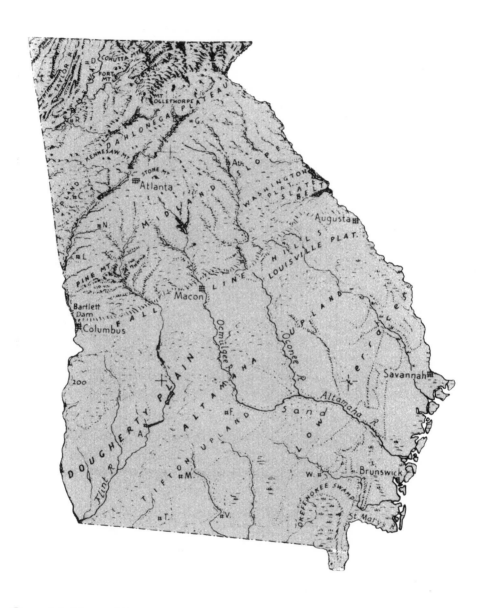

Georgia's Natural Environment. Used with permission. Thomas W. Hodler and Howard Schretter (eds.). 1986. *The Atlas of Georgia.* Institute of Community and Area Development (ICAD), The University of Georgia, Athens.

Georgia has 159 counties, more than any state except Texas. Courtesy GeorgiaInfo, University of Georgia, GALILEO.

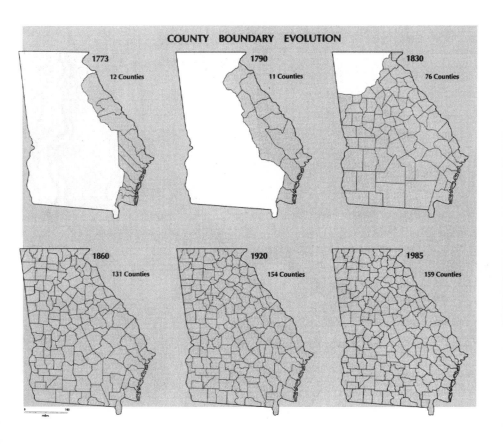

The evolution of Georgia's county boundaries. Used with permission. Thomas W. Hodler and Howard Schretter (eds.). 1986. *The Atlas of Georgia*. Institute of Community and Area Development (ICAD), The University of Georgia, Athens.

INDIAN CESSIONS

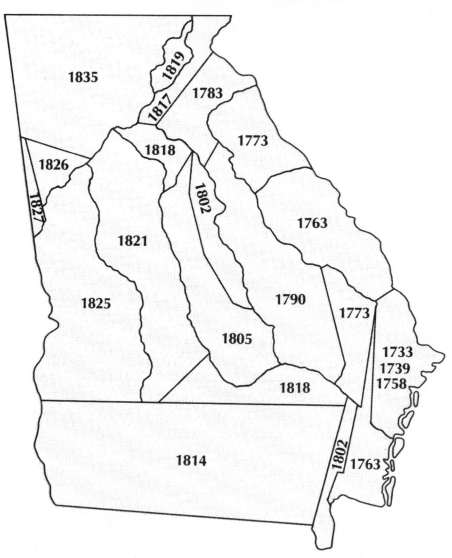

This map shows the cession of Indian lands to the state of Georgia. Used with permission. Thomas W. Hodler and Howard Schretter (eds.). 1986. *The Atlas of Georgia*. Institute of Community and Area Development (ICAD), The University of Georgia, Athens.

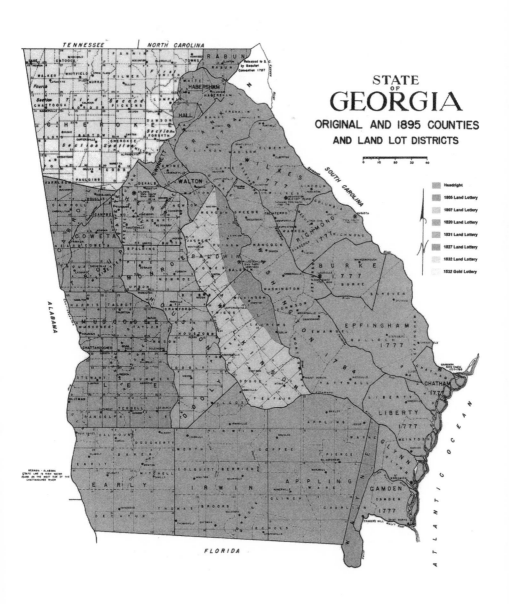

Georgia distributed most of the land it acquired from the Native Indian Nations in a lottery system. The state held six lotteries, in 1805, 1807, 1820, 1821, 1827, and 1832. Courtesy Georgia Archives.

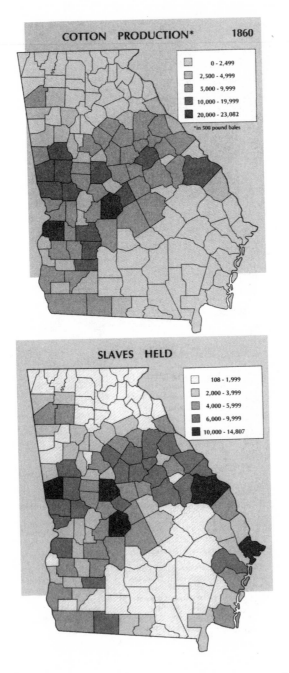

The distribution of slaves and the cotton growing areas of Georgia in 1860. Used with permission. Thomas W. Hodler and Howard Schretter (eds.). 1986. *The Atlas of Georgia*. Institute of Community and Area Development (ICAD), The University of Georgia, Athens.

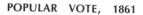

POPULAR VOTE, 1861

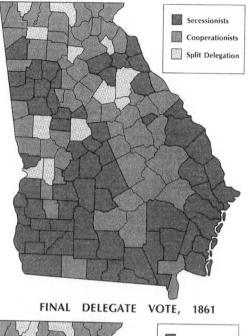

	Secessionists
	Cooperationists
	Split Delegation

FINAL DELEGATE VOTE, 1861

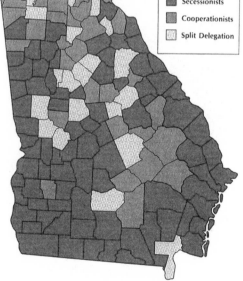

	Secessionists
	Cooperationists
	Split Delegation

This map depicts the relative support for secession in Georgia's counties in 1861. Used with permission. Thomas W. Hodler and Howard Schretter (eds.). 1986. *The Atlas of Georgia*. Institute of Community and Area Development (ICAD), The University of Georgia, Athens.

PERCENTAGE TENANCY BY COUNTY, 1930

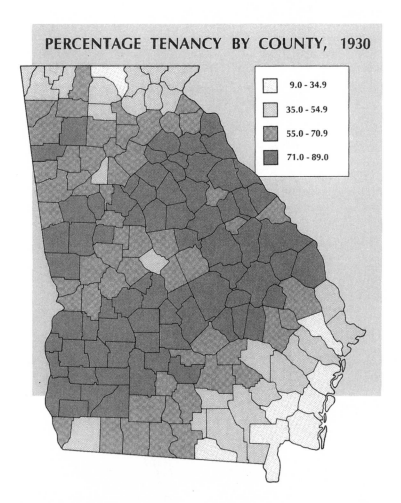

☐	9.0 - 34.9
☐	35.0 - 54.9
▨	55.0 - 70.9
■	71.0 - 89.0

This map depicts the rate of tenancy in Georgia's counties in 1930. Used with permission. Thomas W. Hodler and Howard Schretter (eds.). 1986. *The Atlas of Georgia*. Institute of Community and Area Development (ICAD), The University of Georgia, Athens.

SPREAD OF BOLL WEEVIL, 1892 - 1922

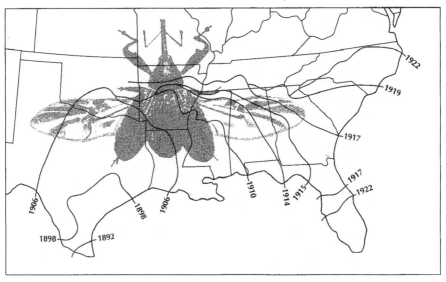

This map traces the progress of the boll weevil from Texas. It arrived in Georgia in the 1910s. Used with permission. Thomas W. Hodler and Howard Schretter (eds.). 1986. *The Atlas of Georgia*. Institute of Community and Area Development (ICAD), The University of Georgia, Athens.

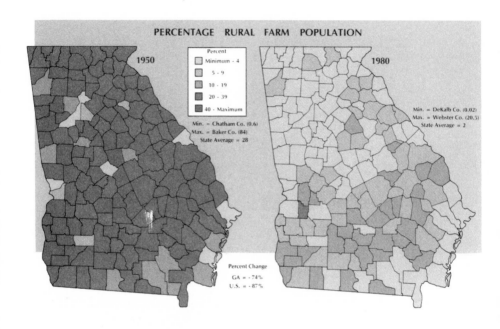

PERCENTAGE RURAL FARM POPULATION

This map compares Georgia's rural population in 1950 and 1980. Used with permission. Thomas W. Hodler and Howard Schretter (eds.). 1986. *The Atlas of Georgia*. Institute of Community and Area Development (ICAD), The University of Georgia, Athens.

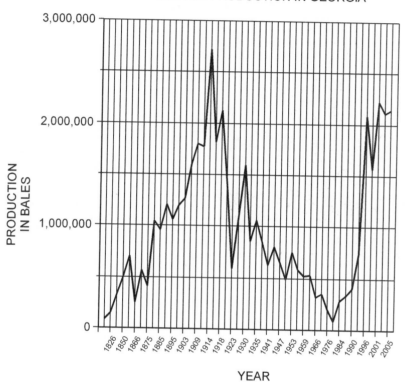

Cotton production in Georgia. Chart by the authors.

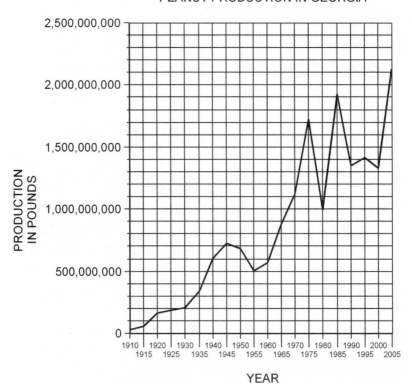

Peanut production in Georgia. Chart by the authors.

Chapter 1

Natives, Europeans, and the Founding of Georgia

Pre-Columbian Georgia

As North America lay in the grip of our planet's most recent Ice Age, the first humans known to inhabit the continent migrated from Asia. By at least 13,000 years ago they arrived in what is today Georgia. These Paleo-Indian (Old Indian) peoples were hunter-gatherers, living in small bands of twenty to thirty, who followed large herds of migratory game animals such as woolly mammoth, mastodon, and giant bison.

With the end of the Ice Age 12,000 to 10,0000 years ago came a warmer climate and extinction of the large beasts upon which Paleo-Indians had depended for their survival. They adapted well to their changing environment during this two-thousand-year transitional era, ushering in a new phase called the Archaic period that stretched from 10,000 to 3,000 years ago. Archaic Indians used new hunting tools and techniques aimed at bringing down smaller game such as deer, rabbit, possum, and squirrel. The spear-throwing stick (*atl-atl* by its Aztec name) and bow and arrow became essential, as did hooks, nets, and baskets for catching fish. But most of their food came from more easily gathered sources like nuts, acorns, and fresh-water shellfish called mussels. Twice-yearly migrations were common among Georgia's Archaic Indians, spending spring and summer at base camps along rivers and streams taking advantage of abundant mussels, then moving to upland areas in the fall and winter where they harvested nuts and acorns. Along the coast, where mussels, clams, and fish

* Clovis Points - found in Clovis, Mexico
* Paleo Indians - Gatherer Hunters

were plentiful, people developed more permanent villages. Some of their remains can be seen to this day on Sapelo Island, where for thousands of years Archaic Indians piled huge rings of discarded shells around their settlements.

Toward the Archaic period's close, the development of pottery led to a significant change in lifestyle. Now easily able to boil water, people could leech tannic acid out of acorn meal, produce and store more food, and remain more settled. They also began to cultivate natural stands of local fruits, berries, and grain, pulling weeds to increase yields and saving seeds to ensure the next year's harvest. Plowing and planting (all by human power since there were no horses or cattle until the coming of Europeans) made food production even more stable and abundant, completing the change to an agriculturally based lifestyle, still supplemented by hunting and gathering, called the Woodland period.

Lasting from about 3,000 to 1,000 years ago, the Woodland era saw Indians developing domestic varieties of vegetables and grains such as maize (corn), beans, squash, and melons that were much larger and more productive. More food meant that villages could support populations of several hundred. And it meant people could spend more time on non-agricultural activities—spinning and weaving cotton cloth, making jewelry, fashioning specialized tools, and producing new forms of pottery both for utilitarian and ceremonial purposes. Much of their time was also devoted to spiritual activities and the construction of ceremonial sites such as Rock Eagle in Putnam County and Fort Mountain in Murray County. Most common of these communal projects were burial mounds containing dozens of bodies, usually centered around higher-status individuals, both men and women, who may have served as chiefs or priests.

- Transitional Period
  12,000 – 10,000 years ago
- The game size is gettin smaller

So skilled were Woodland farmers and artisans that they usually produced more than their villages could use. This surplus encouraged trade from one village to the next across routes that stretched the length and breadth of the continent. Cotton was traded from the southeast. Copper came from the Great Lakes region; red pipe stone from Wisconsin and Minnesota; abalone from the Pacific coast; obsidian (a volcanic glass) from the Rockies; crystalline mica and steatite (soapstone) from Appalachia. Pearls came from coastal regions and jewelry made its way from all points of the compass. As trade increased, villages located at the intersection of trade routes attracted merchants and artisans from surrounding areas and saw their populations rise to many thousands. Over time, these larger towns came to exert not only economic influence over smaller regional villages, but cultural and political influence as well. In effect, they became the capital cities of chiefdoms that encompassed hundreds of square miles and dozens of towns. The first of these large chiefdoms came to prominence along the Mississippi River and gave rise to a new cultural phase called the Mississippian period.

By a thousand years ago Mississippian culture had become the dominant lifestyle among Georgia Indians. It was an agriculturally based culture in which large amounts of surplus food, in addition to trade goods, flowed into larger towns to support their huge populations. A hierarchical elite class of chiefs and priests, developed mainly around kinship ties, organized the storage and redistribution of this surplus, ensuring that no town within the chiefdom suffered unduly during times of drought or pestilence. Elites were also responsible for conducting rituals and ceremonies, interceding with the spirit world for continued blessings of abundant harvests. The most important of these rituals were performed atop large platform or temple mounds, so called because they were flattened on top with temples built on the elevated surfaces. These were much larger than the burial mounds of the Woodland era. Some reached heights of sixty feet or more and covered as much as an acre or more at the base. Though most were destroyed by European settlers seeking buried treasure, some still remain. The best preserved in Georgia, all state or national historic sites, are the Etowah Mounds near Rome, the Ocmulgee Mounds in Macon, and the Kolomoki Mounds near Blakely in southwest Georgia.

Around the twelfth century, Mississippian rituals began to fail as the Earth entered a series of cooling phases known as the Little Ice Age that lasted several centuries. Global temperatures on average dropped by only two to three degrees Fahrenheit, but the impact was far-reaching. Shorter growing seasons brought famine to northern Europe. They destroyed the Anasazi culture of the American Southwest. In Georgia and the Southeast, large Mississippian chiefdoms broke into smaller regional chiefdoms, though they retained much the same social structure and agricultural economy. What might have developed from this later Mississippian culture will never be known, for that world was devastated in the sixteenth and seventeenth centuries by invading Europeans.

Coming of the Spaniards

The first Europeans to set foot in Georgia were Spanish slave traders from the Caribbean who raided coastal communities, taking captives as they went. In 1526 Lucas Vazquez de Ayllon, a financial backer of these slave raids, tried to establish a permanent settlement on the Georgia coast called San Miguel de Gualdape, believed to be near Sapelo Sound. The colony of six hundred included the first known African slaves brought to what is now the

De Allyon : brought 1st Black Boat

United States. Starvation, disease, attacks from local Indians, an uprising among the African slaves, and the death of Ayllon himself all brought an end to the venture after just six weeks. Only one hundred and fifty survivors returned to the Spanish Caribbean.

In 1539 a Spanish army of nearly seven hundred led by Hernando de Soto landed near Florida's Tampa Bay. The next year it made its way through the Georgia chiefdoms of Capachequi, Toa, Ichisi, and Ocute looking for gold, plunder, and slaves. The Spaniards continued in a long loop through the Carolinas and Tennessee before turning back south into northern Georgia and the Coosa chiefdom. They continued toward the Mississippi River, where de Soto died of fever. His men went as far as Texas before turning back toward the Mississippi, where they built seven boats and floated down river, harassed by local Indians as they went. They reached the Gulf Coast in 1542 and headed for Mexico with fewer than half the men who began the journey three years earlier.

Other than to make them wary of Europeans, de Soto's men had little immediate effect on Native Americans. But they brought invisible enemies whose long-term impact would be devastating. Old World diseases such as bubonic plague and small pox, to which the Indians had no immunity, spread from one town to the next along a well-established network of trade routes. Within a generation, tens of thousands were dead. The Southeast's native population, believed to have been as much as five million at the time of European contact, was reduced by more than ninety percent by the late seventeenth century.

In 1559 fifteen hundred Spaniards under Tristan de Luna established a colony near modern Pensacola, Florida. In need of food, they set out into the interior looking for the great towns described in the de Soto journals; they did not find what they had

Ponce De Leon : St. Augustine
Gold + Slaves
Columbian Exchange: Hogs, Horses, Bacteria

expected. After an arduous journey through Alabama and into northern Georgia, they found the once thriving Coosa chiefdom in decline with little food to spare. Its capital, the site of at least five hundred households twenty years earlier, now had fewer than fifty. The temples atop its earthen mounds were in decay. Most of the surrounding cornfields were overgrown and deserted. De Luna's men headed back to the Gulf Coast and abandoned their colony.

The first enduring Spanish presence in Georgia actually began in Florida. In 1565 Pedro Menendez and his men destroyed the French outpost of Fort Caroline at the mouth of the St. Johns River where modern Jacksonville is now located. To ward off further French incursions on Spanish territorial claims, just to the south Menendez built what would become the oldest surviving European settlement in the United States, the town of St. Augustine. The next year, during an exploration up the coast, Menendez landed on the island of Santa Catalina (St. Catherines) and met the principal head man of a chiefdom that covered much of Georgia's coastal region and perhaps many miles inland. The chief's name was Guale, pronounced "Wally" by the Spanish. They began referring to much of the coastal region of Georgia as Guale.

Over the next few years, Menendez sent soldiers to establish small forts called presidios in the interior of north Florida and south Georgia among the Timucua and Appalachee Indians as well as along the Georgia coast among the Guale Indians. The soldiers were accompanied by Catholic priests whose job it was to set up missions, convert the Indians to Christianity, and make them more compliant to Spanish demands. As Spanish subjects, the Indians were expected to pay taxes in the form of food and other goods to support the missions and presidios. Some natives, hoping for trade with the Spanish or fearing their soldiers, paid the taxes. Others saw little benefit in cooperating with the invaders.

A Brief History

Sporadic rebellions occurred, the most significant of which was the Guale or Juanillo Revolt of 1597. The trouble started when two priests intervened to prevent Juanillo, the son of a Guale chief, from succeeding his father. They deemed Juanillo too uncooperative and favored a more submissive chief. Guale Indians who opposed Spanish rule flocked to Juanillo's cause. They attacked the coastal missions, killing several priests, and seemed bent on driving the Spanish all the way back to St. Augustine. They were finally stopped on San Pedro (Cumberland) Island when a Spanish-supporting chief ordered his men to turn back the attackers. Still, the mission system north of Cumberland Island was entirely broken.

Florida's Spanish governor responded with a series of raids along the coast and into the interior, burning crops and villages and killing so ruthlessly that soon the Guale Indians were begging for the priests and their missions to return. With neither guns nor powder and no way to get them, the Indians had little choice but to comply. In 1606 the bishop of Cuba toured Guale missions and reported that the Indians were fully subdued.

The following decades saw Spain expand its presidio and mission system west from the coast into southern Georgia, establishing outposts near Folkston, Valdosta, and Lumber City. They also pushed north from their strongholds near Tallahassee, Florida, setting up missions in southwestern Georgia along the lower reaches of the Flint and Chattahoochee rivers. The threat of Spanish raids kept rebellion suppressed, but a greater threat to Spanish control was looming far to the north.

Coming of the British

In 1607 England established the Virginia colony with its first permanent settlement at Jamestown. From Spain's perspective, this was an invasion of its territory since it claimed all of North America. But Spain did not press the claim. Neither did the British immediately press their own claims any farther south. Then in 1663 Parliament granted a charter for a colony south of Virginia to be called Carolina. Two years later the new colony's southern boundary was, at least on paper, extended well south of St. Augustine, nearly half way down the Florida peninsula.

Spain at first ignored British claims since there were no actual settlements in Carolina, but that changed in April 1670 with the founding of Charles Town (modern Charleston). In May, Spain and England signed the Treaty of Madrid in which each side recognized the possessions of the other. But there was a problem. At the time, Spain had no knowledge of Charleston. Some Spanish officials urged an attack. Others, the viceroy of New Spain included, argued against such a move. Although the English may have been deceptive, technically the treaty still covered Charleston. Spain finally decided to launch an expedition against Charleston but was turned back by rough seas.

The British soon moved to undermine Spain's regional dominance by establishing trade with the Indians west and south of Charleston into what is now Georgia. Dr. Henry Woodward made an agreement with the Westoes under which Charleston would supply them with guns, powder, ammunition, and metal tools in exchange for Indian slaves and deerskins. British traders made similar agreements with the Yuchis, Savannahs, Yamasees, and "Chiluques" (believed to be Cherokees). Many of the Indians had long sought firearms, denied them by the Spanish, both to combat Spain's control and to break the influence of its Indian allies.

In 1680 Chief Altamaha led his Yamasees in a major slave raid against Spain's northernmost mission on St. Catherines Island.

More raids by Indian slave catchers and free-lance pirates, who were often employed by the British, forced Spain to abandon all of Guale by 1686 and withdraw south of the St. Marys River, the modern tidewater boundary between Georgia and Florida. Spain tried to shore up its regional claims with the establishment of Pensacola in 1698 but were cut off by the French who had made their way down the Mississippi from Canada, established an outpost at Biloxi in 1699, and in 1702 set up a fort on Mobile Bay.

The Spanish suffered another series of blows with the outbreak of Queen Anne's War (War of Spanish Succession) in 1702. In August, Carolina's Governor James Moore and Deputy Governor Robert Daniell sailed an army of nearly five hundred soldiers and 370 Indians, mostly Yamasees, down the coast. Their intent was to drive the Spanish out of Florida. They destroyed the missions around St. Augustine, burned the town itself, and laid siege to its fort, the Castillo de San Marcos. The Spanish defenders were saved only by a relief expedition from Havana, Cuba, that arrived on 30 December.

In 1704, during a massive raid that came to be called the Appalachee Massacre, fifty Carolinians and a thousand of their Indian allies swept down the Flint River, destroyed nearly all the Spanish missions in southern Georgia and northern Florida, killed most of the region's Appalachee inhabitants and sold hundreds into slavery. Continued raids over the next few years almost depopulated the area of its native peoples, leaving only a few Appalachee, Timucua, and Calusa survivors huddled around St. Augustine for protection.

The Treaty of Utrecht in 1713 brought an end to Queen Anne's War, in part reiterating the 1670 Madrid Treaty's agreement that each side recognize the other's colonial possessions. But the war's end brought only more misery for the Indians.

Increasingly dependant on trade with the British, they became more vulnerable to being cheated and abused. Whites set the terms of trade, and prices were going up. They demanded more deerskins and slaves for fewer goods. Upwards of one hundred thousand skins were exported from Charleston annually, and the Indians were in debt to the traders for as many more. A census from the period showed that Indian slaves accounted for 15 percent of Carolina's population, not including those exported to New England and the West Indies.

The Indian slave trade was not without controversy among British colonists. Supporters argued that slavery was the best way to Christianize Indians. They also saw slavery as saving Indians from the Spanish, the French, or each other. But an opponent of Indian slavery lamented that white traders generally, and white slave catchers especially, endeavored "to ravish the wife from the Husband, kill the Father to get the Child and to burne and Destroy the habitations of these poore people into whose Country wee were Charefully received by them, cherished and supplyed when Wee are weake, or at least never have done us hurt; and after we have set them on worke to doe all these horrid wicked things to get slaves to sell the dealers in Indians call it humanity to buy them and thereby keep them from being murdered."

Finally the Yamasees had had enough. In 1715, joined by the Cherokees and a collection of other groups, some of which would soon form the Creek Nation, the Yamasees led a coordinated assault on Carolina. They killed South Carolina's Indian agent and dozens of traders. They burned the trading posts then moved east to sack tidewater plantations. Charleston was flooded with refugees, and it seemed that the city might fall. Carolina whites soon gained the upper hand by resorting to their old tactics of setting the Indians against each other. They bribed the Cherokees with gifts and favorable trade agreements then set them against their former allies. When a band of Creeks came to confer with the Cherokees, they were put to death, an incident that caused mistrust between the two nations for years. In 1717 Charleston made peace with most of the Indians, bringing the Yamasee War to a close. The Yamasees themselves fled to Spanish Florida, but were hunted down by English slave catchers. Most were killed or captured and enslaved.

The Yamasee War taught Indians a hard lesson about safety in numbers, and most of them took that lesson to heart. Beginning with the Coweta and Cusseta bands on the Chattahoochee River near modern Columbus, groups including the Hitchiti, Yuchi, Eufaula, Tuskegee, and Alabama formed a political and military alliance that whites called the Creek Nation, after the Ochese Creek Indians who had a major trading post near Macon. The alliance soon encompassed nearly all native peoples of central and southern Georgia and eastern Alabama. Most were native speakers of the Muskogee language, but the alliance included other linguistic groups. With such an alliance, numbering at its outset around ten thousand people (roughly the same population as British Carolina), the Creeks could ward off white British slave catchers and negotiate from strength with the British, French, and Spanish for more favorable trade agreements.

Charleston learned a lesson too. The vast southwestern claim of South Carolina, that region later to become Georgia, was at the center of a three-way international tug-of-war. It was, as historians have called it, the Debatable Land. During the Yamasee War, with the British distracted, Spain began to push out from St. Augustine and re-establish presidios and missions. The French moved into the heart of Alabama and built Fort Toulouse near the present city of Montgomery. What Charleston needed was a militarized buffer zone to protect itself and help populate the colony.

In 1717 Sir Robert Montgomery, an ambitious Scotsman, proposed the establishment of a province or "margrave" between the Savannah and Altamaha rivers to be called Azilia. Carolina's governing proprietors agreed to Montgomery's plan provided he could have the "Margravate of Azilia" populated and functioning within three years. But Britain's attorney general ruled that the proprietors had no authority to establish a margravate. It may have attracted few settlers in any case. Memories of the Yamasee War were still fresh, and the lucrative Indian slave trade had declined accordingly. Britain did, however, agree to fund a small fort at the mouth of the Altamaha River. In 1721, three miles inland from Sapelo Island, construction began on Fort King George, the first permanent British outpost in what would soon be Georgia. A reconstructed Fort King George now stands at its original location in Darien, together with a museum containing artifacts recovered from the site.

Spanish envoys arrived at Fort King George in 1724 to protest the presence of British troops on what they considered their territory, but Spain never attempted to dislodge them by force. Still, the soldiers faced difficulties. Their fort was isolated and under-funded. They constantly battled hunger and disease. A fire of mysterious origin nearly destroyed the fort, probably set by the soldiers themselves hoping to see their outpost abandoned. As one officer reported, his men were certainly in no hurry to extinguish the flames. Finally in 1727 Britain sent most of the garrison to Port Royal, closer to Charleston, but left two soldiers at Fort King George as lookouts to warn of any threatening moves by the Spanish. Though support for settlement south of the Savannah River seemed to have been lost, events were unfolding in distant

London that would soon lead to the establishment of an entirely new British colony in the Debatable Land.

Oglethorpe and the Founding of Georgia

James Edward Oglethorpe was a Member of Parliament in the 1720s, widely known for his reform efforts. His service on two committees in particular reflected his reforming tendencies. One dealt with relief for debtors, the other with conditions in British jails. Oglethorpe had a personal interest in both areas; a close friend had recently died in debtors prison from exposure to small pox. Oglethorpe himself had spent several months in a filthy jail after killing a man in a brawl.

The over-crowded and disease-ridden conditions of British prisons were closely associated with the Industrial Revolution, particularly the woolen textile industry. The landed nobility increasingly forced peasant farmers off the land to fence it in and raise sheep, a process called the Enclosure Movement. Displaced people flooded into industrializing cities looking for work, but there were not enough jobs for the huge numbers. Many went deep into debt trying to survive until they could find work. Those who could not usually found themselves in debtors prison. To relieve the crowded jails, courts frequently sentenced debtors to "travel," meaning exile to the colonies as indentured servants. But some, like Oglethorpe, saw little justice in making criminals of people whom the landed gentry had forced into poverty. He proposed setting up a charity colony south of the Savannah River where these unfortunates could make "a comfortable subsistence" for themselves and help relieve Britain's unemployment problem.

In 1730 Oglethorpe and twenty other prominent men, most of them former members of Oglethorpe's jail committee, requested a royal charter for a new colony to be called Georgia after King

George II. They proposed to govern it themselves as a board of Trustees. Georgia would be populated mainly by small farmers, together with merchants and craftsmen, who could also serve as a militia force. Toward that end, no one, including the Trustees, could own land outright, meaning that land grants could not be mortgaged or sold. Such grants would be limited to fifty acres for most colonists, though about half the land granted by the Trustees went to a class of affluent "Adventurers" who could receive up to five hundred acres each (raised to two thousand acres in 1740). The Trustees would rule by decree, though none could hold any title of office in the colony. Local magistrates, usually constables and justices of the peace, would enforce Trustee rule, answerable only to the Trustees. And since the Trustees were the law, no lawyer would be allowed to practice in the colony.

Oglethorpe and the other Trustees built support in Parliament by promoting Georgia as an inexpensive military buffer colony. Colonists themselves, serving as militiamen, would ward off attacks from the Spanish or the Indians. Though seed money would be necessary—some of which had been raised already by Dr. Thomas Bray—Oglethorpe stressed that Georgia would quickly become a self-sustaining enterprise by supplying the empire with products not found in other colonies. Oglethorpe and the Trustees pushed silk and wine as items Georgia could contribute to Britain's imperial economy.

After some revisions that replaced the idea of helping debtors specifically with the more general "deserving poor," Prime Minister Robert Walpole and the Privy Council, Parliament's executive body, finally issued Georgia's charter in the summer of 1732. Over the next few months the Trustees selected about 120 charity colonists and made preparations for their upcoming voyage. At least one, John West, and probably a number of others had spent

1. Military Buffer
2. Econ Buffer
3. Restr. aimed @ Social Improvement

time imprisoned for debt. Oglethorpe took charge of the expedition, the only Trustee ever to make the trip to Georgia. They set sail on 17 November aboard the ship *Anne*, arriving in Charleston two months later.

Over the next few weeks, Oglethorpe searched down the coast for a suitable town site. Particularly attractive was a patch of high ground overlooking the Savannah River called Yamacraw Bluff after a small band of local natives related to the exiled Yamasees. Oglethorpe asked their chief, Tomochichi, for permission to settle there. Owing at least in part to the intercession of Indian trader and interpreter James Musgrove and his half-Creek wife Mary, Tomochichi agreed for the time being. The matter would eventually have to be taken up with the Creek National Council.

Oglethorpe returned with his colonists on 12 February 1733 and set them to work laying out town lots and constructing Savannah's first houses. Families were assigned lots of sixty by ninety feet for their town dwellings, a five-acre garden plot on the edge of the settlement, and a forty-five-acre farm plot in the surrounding countryside.

In May, with Tomochichi's support, Oglethorpe negotiated his first treaty with the headmen of Coweta and Cusseta towns representing the Creek Nation. The resulting "Articles of Friendship and Commerce" made clear that trade would be conducted with set rates and prices. The treaty also stipulated that "though this Land belongs to us [the Creeks] ... [we] do consent and agree that they [the British] shall make use of and possess all those Lands which our Nation hath no occasion for to use ... provided always that they upon Settling every New Town shall set out for the use of ourselves such lands as shall be agreed upon ... and that those Lands shall remain to us forever."

As the Creeks saw it, the treaty was not a land cession but an expression of willingness to share what they had with their British neighbors. They issued no land titles and viewed land as held collectively, never individually. Georgia's charter, on the other hand, gave the colony all lands between the Savannah and Altamaha rivers, northwest to their headwaters, then west all the way to the Pacific Ocean. At the time, eastern Georgia was populated by so few Creeks and even fewer colonists that there were no immediate land disputes. But the treaty represented a growing economic dependence on the part of Indians and a pattern of deception on the part of whites that would eventually lead to the Indians losing all their lands in Georgia.

British Settlement of Georgia

Savannah's construction, with the help of African slaves hired from South Carolina, continued into the summer of 1733. By June there were eleven houses, a blacksmith forge, and two blockhouses defended by six cannons overlooking the river. Things seemed to be going well for the settlement until Oglethorpe returned from a trip to Charleston and found the colonists in a state of "idleness and drunkenness." Rum turned bad had incapacitated many of the settlers, and the slaves were doing most of the work. Oglethorpe took quick action. He sent the slaves back to South Carolina, smashed all the rum kegs he could find, and prohibited any further rum in town. He informed the Trustees of his actions, and they backed him whole-heartedly. They soon outlawed both slavery and hard liquor, though wine and ale were permitted.

The prohibition on slavery was more practical than altruistic. Oglethorpe never argued against slavery in other colonies. As a director and later deputy governor of the Royal African Company, Oglethorpe promoted the institution and profited by it. But in

Georgia, slavery would not do. Oglethorpe needed militiamen, and slaves could not serve that purpose. They might seek freedom among the Spanish or, worse yet, they might rise in bloody insurrection. Already slaves from South Carolina were using Georgia as an escape route into Florida. In 1739, during the Stono Rebellion, an armed band of South Carolina slaves killed several dozen whites and headed for the Savannah River before Carolina militiamen cut them off. Oglethorpe wanted no such trouble in Georgia.

Another problem Savannah faced in the summer of 1733 was rampant disease, due at least in part to tainted rum. Oglethorpe wrote that "burning fevers" and "bloody fluxes attended by convulsions" were among the symptoms. By mid-July twenty people were dead, including the town's only doctor, and sixty more seemed to be at death's door. Then quite unexpectedly, a schooner arrived from England with more than forty Jewish passengers, most of them recent refugees to London who had fled the Inquisition in Portugal. Among the group was a Lisbon doctor named Samuel Nunes (or Nunez). Oglethorpe wrote to the Trustees that Dr. Nunes "immediately undertook our people and refused to take any pay for it. He proceeded by cold baths, cooling drinks and other cooling applications. Since which the sick have wonderfully recovered, and we have not lost one who would follow his prescriptions."

But there was a problem. The three Jewish commissioners in London who arranged transport had no permission from the Trustees to send immigrants. Part of the justification for Georgia's founding had been that it could provide a haven for persecuted Protestants from mainland Europe who had for years been fleeing to Britain. No concern for persecuted Jews was mentioned. The Trustees sent word to Oglethorpe that the Jews must be expelled.

But Georgia's charter guaranteed that all who "shall come to inhabit in our said colony ... except Papists [Catholics] ... shall have a free exercise of their religion." There was no prohibition against the practice of Judaism, so Oglethorpe ignored the Trustees and let the Jews stay.

Other religious refugees soon followed. In early 1734 a band of Lutherans from the principality of Salzburg in modern Austria founded Ebenezer on the Savannah River about twenty-five miles above Savannah. Jerusalem Church, which the Salzburgers built in 1767, stands today as the oldest church building in Georgia.

In 1736 there arrived in Savannah a congregation of Moravians, German-speaking Protestants from the modern Czech Republic. They were largely viewed with suspicion by their mostly Anglican neighbors for several unusual practices, among them allowing women to preach and hold religious office. One who admired the Moravians was John Wesley, then an Anglican minister who happened to be on the same boat during their trip from England. The Moravian influence would have a lasting effect on Wesley's ideas as he helped shape Methodist theology on his return home.

Refugees of a different sort founded Darien in 1736. A year earlier the Trustees had received a letter from Daniel McLachlan telling of misery among Highland Scots. Land rents were going up and cattle prices were going down, reducing many Highlanders to "a poor, starving condition." He and others were ready to get out, and they wanted to go to Georgia. Oglethorpe and the Trustees, eager for men to help fortify their colony, sent two recruiters, Hugh Mackay and George Dunbar, into the Highlands. It was the first of three successful recruiting trips that would take place over the next four years. On 18 October 1735, the *Prince of Wales* left Inverness with 177 Highlanders aboard.

The Scots settled on the Altamaha River near Fort King George and named their town New Inverness. In a defiant gesture aimed at the Spanish, they called the river stronghold guarding the town Fort Darien after an earlier Scots settlement in Panama that had been destroyed by Spain. Eventually the town would be called Darien as well.

Georgia in the War of Jenkins' Ear

With help from the Highlanders, Oglethorpe began building a series of fortified outposts on Georgia's coastal islands. At the northern end of Cumberland Island, guarding the inlet between Cumberland and Jekyll, was Fort St. Andrew. Fort William, on the southern tip of Cumberland, held the inlet between Cumberland and Amelia islands. Oglethorpe even began construction on Fort St. George near present-day Jacksonville, just thirty-five miles north of St. Augustine. Spanish threats forced him to abandon Fort St. George but, for the time being, Spain did not contest his forts further north.

Oglethorpe's largest and most important stronghold was Fort Frederica, built in 1736 on the back side of St. Simons Island, opposite the future site of Brunswick. A smaller post, Fort St. Simons, was planted on the island's southern end to warn of any Spanish approach. A lighthouse built in the nineteenth century, along with a museum, is now located there.

Frederica was named for the son of King George II, Frederick Louis, Prince of Wales. Far more than an outpost, it was a fortified town surrounded by a moat on the north, east, and south sides, and protected by the Frederica River on the west. It was garrisoned by several hundred regular British troops, sent by the Crown at Oglethorpe's urging. Along with the soldiers and their families Frederica was home to merchants, craftsmen, and farmers totaling around one thousand people at its height. For the next several years, Oglethorpe spent much of his time at Frederica directing the construction of its defenses. So did Mary Musgrove who, after her husband's death in 1735, served as Oglethorpe's interpreter and chief liaison among the Creeks.

Oglethorpe's effort to fortify Britain's claim along the Georgia coast was well timed. Trouble was brewing with Spain not only over land disputes but also over Britain's right to the slave trade in Spanish America. British smuggling in Spanish waters served only to increase tensions. Oglethorpe anticipated war with Spain and meant to take St. Augustine when the time came. He hoped to have help from the Creek Indians. At the Coweta Conference in 1739, Oglethorpe and Mary Musgrove tried to bring the Creeks into a military alliance with Britain. The Creeks refused, but promised that they would not ally with the Spanish or French either.

That same year, the conflict came to a head. Members of Parliament who supported war latched on to an incident that had occurred a few years earlier when British sea captain Robert Jenkins had his ear cut off by a Spanish officer who accused him of piracy. Jenkins was summoned to Parliament and displayed his ear, preserved in a jar, for all to see. This affront to British honor became the excuse for a declaration of war on Spain. The conflict, sometimes known as King George's War, which later became part of Europe's War of Austrian Succession, was most commonly called the War of Jenkins' Ear.

Oglethorpe gathered a force of about fifteen hundred men in May 1740 and sailed for St. Augustine. He planned a combined land-sea assault against the town, but Spanish ships blocked the water approach. Oglethorpe suffered another blow near Fort Mose, an outpost just north of St. Augustine settled by free blacks

A Brief History

who had escaped slavery in Carolina. On 15 June a band of blacks and Spaniards wiped out a nearby British camp. With word that Spanish reinforcements were coming and that his naval support would soon depart, Oglethorpe withdrew to Frederica.

Now St. Augustine took the offensive. Governor Manuel Montiano amassed an army of two thousand and in June 1742 landed on the southern end of St. Simons Island. He occupied Fort St. Simons, but did not move against Oglethorpe's main force at Fort Frederica for a week. That gave Oglethorpe time to lay his own plans and to call for reinforcements from Darien. With his regular forces supplemented by the Highlanders, Oglethorpe blocked the Spanish advance at Gully Hole Creek and ambushed a Spanish relief force at the Battle of Bloody Marsh. Montiano made probing forays over the next few days, but when British ships appeared on the horizon he quickly set sail for St. Augustine.

Oglethorpe tried to get more British troops for another expedition, but his requests went ignored. Still, he mounted a second campaign against St. Augustine in early 1743. His strategy this time was to draw the Spanish out of their defenses, but they refused to take the bait. Again, Oglethorpe withdrew to Frederica. Discouraged and angered by lack of support from London, Oglethorpe returned to England in July never to set foot in Georgia again.

Though the war in Europe dragged on for another five years, there was no further action on the Georgia coast. The troops left Frederica, and a few years later the town was abandoned. Archaeologists began excavating the site in the 1940s and Congress declared it a national historic site. Today, Frederica's ruins and its adjoining museum are open to the public.

9 years
1748

- Oglethorpe ignored Trustees
- William Stevens opped Oglethorpe
- In 1742 Trustees divide GA North of Altamaha / South of Alt.
- North would be Savannah / South: Frederica

William Stevens   William Stevens

21

Society and Economy Under the Trustees

Thanks mostly to Oglethorpe's efforts, Georgia successfully served one of the major functions that had justified its founding— to stand as a military buffer between Charleston and St. Augustine. However, as a charity colony designed to get debtors and other impoverished people back on a sound financial footing, Georgia failed miserably. The main problem for most of these people was the same that they had faced in Britain—deep and continuing debt.

Of the 2,831 colonists transported to Georgia during Oglethorpe's time in the colony, at least a third came with unrelieved debt hanging over their heads. Most of the rest became indebted the moment they set foot in Georgia. The majority of colonists had no way to pay for their passage from Britain, and the Trustees would not transport them for free. Nor would they take steps to relieve their prior debts. So immigrants indentured themselves for years of service. Some were indentured to ship captains who auctioned their services to the highest bidder when they reached Savannah. Others came indentured to large-land-holding men called "Adventurers," who paid their own way and that of their servants. In most cases indigent settlers were indentured to the Georgia Trust itself and worked under the direction of overseers appointed by the Trustees. Adults were ordinarily bonded for around five years, but terms could run much longer, especially for children. Donald Rose, a seven-year-old, was indentured for seventeen years. Four-year-old Anne Macgruer was bound to service for twenty years in payment of her passage.

The Salzburgers were an exception to the general rule. Their passage was paid for mainly by the Society for the Promotion of Christian Knowledge, which helped hundreds of European

Protestants escape persecution. Others were not so fortunate. Almost all the Moravians were debtors, as were many of the Scots. In 1734 forty people arrived from Ireland already indentured servants or soon to be so, and the same was true for Welsh settlers. The Jews who arrived in 1733 were impoverished as well. According to historian Malcolm Stern: "From the outset, the three Jewish commissioners had as their one aim the lifting of some of these poor Jews from the relief rolls of London Jewry."

To work for themselves and profit from their own labor had been the hope of Georgia's early immigrants, but few found that hope fulfilled. In June 1736, Oglethorpe reported that in and around Savannah there were "about 300 debtors … who walk about discontented & will not work because they say their improvements will go to their creditors," the Georgia Trust included. So despondent were most, especially indentured servants, that they ran away from Georgia to avoid that very financial condition, perpetual indebtedness, that many had tried to escape by coming. In September 1738, Oglethorpe wrote to the Trustees that, "the northern division of the province has lost near three forth parts of the people."

For those who stayed, restrictions on land use, small plots granted, and generally poor soil made life difficult. Much of the coastal lands were flooded at high tide, and the rest was too sandy for most crop varieties. The inland pine barrens region was good for little more than growing trees. Food was so scarce during Georgia's first decade that crops had to be imported from other colonies. By 1738, though nearly 59,000 acres had been granted, only about one thousand were under cultivation.

For what land was being worked, the Trustees required colonists to plant one hundred mulberry trees for every ten acres. But most farmers could not afford to devote that much land to feeding silk worms. They had enough difficulty feeding themselves. For those who tried, a late frost could kill the early leaves, which led to starvation for the hatchling worms and sometimes for their owners. One bad year could ruin an already debt-ridden farmer. Except among the Salzburgers, whose initial lack of indebtedness made silk production more commercially viable, few Georgians prospered as silk producers.

The Trustees' vision of Georgia as a wine making colony fared no better than their plan for silk, and for many of the same reasons. European grapes did not adjust well to coastal Georgia's soil and climate, and the native wild grapes produced a wine that was too bitter for most palates.

If the land did not easily support the Trustees' dream of silk and wine, it could support cattle. There was good pastureland on the barrier islands as well as the mainland. Canebrakes, bottomlands, and even scrub brush in the pine barrens could sustain large, free-range herds. Many who tilled the soil also supplemented their income by raising cattle. Some relied mainly on their herds. They grazed cattle not only on their land grants, but also used the vast inland stretches of ungranted land. Salted beef soon became a primary staff of life in the young colony. So much cattle roamed Georgia by the 1740s that confusion over ownership was inevitable. A variety of cattle brands were developed to address the problem, but disputes remained constant.

A fledgling timber trade also began to develop as a supplement to farming. Barrels, staves, tar, pitch, planks, shingles, and firewood were constantly in demand. Some charity colonists became woodcutters, but few could afford the equipment needed to supply more than firewood. Some of the more affluent Adventurers, with their land grants running into the hundreds of acres, put indentured servants to work in their forests and small lumberyards producing planks and shingles. Even the Adventurers usually lacked enough capital to make lumbering more than a sideline, but within a few decades the industry became one of Georgia's leading economic forces.

Some Georgians abandoned their unproductive land grants entirely and turned to the Indian trade for support. Deer, otter, and beaver skins were in high demand among the British, as were guns and other manufactured goods among the Indians. Earlier Scots immigrants to Carolina as well as more recent Scots arrivals to Georgia were among the most active Indian traders. Many took wives among the Creeks and Cherokees. Because native societies were matrilineal, the children identifying with their mother's extended family, men with names like McIntosh, McGillivray, and Ross became some of the wealthiest and most influential among the natives.

Most of Georgia's Indian trade was at first funneled through Charleston, following routes dating back to the 1670s. But the Trustees began diverting the trade by requiring that all traders operating west of the Savannah River travel to Savannah and secure a license. South Carolina protested, but the license requirement remained in place. Georgia's new trading town of Augusta, at the head of navigation on the Savannah River, soon became the largest Indian trading center in the southern colonies. At the height of the trading season, as many as six hundred British traders and two thousand pack animals crowded its streets. From there the riches of Indian country floated down river to Savannah for transport to other colonies and to Britain.

In addition to dry goods, rum was regularly traded to the Indians. Although rum was forbidden in Georgia, the ban was almost entirely ignored. Many Savannah merchants, some of the colony's leading men among them, made huge fortunes from rum smuggling. It was easy enough to obtain since rum was a major export from British colonies in the Caribbean. Rum also flowed freely from Carolina. Georgia colonists as well as Indians were among rum smugglers' best customers. In 1737 William Stephens reported from Savannah on the "abundance of unlicensed tippling houses in all parts of the town where spirits are sold," rum included. Finally, in 1742, the Trustees gave in and relaxed the ban on rum importation.

Georgia and the Slavery Debate

The Trustees had long found Oglethorpe to be a poor correspondent, so they hired William Stephens, a Cambridge graduate and former Member of Parliament, as their reporting secretary. The Trustees' relations with Oglethorpe, whom they saw as increasingly dictatorial, continued to sour until in 1741 they divided Georgia into two counties, Savannah in the north and Frederica in the south. Each would be governed by a president and a council of four assistants. The Trustees made Stephens president in Savannah. They asked Oglethorpe to recommend a suitable candidate to serve as president of Frederica, but he never responded. Though as a Trustee he could hold no title of authority, Oglethorpe had been from the beginning Georgia's only resident Trustee and had largely directed Georgia's affairs. He continued to do so in Frederica until he left Georgia for good in 1743. With Oglethorpe gone, the Trustees made Stephens president of the entire colony.

The Trustees also gave Stephens and his council authority to grant land, marking a major shift away from the notion of Georgia as a charity colony. More than 85 percent of all land grants to charity colonists, issued by the Trustees or Oglethorpe, were made before 1741. Beginning that year, Stephens and his council made clear that they favored larger land grants and wealthier immigrants. Within a few years plantations were established by Noble Jones, James Habersham, and others who would become some of Georgia's richest and most influential men. Stephens himself soon had a plantation just outside Savannah.

Along with larger land grants came increased pressure on the Trustees to lift their ban against outright, or fee-simple, land ownership and slavery. For years South Carolina rice planters had sought land in Georgia, and they wanted to bring their slaves with them. Now many Georgia grant holders, especially those with larger estates, wanted the ability to sell portions or mortgage it all to raise cash. And they wanted to use that cash to buy more land and slaves. Pressure also came from the "Malcontents," a group of Adventurers and merchants from the Savannah region who hoped to enhance their fortunes by trading in slaves or becoming slaveholding planters themselves; they were led by four Lowland Scot Adventurers: Patrick Tailfer, David Douglass, Patrick Houstoun, and Andrew Grant—and an English merchant, Robert Williams. In 1738 they and more than one hundred Savannah-area Malcontents sent a petition to the Trustees demanding fee-simple ownership of land as well as slavery.

The Malcontents were opposed by Georgians who were just as determined to keep slavery out of the colony. Georgia's free laborers had among the highest wages in colonial America, mainly because they were not competing with slaves. Working class women who earned a living as cooks, laundresses, and housekeepers worried that slavery would end their employment. Artisans and craftsmen, too, feared what slavery might mean to their trades. John Martin Bolzius, a leading pastor at Ebenezer, rallied the Salzburgers to oppose slavery, calling the institution a perversion of Christianity. He ridiculed the argument that free white labor could not produce rice, pointing to a bountiful crop grown in 1739 by the Salzburgers.

The Scots Highlanders at Darien opposed slavery as well and countered the Malcontents's petition with one of their own. After listing various disadvantages of slavery, they concluded by stressing: "It is shocking to human nature that any race of mankind and their posterity should be sentenced to perpetual slavery; nor in justice can we think otherwise of it, than that they are thrown amongst us to be our scourge one day or other for our sins."

Much to the relief of nearly all but the Malcontents, the Trustees left the ban on slavery in place. But slavery's supporters continued to push for change, and over the next few years they began to ignore the ban altogether. Though William Stephens publicly maintained his support for the Trustees, he and the council made little effort to enforce their slavery ban. On the contrary, the Stephens administration encouraged slavery by issuing Georgia's best land to wealthy men in grants of hundreds of acres. In 1745 John Martin Bolzius complained that poor people were being crowded out and pushed onto marginal lands. "Merchants & Other Gentlemen," he pointed out, now had in their hands "all good & Convenient Ground at the Sea Coasts & Banks of Rivers." Poorer folk were "forced to possess Lands remote from the Conveniency of Rivers & from Town."

Despite its illegality, slavery soon followed in the wake of large land grants. Under Stephens, Carolina planters began to get land grants in Georgia, and they brought slaves with them. Georgia planters brought in more slaves. Finally in 1750, with so many slaves already in Georgia, the Trustees relented and lifted their ban on slavery and on fee-simple land ownership. Stephens and the council quickly tied large land grants to slave ownership: The more slaves a man owned, the more land he could get.

In January 1750, the non-slaveholding residents of Ebenezer complained when a planter "with many Negroes" was granted a huge tract of nearby land where their young people had hoped to establish farms. After repeated inquiries, James Habersham, a member of the council, told the Salzburgers that without slaves they could never hope to get significant land grants. The people of Abercorn, a small village fifteen miles above Savannah, were having similar problems with planters. In mid-1750 they sent a plaintive letter to the Trustees telling how they were being "eaten up" by the five-hundred-acre grants surrounding their settlement. "Being confined to our 50 acre lots we shall have but little range or food for our few cattle." But there was no going back. The age of the planter and slavery had arrived.

Chapter 2

Royal Colony and Revolution

Georgia Becomes a Royal Colony

The lack of relief for debtors together with a shift toward larger land grants for a few wealthier grantees contributed to making Georgia the poorest and least populous of Britain's American colonies. By 1750, when slavery became legal in Georgia, the colony contained only seventeen hundred whites and four hundred blacks. A minority population of rice planters was beginning to dominate the coastal regions while the majority was increasingly pushed onto marginal lands. Many turned to day labor or left the colony altogether. The Trustees' original plan to make Georgia an economically self-sustaining charity colony had been undermined by their own policies, that virtually guaranteed continued indebtedness for most residents.

In 1751 the Trustees, as was their annual habit, asked Parliament for more money. This time Parliament refused. It had already given Georgia more money than anticipated, and many of its members saw further funding as throwing good money after bad. Parliament's lack of support sparked fear, especially among larger landowners, that Georgia might be handed back to South Carolina. If that occurred, South Carolina might not recognize existing land grants, as some in the Charleston legislature had never recognized Georgia's legitimacy as a separate colony. The Trustees' charter was set to expire in 1753, leaving Georgia's future uncertain.

Frustrated with funding problems, the Trustees relinquished their charter a year early, in 1752. To shore up the colony's claim to legitimacy, they established Georgia's first elected assembly. It had no power to legislate, only to make recommendations, but it did ensure that there would be a representative body in place when the Trustees left. In their letter turning Georgia over to the crown, they related the fear among Georgians that South Carolina would assume control and that they would be "Ousted from their Settlements, cultivated at a great Expense, under pretense of old Grants, which were totally neglected, and indeed forfeited before the Georgia Charter, and absolutely set aside by it."

Parliament allowed Georgia to remain a separate colony, a royal colony, with its own legislature, court system, and governor. The legislature, or General Assembly, was composed of two houses, and membership was limited to the relatively wealthy. Voting was restricted as well. The lower house, or Commons House, had nineteen members, each of whom had to own at least five hundred acres of land. They were elected by voters who had to own at least fifty acres.

The fifty-acre requirement prevented many poorer folk from voting. Though most had been granted fifty acres as charity colonists, they tended to sell as much land as they could to pay off debts as soon as fee-simple ownership went into effect. The property requirement for voting also shut out town dwellers. Wealthy merchants were upset about their lack of representation in the Commons. The law was soon changed to allow voting by those who paid tax on property equal to fifty acres. Those who paid tax on property worth three hundred pounds sterling could be elected to a seat in the Commons.

The Upper House of the General Assembly was not elected. It was composed of twelve men appointed in the name of the king.

It served as the Governor's Council, the colony's supreme court (the governor was chief justice), and acted with the governor to grant lands. The governor himself had extraordinary powers, more than was usual in most colonies. He could convene, adjourn, or even dissolve the Assembly at will, and he could veto any act of the Assembly. Technically, most other royal governors could do the same but rarely did so since their salaries were paid by the legislature. In Georgia, the governor's salary was paid from London, making his office much more independent of the Assembly.

Still, the Assembly had some influence, as it demonstrated with the first man to hold the title of governor in Georgia, John Reynolds, who took office in 1754. Reynolds, a captain in the British Royal Navy, was a man used to having his way. He laid elaborate plans for Georgia's defense that proved both impractical, considering the colony's small militia force, and expensive. His demand for excessive funds put him at odds with the Commons House, which was responsible for originating monetary legislation. The Governor's Council tried to mediate, but Reynolds did not take advice well. Instead he tried to ignore the Assembly, an effort that alienated both houses. He even tried to move the capital out of Savannah. The Assembly complained so loudly about Reynolds's dictatorial and spendthrift ways that the British Board of Trade, responsible for overseeing colonial affairs, removed Reynolds in 1757.

His replacement, Henry Ellis, was a different sort of man entirely. A competent administrator, willing to take advice and work with the Assembly, he was just as interested in science and natural history. A well-traveled man of the Enlightenment, it was not unusual to see him in the streets of Savannah making notes on weather and taking readings with his thermometer. Though popular with the Assembly, ill health forced Ellis to resign in 1760.

James Wright assumed the governor's office that year and remained Georgia's royal governor until American independence was established more than two decades later. His long tenure in office reflected not only his political skill but also his financial stake in the colony. By the time of the Revolution, Wright owned eleven plantations and 523 slaves, making him the wealthiest man in Georgia.

Wealthy slaveholders dominated Georgia politics during its period as a royal colony. Rice planters of the coastal region were the most influential. This elite class contained about sixty men, each holding at least 2,500 acres and a minimum of forty slaves. Men from this select group normally formed the Governor's Council. They controlled land regulation and distribution, and they tended to favor slaveholders. Though under this "headright system" each head of household coming into Georgia was granted one hundred acres of land by right, an additional fifty acres was allowed for each family member or slave. Such allowances most often went to slaveholders, and more slaves equaled more land.

The tie between slaves and land granting in Georgia helped drive the price of slaves to new heights throughout the southern colonies. In Charleston, the largest slave-trading port in the South, prices rose from twenty to sixty pounds and more. Few among the common folk could afford such prices, and to borrow money to buy slaves was much too dangerous. The death or escape of a single slave could ruin a small farmer. Most people coming into Georgia during the 1750s owned no slaves. They were generally granted poor lands of sandy soil in pine barrens beyond the tidewater, where they tried to eke out a meager living as subsistence farmers.

Many of those who found their lands too poor to produce a crop made their way to Savannah in search of work. But slavery had driven prices up and wages down. John Martin Bolzius observed that common folk in the city needed several skills to survive. A single trade could not produce enough income to maintain a household. Increasingly, white labor was being pushed aside in favor of slavery.

It was in part rising poverty rates that led Governor Ellis to divide Georgia into eight parishes, much like later counties, in 1758. Wardens of the government-supported Anglican Church collected taxes from parishioners to support poor relief. They also petitioned the Commons for relief funds. Worsening poverty led the Assembly to pass a vagabond law designed to discourage poor people from coming to Georgia. Those who could not support themselves were subject to imprisonment or impressment into the British navy.

Still, the colony needed more men for the militia. The Seven Years War had broken out in 1756 between Britain and France, and Spain allied itself with the French. So did most of the Indians, which is why British settlers called it the French and Indian War. Natives tended to favor the French mainly because they came to trade, whereas the British came not only to trade but also to take Indian land. Governor Ellis's diplomatic skills helped keep peace with the Creeks. Not so with the Cherokees. In 1758 land disputes in the Carolinas and Virginia led to the Anglo-Cherokee War, which lasted until 1761. Cherokee resistance, together with French and Spanish raids along the coast, made clear to the incoming governor, James Wright, that he needed a stronger militia.

To attract more settlers for his militia Wright needed land. But the Creeks were reluctant to give up more land. That changed when the Treaty of Paris of 1763 ended the Seven Years War. France lost its claims in North America, and Florida passed from Spain to Britain. Now the Indians were more dependent than ever on British trade, and Wright took full advantage. With the Treaty of Augusta, also signed in 1763, Wright and the three other Southern governors forced major land cessions from the Indians. Georgia got 2.4 million acres of Creek land in two sections; one stretching south from the Altamaha to the St. Marys River and inland for roughly forty miles, and another between the Savannah and Ogeechee rivers running north to just above Augusta.

Wright immediately began issuing land grants in the 1763 cession. Coastal regions went in large tracts to rice planters, but inland areas, especially between the Savannah and Ogeechee, went mainly to small farmers who agreed to militia service in exchange for their lands. By the early 1770s, this influx of farmers, planters, and enslaved blacks brought Georgia's population to just over twenty-three thousand people, about eleven thousand of whom were slaves. Though making up nearly half the colony's number, slaves were concentrated in relatively few hands. Only about 5 percent of white Georgians owned any slaves, and half of all slaves were owned by just sixty planters—fewer than 1 percent of the white population.

The Tax Controversy

The French and Indian War secured Britain's claim to North America east of the Mississippi, but it left the royal treasury exhausted. Continued conflict with the Indians over land threatened to further drain the empire. Britain acted on these difficulties in two ways. First, to secure peace with the Indians, it announced the Proclamation of 1763 establishing a boundary running down the Appalachian Mountains, then cutting across

Georgia's backcountry to the St. Marys River. All areas west and south of that line would be reserved to the Indians. Second, to rebuild the treasury, Parliament for the first time began imposing direct taxes in the American colonies.

Colonial elites generally resisted both these moves. Some had already granted themselves land beyond the Appalachians and hoped either to sell the land or move settlers there who would pay them rent. They balked at the taxes as well with the refrain "no taxation without representation." Since the colonies were not directly represented in Parliament, then that body should have no power to impose taxes on them. Parliament responded with the doctrine of virtual representation, arguing that every Member of Parliament represented the interests of the empire, and America was part of that empire. Besides, the colonies had benefited enormously from the recent Seven Years War by having the French and Spanish threats removed. They should help pay the war's cost as well as the cost of maintaining British armed forces in America. And the cry of "no taxation without representation" rang hypocritical in any case. Colonial legislatures had for generations been taxing people who had neither land nor wealth enough to vote or hold office.

Those with money complained the loudest because the new taxes were aimed mainly at them. The first tax, the Revenue Act of 1764, targeted sugar, a relatively expensive import. It was followed in 1765 with the Stamp Act, which required that all kinds of written material—books, newspapers, legal documents, bills of lading, permits—be printed on embossed paper bearing a royal seal. The tax had little direct effect on most colonists because illiteracy rates were so high. In Georgia there were no public schools. A few locally supported schools existed in towns like

Savannah, Sunbury, Ebenezer, and Augusta, but the funding was so meager that good teachers were hard to keep.

Most colonial legislatures protested the new taxes, and all but one governor refused to enforce the Stamp Act until protests against it could be heard in London. Only James Wright tried to enforce the Stamp Act. He refused to call the Assembly into session to discuss the issue, and for several weeks closed the port of Savannah until the stamped paper arrived. A mob composed mainly of Savannah merchants, along with Stamp Act opponents from Charleston who had come to egg them on, hanged and burned a stamp master in effigy. They demanded that the port be opened with the Stamp Act ignored. Wright opened the port, but cleared shipping only with stamped paper. So eager were they to get the ships moving that most merchants and planters supported Wright's action. Georgia thus became the only colony of the future thirteen original United States in which the Stamp Act was enforced.

Parliament repealed the Stamp Act in 1766 and reduced the tax on sugar, but a year later imposed new taxes with the Townshend Acts. These acts placed taxes on a variety of imported goods such as paper, paint, lead, glass, and tea. In response, the lower house of Massachusetts's legislature sent a circulating letter to all the colonies asking them to resist the Townshend Acts and boycott British goods; Virginia sent out a similar letter. In 1768 the Georgia Commons House passed resolutions supporting the right of protest and called the Townshend Acts a violation of British constitutional principles, but stopped short of imposing a boycott. Still Governor Wright, who had warned the Commons against considering the Massachusetts and Virginia letters at all, promptly dissolved the Assembly. The next year Savannah merchants held two meetings calling for a boycott, but little came of the move.

Other colonies had more success with their boycott movements. In 1769 British imports dropped by 38 percent. The next year Parliament again relented and dropped most of the taxes, but retained the tea tax as an assertion of its right to tax the colonies. Throughout the crisis over the Townshend Acts, only in Georgia did British imports continue to flow freely. Legislators in South Carolina were so upset with their neighbor to the south that some suggested invading the colony and closing its ports. They settled for a boycott of Georgia instead.

Carolina's upper crust also responded to the Townshend taxes by passing higher costs on to lower class folk. Their taxes and land rents were going up as well, mostly on backcountry tenant farmers who did not qualify for voting or office holding. The situation was similar in other colonies. In North Carolina backcountry farmers refused to pay increased taxes and rents, organized themselves into armed bands of "regulators," and drove off tax and rent collectors-- sometimes wearing tar and feathers. At its height, in the three western counties where it was concentrated, the Regulator movement enjoyed around 80 percent support.

In 1771, with backing from the North Carolina legislature, an eastern militia led by Governor William Tryon invaded the backcountry and crushed the rebellion, hanging several of its leaders. Refugees scattered across the southern backcountry, many fleeing to Georgia. Some became squatters on ungranted lands in the 1763 cession. Others ventured further onto lands not yet ceded by the Indians. In 1773 Governor Wright met with Creek and Cherokee leaders and secured the land for Georgia in exchange for relieving Indian debts to white traders. The deal would be funded by land sales in the newly ceded areas, but resident settlers found it difficult to pay. There were difficulties, too, with the Indians. Many had opposed the new land cessions, and some formed raiding parties that killed several whites. No general war resulted, but tensions remained high along the upper Ogeechee.

Georgia Joins the Revolution

Tensions were also brewing in far-off Boston that would have consequences for all of the colonies. In 1773 the British East India Company lowered prices on its tea, making it cheaper than tea smuggled in by Boston merchants trading illegally with the Dutch. The smugglers and their supporters, some disguised as Indians, dumped their competitor's tea in Boston Harbor and called it a protest against the tea tax. Parliament responded the next year with a series of laws known in America as the Intolerable Acts. They temporarily closed the port of Boston and dissolved the Massachusetts legislature, allowing the royal governor direct rule.

Merchants and political leaders in Massachusetts and other colonies howled in protest against the Intolerable Acts. Reaction was more muted in Georgia. As the youngest of the thirteen colonies, Georgia's most prominent families still had strong family and economic ties to Britain. They had religious ties as well, most being members of the Anglican Church.

A major exception was St. Johns Parish, centered around the Midway settlement, which was populated mainly by South Carolina immigrants whose families had largely come from New England and had been in America for generations. Though nominally Congregationalist, nearly all of their ministers were Presbyterian. Presbyterians also dominated in Darien, as did Lutherans at Ebenezer. Baptists, many of them part of the recent wave of refugees from Carolina, were most influential in the backcountry and had long advocated separation of church and state. These groups would play pivotal roles in opposing Britain's colonial dominance.

Savannah merchants most directly affected by the tax issue were early leaders of the resistance in Georgia. They called themselves Whigs after Britain's liberal Whig Party, which generally opposed the more authoritarian Tories. Four of the most active Whigs—Noble W. Jones, Archibald Bulloch, John Houstoun, and George Walton—called for decisive action. In July and August of 1774, they and other Whigs met in Savannah at Peter Tondee's tavern and drew up the Tondee's Tavern Resolutions. They protested the Intolerable Acts and denied Parliament's right to tax the colonies. However, because support for the resistance movement was still relatively weak in Georgia, they sent no delegates to the First Continental Congress meeting that September in Philadelphia. Georgia was the only one of the thirteen colonies not represented.

In January 1775, the Whigs formed Georgia's First Provincial Congress and again tried to bring Georgia into the Continental Association, a general boycott of British trade, but support was still too weak. That spring Georgia Whigs became more aggres-sive. When news of April's fighting at Lexington and Concord in Massachusetts reached Savannah, some of the more rebellious Whigs stole six hundred pounds of gunpowder from the royal magazine. In May, St. Johns Parish sent Lyman Hall to the Second Continental Congress, though not as a voting member since he did not represent the whole colony. Hall took with him more than 150 barrels of rice and cash donations for the relief of Boston. Rumors circulated that he also carried some of the stolen gunpowder.

In June, Whigs spiked cannons in Savannah so they could not fire a salute at the upcoming birthday celebration of King George

III. On 5 June, as Wright and his supporters toasted King George, Whigs paraded through the streets of Savannah and erected a liberty pole on the public square. A few days later they broke into a royal storehouse and stole guns and ammunition. At the port of Sunbury, twenty-five miles south of Savannah, Whigs freed two ships carrying smuggled cargo that had been seized by royal customs officials.

On 4 July, Whigs met at Georgia's Second Provincial Congress in Savannah. With more than one hundred delegates from all but two parishes, it set itself up as an opposition government. It declared Georgia no longer subject to acts of Parliament, though still nominally loyal to King George, placed a ban on trade with Britain, and made Lyman Hall Georgia's delegate to the Continental Congress. To draw support from common folk, and over the objections of more conservative Whigs, the Provincial Congress extended voting rights to all adult white males who paid any taxes. Support for the rebellion swelled to such an extent that Governor Wright soon confessed that he had no real authority in Georgia. He called those active in the movement "a parcel of the lowest people." They were led, he admitted, by "some better sort of men and some merchants and planters" but contained "many of the inferior class."

Before the Provincial Congress adjourned, it established a fifteen-man Council of Safety to act as an executive body and to enforce the ban on British trade. Like the Provincial Congress itself, the Council of Safety was made up mostly of more radical Whigs—Noble W. Jones, Archibald Bulloch, and George Walton among them—who were willing to go to extremes. Through late 1775 and into 1776 the Council set up local committees through which they instituted a reign of terror. Georgians suspected of loyalty to Britain, generally called Tories, were forced to sign an oath of allegiance to the Continental Association; most complied to preserve their lives and property. "If a Tory refused to join," recalled Savannah resident Elizabeth Johnston, "he was imprisoned, and tarred and feathered." In January 1776, the Council announced that Georgians must either sign the oath or forfeit their property and leave the colony.

That same month British naval vessels arrived at Savannah and tried to purchase provisions. Governor Wright urged the Council of Safety to suspend the embargo but was threatened with imprisonment. Wright and several of his officials fled to the British ships. Still, the navy wanted provisions, especially the rice cargo on several ships anchored above Savannah. Colonel Lachlan McIntosh, commanding Savannah's Whig forces, called for volunteers to defend the city. On 3 March, after a standoff lasting several weeks, McIntosh ordered troops to unrig the rice boats but discovered that the British had boarded them the night before. In the Battle of the Rice Boats, McIntosh sent a fire ship into the flotilla, destroying three or four vessels, but the British successfully ran most of the boats down river with sixteen hundred barrels of rice. The British fleet then left, taking Governor Wright with it.

Whigs now firmly held Georgia's government, though not entirely the loyalty of its people. The Whig reign of terror had left a bitter taste in the mouths of many Georgians, and latent British sentiment remained.

Radicals and Conservatives Struggle for Control

Georgia's Provincial Congress convened again on 8 March 1776, this time in Augusta. Upcountry response to the recent call for troops had been weak, and Whigs wanted to make clear that they were in control. In April they drew up Georgia's first independent governing document, the Rules and Regulations, which established a judiciary, a one-house legislature, and a Council of Safety headed by a president, who would serve as chief executive and commander-in-chief of Georgia's armed forces. When the document took effect on 1 May, the delegates elected Archibald Bulloch president.

On 12 June 1776, the Provincial Congress declared Georgia formally independent from Britain. Three weeks later, on 2 July, the Continental Congress did the same for the United States. The Declaration of Independence was adopted on 4 July, with Lyman Hall, George Walton, and Button Gwinnett signing on behalf of Georgia.

The Provincial Congress began work on a permanent constitution that would take effect in May 1777. Under this document, a one-house legislature, or House of Assembly, would be elected annually, and the Assembly would choose the governor and his council. Eight counties replaced the old parish system. To secure separation of church and state, Whigs disestablished Anglicanism as the official church, declared that no taxes could be used to support any religious activity, and wrote into the new constitution that "no clergyman of any denomination shall be allowed a seat in the legislature."

As to who could sit in the legislature and elect its members, radical and conservative Whigs disagreed. Conservatives wanted to keep voting and office holding restricted to men of substantial property; radicals insisted on broader political rights. In something of a compromise, voting was opened to all white males over age twenty-one who paid taxes on ten pounds of property or was a skilled artisan practicing a "mechanic trade." The right to hold office was limited to men who owned 250 acres of land or owned property worth 250 pounds, a small fortune at a time when school teachers might earn sixty pounds annually and unskilled workers considerably less.

Still, conservative Whigs were far from satisfied. Joseph Clay, Savannah merchant and deputy paymaster for Continental troops in Georgia, complained that the new constitution was too "democratical" in giving political voice to "those whose ability or situation in life does not intitle them to it." Political differences sometimes became personal, even deadly. In February 1777, when British troops in Florida threatened Georgia, the Council of Safety handed all executive powers to the radical President Bulloch, making him practically a dictator. Just two days later, he died under mysterious circumstances. Some suspected that conservatives had poisoned Bulloch rather than see him wield such power.

Button Gwinnett, another radical leader, replaced Bulloch and ordered an invasion of Florida. When the invasion failed, Gwinnett blamed General Lachlan McIntosh, commander of Georgia's militia. McIntosh, a leading conservative, called Gwinnett "a scoundrel and lying rascal." A duel followed in which both men were wounded. Gwinnett died three days later.

Disagreements between McIntosh and Gwinnett certainly hampered military operations, but the main problem was a lack of men. In July 1776, Georgia began offering one hundred acres for volunteers. Men came from as far away as Pennsylvania in response. A few of them were black, though Austin Dabney was the only African American to whom Georgia granted land for military service, and then only fifty acres. Blacks were far more often used to entice whites to join the Whig ranks. In addition to land, Georgia's Whig government offered new recruits slaves confiscated from British loyalists.

Promises of land and slaves brought some volunteers, but they came in small numbers. When Gwinnett ordered the Florida invasion in March 1777, Georgia had only four hundred state troops on hand. He tried to get more men from General Robert Howe, commander of Continental forces in the South, but Howe refused to support the operation. What men he could spare would not be enough to do the job.

Governor John Treutlen of Ebenezer, the first man to hold that office under the new state constitution, was too busy trying to keep peace among the Whigs to concern himself with the British in Florida. Treutlen, a radical, had been strongly opposed by the conservatives. When they failed to keep him out of the governor's seat, some conservative leaders supported a proposal to rob Treutlen and the dominant radicals of their power by having Georgia annexed to South Carolina. South Carolina's legislature agreed to the plan, but the Georgia Assembly voted it down.

In the spring of 1778, Georgia's next governor, John Houstoun, a man of more conservative leanings and more broadly supported in the Assembly, led another invasion of Florida. This time Georgia was better prepared, having issued volunteers promises of more land taken from Tories under the Confiscation Act of 1778. The state also offered land in Florida itself. General Howe contributed troops to the effort, bringing the total Whig force to about two thousand. But disagreement over who should command led Howe to abandon the invasion. Without Continental support, Houstoun gave up as well.

Georgia's lack of military preparedness would soon have dire consequences. Up to this point, British campaigns against Whig forces had been concentrated in the North. Then in October 1777 came Britain's first major defeat at the Battle of Saratoga in New York. With this hint that the Continentals could win, France entered the war on the side of the United States. In response, Britain shifted its attention to the South, where Tory support tended to be greater. In December 1778, British troops launched a surprise attack on Savannah and took the city almost unopposed. By the end of January 1779 British troops had pushed up the Savannah River and Augusta was in Tory hands. Fourteen hundred Georgia men joined the Tory militia, and Georgia was once more a royal colony.

Blacks generally welcomed British forces. Hundreds escaped to British lines believing that doing so meant freedom. On 30 January, ninety enslaved blacks from one plantation joined the British army as it marched toward Augusta. From the war's outset, Whigs had warned Georgia slaveholders that should the British return, they would offer blacks freedom in exchange for military service as they previously had in Virginia with the Dunmore Proclamation, so called after Virginia's royal governor, Lord Dunmore, who issued the document.

In June 1779, Sir Henry Clinton, commanding general of royal forces in America, expanded Dunmore's efforts with his own Philipsburg Proclamation. This document declared that all Whig-owned slaves in America were free. Thousands of enslaved people responded to the call. One was David George, a black preacher who fled to Savannah and helped found Georgia's first African American Baptist church. Two companies of black soldiers, now as free men, were mustered into British service and helped fight off an assault by Continental forces against Savannah in October 1779.

The British also tried to establish a standing alliance with the Cherokees and Creeks to supplement their forces in the backcountry. Most Indians tended to favor continued British control since Parliament had promised to limit settlement to areas east of the 1763 Proclamation line. Should British authority be defeated, that line would disappear. Indians in the Georgia backcountry mostly adopted a neutral stance early in the war, not knowing who might win and not wishing to alienate any trading partners. But fear of a British-Indian alliance led to several Whig attempts to drive both Cherokees and Creeks further into the backcountry during 1777 and 1778. The loss of Indian crops and resulting famine spoiled British plans to ally with the Indians and make them an effective fighting force. Still, some Cherokees and Creeks did later join Tory bands in their raids against Whig militia.

Whigs, Tories, and Shifting Loyalties

Georgia Whigs, supported by North Carolina militia units, quickly regrouped after Augusta fell to the British. On 14 February 1779 they defeated seven hundred Tories at the Battle of Kettle Creek in Wilkes County. British troops abandoned Augusta that same day and withdrew toward Savannah, but on 3 March beat back the Whigs at Briar Creek in Screven County. For more than a year Georgia remained divided, with Whigs controlling the upcountry and Tories, under a reinstated Governor James Wright, dominating Savannah's environs and most of the tidewater. General Benjamin Lincoln, Continental commander in the South, with French support under Count Charles Henri d'Estaing, tried and failed to take Savannah in October 1779. Allied troops suffered more than eight hundred casualties, five times more than the British. One of those killed was a Polish cavalry general in the Continental army, Count Casimir Pulaski. Fort Pulaski, guarding the mouth of the Savannah River, and Pulaski County were later named for him.

Georgia Whigs re-established their capital at Augusta and prepared for a new offensive. To attract more settlers who could serve as militiamen, the Whig Assembly again promised land—this time offering two hundred acres to each family head. But in May 1780 when the British captured Charleston, General Lincoln withdrew forces from Georgia to defend South Carolina, leaving Augusta vulnerable. Governor Wright and Georgia's British loyalists took full advantage. Within days of Continental troops leaving Augusta, British forces surged up the Savannah River and took possession of the town. Thus Georgia became the only one of the rebellious colonies to have British government almost completely reestablished during the war.

Only the area northwest of Augusta, mostly the original Wilkes County, was left to the Whigs. Even in this region their control was questionable. Considerable doubt remains about the location or even the existence of a Whig government between May 1780 and July 1781. Legend holds that it met, if at all, in various spots around Wilkes County, keeping one step ahead of Tory militia. It may have met briefly in South Carolina. Whatever the case, the Whig government was certainly too weak to enforce its will.

Guerilla fighting defined the war in Georgia's upcountry from mid-1780 to mid-1781. Tory and Whig raiders put each other's lives and lands, and those of their less aggressive neighbors, in constant danger. Loyalties shifted frequently depending on which side happened to be locally dominant at the time. Most settlers tried to remain neutral, preferring to stay put and protect their homes from raiders rather than become raiders themselves. But professions of neutrality were nearly always taken as opposition, with both Whig and Tory partisans holding a "with us or against us" attitude. Atrocities were common on both sides. Whig Colonel

John Dooly, operating without orders (as most guerillas did), wrought havoc in the upcountry until a Tory band murdered him in his bed. In the spring of 1781, Whig raiders killed around one hundred suspected British loyalists, both government officials and common settlers.

Women were often the victims of guerilla raids, but not always easily victimized. One of the most popular legends to emerge from the period involved Nancy Hart, whose family lived in what would later become Elbert County. She and her husband Benjamin were strong Whig supporters. Benjamin served as a lieutenant in the Georgia militia, and Nancy sometimes spied for Whig forces. One day while Benjamin was away, six Tories showed up at the Hart cabin demanding to be fed. After her unwanted guests stacked their arms and helped themselves to dinner, Nancy grabbed one of their guns and threatened to shoot anyone who moved. She killed one man who lunged at her, wounded a second, and held the rest at bay while her young daughter went to find her father. When Benjamin arrived with several Whig friends they hanged the Tories from a nearby tree. Hart County was later named for Nancy—the only Georgia county to be named for a woman.

In April 1781, General Nathaniel Greene, now commanding the South's Continental forces, began a major offensive. On his orders, Georgia and Carolina militiamen laid siege to Augusta, which finally fell to the Whigs on 5 June. Greene sent his paymaster general, Joseph Clay, to form a new state government. Dr. Nathan Brownson was placed in charge of the militia. A reconstituted Assembly soon met in August and elected Brownson governor.

Despite this setback, Georgia's Tory loyalists, particularly those driven from Augusta, were hardly ready to give up the fight.

Their mood was reflected in a popular song called "The Volunteers of Augusta" set to the tune "The Lilies of France." A few of the stanzas, as published in Savannah's *Royal Georgia Gazette* that fall, made Tory intentions clear:

Come join, my brave lads, come all from afar,
We're all Volunteers, all ready for war;
Our service is free, for honour we fight,
Regardless of hardships by day or by night.
Then all draw your swords, and constantly sing,
Success to our Troop, our Country, and King.

They've plunder'd our houses, attempted our lives,
Drove off from their homes our children and wives;
Such plundering miscreants no mercy can crave,
Such murdering villains no mercy shall have.
Then chop with your swords, and constantly sing,
Success to our Troop, our Country, and King.

When back through Augusta our horses shall prance,
We'll dismount at the Captain's, and there have a dance,
We'll toss off full bumpers of favorite grog,
Be merry all night, in the morning drink knog.
Then rest on your swords, and constantly sing,
Success to our Troop, our Country, and King.

Tory dreams of re-taking Augusta never materialized. By fall 1781 the impact of French intervention had made itself felt and things were going badly for the British on all fronts. In October at Yorktown, Virginia, George Washington, with the help of French land and naval forces, captured a major British force under Lord

Cornwallis. This freed Continental troops to pressure the British in their remaining strongholds. In January 1782, many of those troops arrived in Georgia and drove Tory forces into their Savannah defenses.

By that spring both sides knew that the war was winding down and took no major military action. But in May the Assembly flexed its muscles by passing the Confiscation and Banishment Act. It named 277 specific individuals guilty of treason, ordering them to forfeit their land and leave the state within sixty days. The act also established broad categories of persons who at any time might have professed loyalty to the British crown during the Revolution. They too could have their property confiscated by the state.

The Confiscation and Banishment Act of 1782 essentially gave the state license to take nearly any land it wanted since few Georgians had remained steadfastly loyal to either side throughout the conflict. Rather than adhering to abstract notions of liberty on the one hand or fidelity to King George on the other, most followed the more practical course of trying to protect what land they had by acquiescing to whichever government seemed dominant at the time. Most Georgians had little difficulty expressing loyalty to the Whigs from 1776 through 1778 when the British had abandoned the colony. Loyalties were more fluid, especially in the upcountry, between 1779 and 1781 when the British held much, and usually most, of Georgia.

In that land had much to do with loyalty, the Whigs held a key advantage. They repeatedly offered confiscated Tory land in exchange for support, making it possible for small landowners to expand their holdings and for non-landowners to acquire small estates. This practice was particularly attractive, especially in the latter stage of the war, to men from other states where land policies were not so liberal. The British took a different approach, promising little more than to reestablish the pre-war status quo. When they regained control of Georgia in 1779, British officials practiced a policy of forgiveness, offering a full pardon to Georgians for past disloyalties and letting them keep their land. The policy worked to pacify most Georgia residents and secured their loyalty for the time being, but it drew no new supporters to the Tory cause.

In July 1782, Governor Wright and the remaining British forces left Savannah, bringing the war in Georgia to a close. At least 3,500 whites and an equal number of blacks, mostly slaves, went with them. Firm numbers for the 1782 evacuation are difficult to determine, but the refugees likely totaled many more. Some Georgia Tories fled as early as 1775 during the Whig reign of terror. Others left between 1776 and 1778 under continued Whig threats.

After the war, Britain set up a Loyalist Commission to compensate exiled Tories for their lost property. As a percentage of population, the number of claims from former Georgians totaled more than those from any other state. Claims from former Savannah residents totaled more than those from any other American city. Clearly Georgians had been divided in their loyalties during the war and remained considerably so even at its end.

Chapter 3

Land Frauds, Lotteries, and Indian Removal

Land Grants and the Headright Scandal

With the Treaty of Paris of 1783, Georgia and the other twelve former colonies became internationally recognized as the United States. Its boundaries stretched east to west from the Atlantic Ocean to the Mississippi River and north to south from the Great Lakes almost to the Gulf of Mexico. On maps of the new United States, Georgia's boundaries reached from the Atlantic and Savannah River west to the Mississippi, encompassing not only what is now Georgia but nearly all of Alabama and Mississippi as well. But the state government controlled only the tidewater region and lands between the Savannah and Ogeechee rivers up to the original Wilkes County. Beyond the Ogeechee, Georgia's land claims were still occupied by Cherokees, Creeks, Choctaws, and Chickasaws. Over the next half-century nearly all these natives would be driven west by whites, or as the Creeks called them, *Ecunnaunuxulgee*, meaning "people greedily grasping after Indian lands."

Hoping to satisfy white greed for land, some Cherokees and Creeks were willing to give up areas along their eastern borders. Many Indians had fled these lands anyway during the Revolution, seeking safety farther west. In May 1783, Cherokees sold more than a million acres north and west of Wilkes County. The region was soon organized as Franklin County.

Later that year, two Creek chiefs released a much larger tract of land between the Ogeechee and Oconee rivers. Whites began moving into the area before it was surveyed, some even beyond the Oconee River boundary. This aggravated an already tense situation in that many Creeks had opposed giving up any land in the first place. The Creeks were led by Chief Alexander McGillivray, the son of a Creek woman and a Scottish trader. McGillivray and his followers threatened war if the ceded lands were not returned, but whites continued to settle in what Georgia was now calling Washington County. Finally, McGillivray's Creeks mounted a series of raids between 1787 and 1789 known as the Oconee War. Whites made raids of their own, burning Creek towns and crops, and more than eighty whites were killed along with an unknown number of Indians.

The issue was settled only after President George Washington invited McGillivray and other Creek chiefs to New York, then serving as temporary capital of the United States. In the resulting Treaty of New York of 1790, Creek leaders, including McGillivray, agreed to give up lands east of the Oconee in exchange for a $1,500 annual payment and a promise that no whites could legally settle west of the river. Elijah Clarke, a former Revolutionary War general, tested that promise in 1794 when he and hundreds of adventurers and land speculators tried to establish their own country beyond the Oconee, independent of the US and loosely allied with France. They built several fortified towns in what they called their Trans-Oconee Republic. But when the Georgia militia moved against them almost all of Clarke's men deserted.

Georgia's General Assembly initially sought to discourage land speculators like those in Clarke's party by distributing land under a headright system similar to that of colonial days. The idea was to get land into the hands of settlers who would cultivate it rather than hold it waiting for higher prices, thus promoting Georgia's economic growth. Every head of household had a right to two hundred acres of land, plus fifty more for each additional family member or slave held up to a thousand acres. Still, wealthy or well-connected men, even land speculators, could get much more with the Assembly's approval. They also needed the governor's support, which usually was not difficult to obtain since, at that time, he was appointed from and by the Assembly. Governor George Walton approved grants of up to fifty thousand acres. His successor Edward Telfair signed off on grants for twice that amount and Governor George Mathews approved even larger grants.

In practice, the headright system favored wealthy slaveholders and land speculators but still gave enough land to most white males to qualify them for office in the General Assembly under the state constitution of 1789. That right became more restricted under the 1798 constitution when Assembly membership became tied to land and property value. It hardly mattered since common folk rarely had the wherewithal to campaign for election to the Assembly. Voting under both constitutions was open to all white men who paid taxes, though the Assembly mandated a statewide poll tax that limited the voting strength of poorer men.

The headright system worked well to draw settlers to Georgia, mostly from Virginia and the Carolinas. The state's population ballooned from a pre-Revolutionary level of just over 23,000 (about half enslaved) to 82,548 (just over one-third enslaved) in 1790. By 1800 that number had nearly doubled to162,686, with slaves still accounting for more than a third of the population. The state capital moved with the center of population: from Savannah to Augusta in 1786, then to Louisville in 1796, and to Milledgeville in 1806, where it remained until 1868 when Atlanta became the capital.

Though the headright system encouraged settlement, as a deterrent to land speculation, legal and otherwise, it was a dismal failure. Legislators frequently took bribes in exchange for approving large land grants to speculators. The problem became even worse after 1789 when headright land granting was placed in the hands of county officials. They regularly drew up titles or warrants to fictitious land lots, listing non-existent creeks and trees as boundary markers. They advertised these warrants for sale in newspapers up and down the eastern seaboard, lining their pockets with cash from individual buyers or, more often, from land speculation companies. Company managers, frequently located hundreds of miles away, would never actually survey their purchases. Their only interest was to resell the land at a profit to the next unsuspecting buyer.

These headright land frauds created enormous tracts of land that existed only on paper. Effingham County at the time contained only 310,440 acres. Yet it distributed lands totaling 1,149,791 acres. Washington County had 416,720 acres but printed warrants amounting to 5,018,048. The worst offender was Montgomery County, which contained 407,680 acres. Its officials put 7,436,995 acres worth of warrants in circulation, representing nearly twenty times more land than actually existed in the county. In total, although Georgia's twenty-four counties as of 1796 contained only 9 million acres, county officials issued warrants for 29 million acres.

Corruption was rampant in the General Assembly as well. Far from trying to rein in fraud at the county level, state legislators jumped on the speculation bandwagon to enrich themselves using Georgia's vast claims between the Oconee and Mississippi rivers. Those lands were still occupied by the Indians, though that was of little concern to the Assembly. Of greater concern was that the southern part of the territory was claimed as part of West Florida by Spain, to which Britain had returned Florida after the Revolution. That claim was settled at the 31st Parallel with the 1795 Treaty of San Lorenzo, or Pinckney's Treaty after US ambassador to Britain Thomas Pinckney, who represented the United States in the negotiations.

The Yazoo Land Fraud

Even before the Treaty of San Lorenzo went into effect, legislators plotted to sell up to fifty million acres of Indian land to four land speculation companies for $500,000, or about one penny per acre, a ridiculously low price even for the time. In return for their votes approving the sale, legislators received bribes in the form of land, slaves, rice, and money. James Gunn, Georgia's senior US senator, was a leading lobbyist for the bill. Those few Assemblymen who refused to cooperate were encouraged to leave Augusta under threats to their lives.

In January 1795, Assemblymen passed the Yazoo Act, named for the Yazoo River in the far west of Georgia's claim. Governor Mathews, himself known for shady land deals, signed the bill.

Those who opposed the act began a public campaign to have it overturned. As word spread that Georgians had been cheated out of any future hope of land grants in areas covered by the Yazoo Act, public outrage built to a fever pitch. Local grand juries allied with Yazoo opponents brought charges against pro-Yazoo legislators. Threats against corrupt legislators became so serious that some fled the state. James Jackson, Georgia's junior US senator and opponent of Yazoo from the start, resigned his seat and ran for the Assembly from Chatham County. Like so many other non-incumbent Assembly candidates, he campaigned on a promise to overturn the Yazoo Act.

Not surprisingly, nearly every member of the old Assembly was turned out. The new Assembly quickly moved not only to overturn Yazoo with the Rescinding Act of 1796 but also to wipe every vestige of it from state records. On the grounds of the new state capitol building at Louisville, members of the Assembly gathered to burn all records associated with Yazoo. As far as Georgia was concerned, the Yazoo sales were now void.

During the year-long process of electing new legislators and rescinding Yazoo, much of the land involved had been sold and re-sold. Though Georgia offered purchasers their money back, many insisted on making a profit and refused the deal. Litigation followed in which buyers insisted that Georgia had no right to take back the Yazoo lands. The situation became so troublesome to Georgia that it finally turned the problem over to Washington. Under the Compact of 1802, Georgia sold the areas that are today Alabama and Mississippi to the federal government for $1.25 million.

Like Georgia's General Assembly, Congress denied the Yazoo deal's legitimacy. Buyers continued to press their claim to ownership through the courts, and their position was finally heard by the Supreme Court in *Fletcher v. Peck* (1810). Land speculator John Peck held title to Yazoo lands and sold parts of his land to Robert Fletcher, also a speculator. In a deal worked out between the two, Fletcher brought suit against Peck, charging that Peck did not have title to the land when he sold it. Fletcher hoped to lose the case, and thus secure both for himself and Peck, as well as other Yazoo claimants, clear title to their lands or a profitable buy-out from Congress.

A unanimous court obliged by ruling that Georgia's Rescinding Act was unconstitutional. The decision authored by Chief Justice John Marshall stated that even though corruption was at its heart, the Yazoo Act was a binding contract under Article I, Section 10, Clause I (the Contract Clause) of the Constitution and that neither party to a contract could alter it without consent from the other. This case was one of the earliest in which the Supreme Court declared a state law unconstitutional, thus upholding Article VI's Supremacy Clause making the

Constitution the "supreme law of the land." With this decision in hand, Yazoo claimants pressured Congress into a buy-out that totaled over $4.25 million. Added to monies paid under the Compact of 1802, it had cost the nation's taxpayers roughly $5.5 million to settle Georgia's corrupt land deal.

In addition to the cash Georgia received under the Compact of 1802, it demanded from the federal government a promise to remove all Indians remaining on state land claims. Even though lands west of the Oconee had been guaranteed to the Indians under the 1790 Treaty of New York, federal representatives agreed to insert into the Compact that "the United States shall, at their own expense, extinguish for the Use of Georgia, as early as the same can be peacefully obtained on reasonable terms ... Indian Title to all the other Lands within the State of Georgia." The phrase "peacefully obtained on reasonable terms" implied that the Indians must agree to give up their lands. Congress further stressed the point in its Indian Trade and Intercourse Act, also passed in 1802, under which no Indian land could be taken without a treaty. Nevertheless, Georgia took the Compact of 1802 to mean that the Creeks and Cherokees would soon be gone one way or another.

As to where they might go, in 1803 the United State purchased from France a huge tract of land west of the Mississippi River that roughly doubled the nation's land mass. As part of his effort to have the treaty ratified in the Senate, President Thomas Jefferson pointed out that a portion of the purchase area could be set aside as a reserve for Indians being pushed out of the East. For that reason, Jefferson is sometimes called the father of Indian Removal.

Soon after the Compact of 1802 was signed, in a vain effort to satisfy the *Ecunnaunuxulgee*, the Creek Nation agreed to sell lands that Georgia had long sought between the Oconee and Ocmulgee rivers. Once those lands were state property, rather than distribute them using the discredited headright system, Georgia tried to end both corruption and speculation by instituting land lotteries, a practice that was unique to Georgia. Under the new lottery system, former Indian lands were organized into counties and surveyed into land lots of usually between 160 and 490 acres depending on the estimated land values in each new county. Citizens could then register for a lottery in which these lands would be raffled off. Each qualified citizen was entitled to at least one chance. Those belonging to designated groups such as military veterans, widows, orphans, or heads of families, could register more than once.

Tickets bearing the names of those registering for the lottery were sent to the state capital at Milledgeville where they were placed in a large rotating wooden drum. Tickets with land lot numbers written on them were deposited in a second drum. Both drums were spun and one ticket from each was drawn. Since there were always several times more people registered than land lots available, most participants won no land. But for those who did, on payment of a nominal fee they became the new owner of a land lot.

Though the system remained in place until the last lottery was held from 1832 to 1833, it ended neither speculation nor corruption completely. Land companies sometimes cheated winners out of their land by offering them undervalued prices before they knew their land's true worth. Many people registered who were not citizens of Georgia. Some claimed to be heads of households that were in fact nonexistent. Others who never served in the military passed themselves off as veterans. State officials were sometimes caught trying to rig the lottery's outcome. But despite its flaws, the lottery never approached levels of corruption seen when the headright system was in effect.

Removal of the Creeks

Indians tended to have a different view of the land lottery. To them it did little to abate the greed for land they had long observed among whites—a greed that had already begun to infect and divide the Indians themselves. Several generations of intermarriage between white traders and native women had produced a class of well-to-do mixed bloods among the Indians. Because of their families' trade ties and wealth, these men exercised great influence and rose to positions of leadership in the Cherokee and Creek nations, especially among the Lower Creeks. They became the conduit by which white customs were introduced among the Indians—customs such as a monetary system, slavery, and private as opposed to communal land ownership. They also introduced a growing economic dependence on, and indebtedness to, the whites, which would make it increasingly difficult to resist their demands for land.

The Upper Creeks of central and northern Alabama were less directly affected since they were more geographically isolated. Upper Creek chiefs and full bloods generally tended to be more resistant to changing customs brought by contact with the whites. But such was the mixed-blood influence among Lower Creeks and on the national council that resistance became increasing futile.

It became more so after Benjamin Hawkins was made US agent to the Creek Nation in 1796. Hawkins encouraged the Creeks to view landholding and farming rather than commercial hunting as the path to economic prosperity. It was a radical change from what whites of a century earlier had done. For nearly three thousand years, southeastern Indians had been communal farmers, developing some of the most productive crop varieties in the world. When the British arrived in Charleston, their demand for deerskins transformed Indians largely into commercial hunters. Now Hawkins sought to reverse that trend, hoping to open huge tracts of hunting grounds for land cessions to Georgia. Lower Creeks, desperate to pay off debts to white traders, more readily acquiesced to white notions of privately owned farms. Upper Creeks, more economically independent of whites, tended to adhere to the old communal ways.

Though becoming more and more divided along geographic, economic, and ethnic lines, the Creeks remained united in their opposition to giving up land. But underlying tensions festered and finally came to a head in 1811 after the United States widened an old horse path through the Creek Nation, making it a major roadway running from Macon to New Orleans. Some Lower Creeks agreed to construction of what was called the Federal Road, seeing in it new opportunities for trade. Most Upper Creeks strongly opposed the road. They saw it as little more than a route to bring more whites and their ways into Creek country. Even Creeks who had supported the Federal Road were dismayed to find the army building forts along the old path. What began as a travel route was starting to look like preparation for an invasion.

Tensions among the Creeks were further strained when a Shawnee chief named Tecumseh spoke to the tribal council in late 1811. In an effort to halt American expansion, Tecumseh hoped to create a vast Indian alliance stretching from the Great Lakes to the Gulf of Mexico. Already many Indians of the Ohio River Valley were on board. Now Tecumseh, whose mother was Upper Creek, invited the Creek Nation to join him. Most Lower Creeks feared provoking the whites, but Upper Creeks largely backed the plan. They were ready to drive the whites from their land with or without support from their Lower Creek cousins.

In early 1812, Tecumseh's supporters, mostly Upper Creeks called "Red Sticks," killed several whites traveling along the Federal Road. Hawkins demanded that the killers be executed or Creek trading posts would be shut down and annuity payments cut off. Mixed-blood Chief William McIntosh of Coweta sent a detachment of "Friendlies," as whites called the more compliant Indians, to hunt down suspected Red Stick killers and executed eleven of their number on sight. Red Sticks retaliated by killing several of the executioners. Reprisals followed reprisals until a civil war was raging in the Creek Nation.

Early 1812 also found expansionists in Congress persuading their colleagues that British Canada, or parts of it, could easily be annexed to the United States. In June Congress declared war on Britain, and Tecumseh quickly allied with the new American enemies. In January 1813, hundreds of British troops and Indians, including Creek Red Sticks, defeated an American detachment in Michigan. Whites feared a similar alliance in the South. That spring and summer, murders along the Federal Road increased, and both Georgia and Tennessee called up their militias.

In August Red Stick Creeks led by William Weatherford, also known as Red Eagle, attacked an outpost near the Federal Road called Fort Mims in southern Alabama. They killed about four hundred whites and "Friendlies," and took one hundred captives. In response, an army of US troops, together with Georgia militia, Tennessee militia, and friendly Creeks, all led by General Andrew Jackson, entered the Creek Nation to subdue the Red Sticks. They were joined by a regiment of Cherokees that included John Ross and Major Ridge, who hoped an alliance with the Americans would help secure Cherokee lands.

In March 1814, the last Red Stick stronghold was wiped out at the Battle of Horseshoe Bend, located in what would soon become eastern Alabama. That August, Creeks as a whole were forced to sign the Treaty of Fort Jackson under which they lost 23 million acres, well over half their nation, in northwestern, west-central, and southern Alabama and south Georgia. Now all they had left were lands between the Ocmulgee and Chattahoochee in west-central Georgia, along with areas of east-central Alabama between the Chattahoochee and Coosa rivers—lands that the Fort Jackson Treaty promised would be theirs forever.

Over the next few years the army rounded up thousands of destitute Creeks, both Red Stick and Friendlies, and drove them from the ceded lands. Some sought refuge in Florida among the Seminoles, most of whom were themselves Creek refugees or their descendants from earlier days, along with escaped slaves and a handful of surviving Appalachee and Timucua natives. Even that refuge became precarious after 1821 when Florida passed from Spain to the US following the First Seminole War (1817–18) and subsequent Adams-Onis Treaty of 1819.

With so much land gone, the Creeks were even more dependent not only on trade but also on government annuities that were supposed to come in payment for their land. But Indian agent David B. Mitchell, a former governor of Georgia, partnered with Chief William McIntosh to siphon off more than a third of those annuities for an illegal slave-smuggling operation. What money did get through went mostly into the pockets of white traders who were cheating the Creeks and running up their debts. In 1821 the US offered to pay off those debts in exchange for more land. McIntosh brokered the deal, receiving a kickback of a thousand acres and $12,000 for his trouble. Under this Treaty of Indian Springs, the Creeks lost five million acres between the Ocmulgee and Flint rivers. With only ten million acres left, the Creek National Council reaffirmed an earlier edict widely known as the Blood Law. If any Creek should sign land over to the whites without permission from the Council, he would be subject to execution on sight.

William McIntosh, robbed of his status as a chief for his secret dealings with the whites, tested that law in 1825. At the behest of Georgia's new governor, McIntosh's own first cousin George M. Troup, McIntosh and several chiefs signed a second Treaty of

Indian Springs without the Council's approval, which relinquished lands between the Flint and Chattahoochee rivers. McIntosh's pay-off for the deal amounted to $35,000. Troup had become Georgia's first popularly elected governor the year before, campaigning on a promise to get more Indian land for another lottery. He kept that promise to the voters of Georgia. Now the Creek National Council would keep its promise as well. In April it sent a party of Creek warriors to enforce the Blood Law against McIntosh.

The Council also declared McIntosh's treaty void and sent word of that decision to Governor Troup. Nevertheless, Troup sent Georgia militiamen to secure the disputed area. The Creeks appealed for protection to President John Quincy Adams, reminding him of the Fort Jackson Treaty's promise of their right to the land. Adams refused to intervene, but did agree to pay the Creeks for their lost land. Under the Treaty of Washington of 1826, the Creeks would get an up-front sum of $217,600 plus a perpetual annuity of $20,000.

A year later, the Creek Council was forced to sign away a small strip of land between the Chattahoochee River and the Alabama state line. By 1836 the Creeks would lose all their remaining lands in Alabama and be driven west to Indian Territory, later to become the state of Oklahoma. With the Creeks driven entirely out of Georgia, the General Assembly turned its attention to the Cherokees.

Gold Fever, Cherokee Resistance, and Worcester v. Georgia

In December of 1828, the Assembly passed an act declaring that on the first day of June 1830, those portions of the Cherokee Nation lying within what the state claimed as its boundary would be subject to the laws of Georgia. All Cherokee laws and customs were to be rendered null and void on that date.

Regardless of Georgia's claim, the Cherokees had no intention of giving up their land. In fact, they had long since adopted many ways of the white man in an attempt at assimilation and as a means of avoiding removal. By the 1820s, the Cherokees were no longer communal farmers or commercial hunters. They were land-owning farmers, merchants, blacksmiths, and carpenters. They had built towns and established networks of trade and commerce within their nation and beyond its borders. Sequoyah, or George Guess by his Anglo name, developed a written form of the Cherokee language, and in February 1828, the first issue of the *Cherokee Phoenix* went to press. This newspaper was printed in both English and Cherokee.

Many Cherokees had also adopted the religion of the white man through the efforts of Christian missionaries who helped set up churches and schools in the Cherokee Nation. In 1827 the Cherokees established a tribal government modeled after the US Constitution and made New Echota their capital. Elias Boudinot, editor of the *Cherokee Phoenix*, pointed to the success of assimilation by quoting from an 1826 census showing the sixteen thousand people of the Cherokee Nation holding 22,000 cattle; 7,600 horses; 46,000 swine; 2,500 sheep; 762 looms; 2,488 spinning wheels; 172 wagons; 2,943 ploughs; 10 saw-mills; 31 gristmills; 62 blacksmith shops; 8 large cotton gins; 18 schools; 18 ferries; and a number of public roads.

For all this, most whites continued to view Cherokees as little more than ignorant savages. Georgia's Governor George Gilmer went so far as to question "whether they are the descendants of Adam and Eve." In early nineteenth-century terms, this was to doubt the very humanity of the Cherokees. Faced with such attitudes on the part of most whites, the Cherokees recognized that their position was precarious. It would shortly become even more so.

A Brief History

In August 1829, a Milledgeville newspaper, the *Georgia Journal*, announced that gold had been discovered in northern Georgia. By autumn a flood of gold-fevered miners were pouring into Cherokee country. Benjamin Parks, who discovered gold along the Chestatee River in what would become Lumpkin County, recalled many years later,

> The news got abroad, and such excitement you never saw. It seemed within a few days as if the whole world must have heard of it, for men came from every state I had ever heard of. They came afoot, on horseback and in wagons, acting more like crazy men than anything else. All the way from where Dahlonega now stands, to Nuckolls-ville [Auraria] there were men panning out of the branches and making holes in the hillsides.

Samuel Wales of neighboring Habersham County wrote that, "no event within my recollection has produced so much excitement among the people as the discovery of gold."

Principal Chief John Ross appealed to the federal government to honor its treaty obligations and expel the intruders, but Governor Gilmer objected, and President Andrew Jackson left the Cherokees at the mercy of Georgia.

With thousands of intruders swarming over their lands and no assistance to be had from Jackson, the Cherokees realized that the only remaining way to challenge Georgia's action was through the judicial system. They employed William Wirt, a Baltimore lawyer, who began to search for a case that might bring the Cherokee cause to the Supreme Court. Georgia itself provided the opportunity when state officials arrested eleven missionaries among the Cherokees for refusing to pledge an oath of allegiance to the state. Nine of the eleven relented, but Samuel A. Worcester and

67

Dr. Elizur Butler refused and were sentenced to four years of hard labor. Their only recourse was an appeal to the United States Supreme Court.

In the case of *Worcester v. Georgia*, Chief Justice John Marshall handed down the court's decision:

> The Cherokee Nation, then, is a distinct community, occupying its own territory, with boundaries accurately described, in which the laws of Georgia can have no force, and which the citizens of Georgia have no right to enter but with the assent of the Cherokees themselves or in conformity with treaties and with the acts of Congress.... The whole intercourse between the United States and this nation is, by our Constitution and laws, vested in the government of the United States.... The act of the State of Georgia under which the plaintiff in error was prosecuted is consequently void.

John Ross and the rest of the Cherokee Nation received the news with overwhelming relief. Under treaty, Congressional law, and the US Constitution itself, their ancestral homeland was safe from the grasping hands of Georgia. Elias Boudinot, in the *Cherokee Phoenix*, proclaimed the decision "a great triumph on the part of the Cherokees so far as the question of their rights [is] concerned. The question is forever settled as to who is right and who is wrong." Two days after announcing the Court's ruling, Marshall issued a formal mandate ordering Georgia to release Worcester and Butler.

The Cherokee's victory was short-lived, for it quickly became clear that Georgia would not abide by the Supreme Court's ruling. Georgia refused to recognize the Court's authority in the case and

Davey Crockett: for the Indians
vs. Andrew Jackson

the missionaries remained in the state penitentiary while Georgia continued to claim authority over Cherokee lands.

Infuriated and distraught that all their efforts might come to nothing, the Cherokees sent a delegation to Washington in a last-ditch effort to obtain President Jackson's cooperation. John Ridge, leader of the delegation, asked Jackson directly whether he intended to carry out his constitutional obligation to enforce the Supreme Court's *Worcester* ruling. Jackson replied pointedly that he had no such intention. Instead, he advised Ridge to return home and tell his people that their only hope for survival as a nation was to abandon their homes and move beyond the Mississippi River.

The Treaty of New Echota and the Trail of Tears

With a promise of non-interference from Jackson, Georgia had a free hand in what was now solidly its northwestern territory. In late 1831, surveyors began partitioning Cherokee lands. Teams consisting of a surveyor, chain carrier, pack carrier, two axe men, and a cook roamed the hills and valleys of north Georgia for months preparing the region for the state's final land lottery.

Though most Georgians were intrigued by the prospect of a lottery in which they might literally win a gold mine, there was considerable opposition to the idea. Many believed it a terrible waste to distribute the state's wealth in such a wasteful fashion. In a vein of classic socialism, Governor George Gilmer himself argued that it would be more beneficial for the state to operate the mines. Through state management of the gold region, taxes could be lowered, improvements on roads and navigable rivers could be made, and revenue could be generated for public education. Said Gilmer, "Mines ... should be managed for the general and not the individual advantage."

This question was hotly debated in the gubernatorial campaign of 1831. Wilson Lumpkin, Gilmer's opponent, enthusiastically supported the lottery. Lumpkin cited as evidence for his position what he contemptuously referred to as the need for "a settled freehold population on every part of our territory ... hitherto the abode of a people wholly unqualified to enjoy the blessings of wise self-government."

By election time the voters of Georgia were, as the *Cherokee Phoenix* put it, "sick with the expectation of Indian land and gold." Wrote another disturbed Cherokee of Georgia's electorate: "This class is numerous, and all ignorant—they do not know anything about writs of error, the constitution of the United States, etc. They know they are poor and wish to be rich, and believe that, if they have luck, they will draw a gold mine, and most everyone expects to have his luck in the lottery." With the additional attraction of such estates as those of Major Ridge, John Ross, and David Vann, it is hardly surprising that the ethical questions of the lottery were given little attention. Said George Paschal, whose family had eleven chances in the lottery, "the immorality ... was so infinitesimally divided among seven hundred thousand people, that no one felt the crushing weight of responsibility." A popular song of the day summed up the general attitude.

> All I want in this creation,
> Is a pretty little wife and a big plantation,
> Away up yonder in the Cherokee nation.

The temptation proved too great for Georgians to overcome. By a slim majority, they sold their votes for a chance at Cherokee land and gold, and Wilson Lumpkin became the new governor.

By September 1832 the surveys were complete and all across Georgia people flocked to register for the lottery. In October the twin drums began to spin and names and tickets were drawn by the thousands in what Cherokees saw as state-sponsored theft of their land.

Cherokees were not the only ones to view the lottery as theft. Many white friends expressed similar disgust at Georgia's greed. Judge William H. Underwood, who had defended the Cherokees in cases brought before local courts in northern Georgia, continued to argue for Indian rights. On one occasion, the judge visited a Baptist preacher in Hall County whom he knew to be an honest and just man. This preacher was very influential in the community and Underwood felt that he might be of some help to the Cherokee cause. In their conversation, Underwood reviewed the long history of injustice inflicted on the Indians. From the initial atrocities of colonial times to Georgia's present attempt to expel the Cherokees, Underwood told of the misery suffered by the Indians at the hands of Europeans and their descendants. "And now," said Underwood in conclusion, "Parson, is not our State doing a grievous wrong, for which God will hold us and our children to fearful accounts?"

"Yes, Judge," replied the reverend, "it looks very much as you say."

"Looks!" said Underwood, "Looks!!" "But is it not so?"

"Yes!" responded the preacher, "I reckon it is as you say. But then, Judge," said this honest man of God, "we want the land!"

Underwood could only shake his head in reply and lament, "Yes, we want the land! Good God Almighty!"

The flood tide of whites entering the region following the lottery proved impossible to stop. Still, most Cherokees refused to leave. But by 1835 a small Cherokee faction led by Major Ridge and his son John was ready to give in. Together with *Cherokee Phoenix* editor Elias Boudinot and others, they signed the Treaty of New Echota in December. Under its terms, the Cherokees would receive $5 million, new lands in the West, and a hollow promise that those lands would never become part of another state or territory. During preliminaries to the signing, Major Ridge spoke of his reason for signing land over to the whites.

> I know the Indians have an older title than theirs. We obtained the land from the living God above. They got their title from the British. Yet they are strong and we are weak. We are few, they are many. We cannot remain here in safety and comfort. I know we love the graves of our fathers…. but an unbending, iron necessity tells us we must leave them. I would willingly die to preserve them, but any forcible effort to keep them will cost us our lands, our lives and the lives of our children. There is but one path to safety, one road to future existence as a Nation.

Despite Ridge's sincere intentions, the Treaty of New Echota was a fraud. No more than a few hundred Cherokees supported the treaty's terms. Neither was it authorized by Principal Chief John Ross nor the Cherokee National Council. "Our hearts are sickened, our utterance is paralyzed," said Ross, "when we reflect on the condition in which we are placed."

> The instrument in question is not the act of our Nation; we are not parties to its covenants; it has not received the sanction of our people. The makers of it sustain no office nor appointment in our Nation, under the designation of Chiefs, Head men or any other title, by which they hold, or could acquire, authority to assume the reins of Government, and to make bargain and sale of our rights, or possessions, and our common country. And we are constrained solemnly to declare; that we cannot… believe It to be the design of these honorable and high-minded individuals, who stand at the head of the Govt., to bind a

while Nation, by the acts of a few unauthorized individuals.

But the United States Senate ratified the treaty in early 1836, insisting that the entire Cherokee Nation move west within two years or be forced to do so; still they refused to leave.

In May 1838, General Winfield Scott arrived in the Cherokee Nation with five thousand troops and began rounding up the terrified natives like cattle. Years later, as one old Cherokee recalled:

Families at dinner were startled by the sudden gleam of bayonets in the doorway and rose up to be driven by blows and oaths along the weary miles of trail that led to the stockade. Men were seized in their fields or going along the road, women were taken from their [spinning] wheels and children from their play. In many cases, in turning for one last look as they crossed the ridge, they saw their homes in flames, fired by the lawless rabble that followed on the heels of the soldiers to loot and pillage.

By the autumn of that year, almost all the Cherokees had been rounded up and the long journey began toward Indian Territory. The forced migration lasted through the winter, which was one of the coldest on record. Of nearly sixteen thousand people who set out on the march, forever to be known as the Trail of Tears, roughly four thousand died along the way. Among them was John Ross's wife Quatie. She gave up her blanket to a sick child and contracted pneumonia. The child lived, but Quatie died and was buried near Little Rock, Arkansas.

For some, the emotional wounds they suffered that winter never healed. In later life one old Cherokee remembered how his father collapsed in the snow and died. He was buried by the trail and the family moved on. Then his mother sank down. "She speak no more," he recalled. "We bury her and go on." Finally his five brothers and sisters all became ill and died. "One each day, and all are gone." Even after the passage of decades, the old man could still hear the cries of his dying family. "People sometimes say I look like I never smile, never laugh in lifetime."

Chapter 4

Planters, Plain Folk, and the Enslaved

The Rise of King Cotton

The push for Indian Removal was driven not only by overt racism but also by the value of Indian land. What gave that land its value was the extent to which it could produce wealth, especially in the form of cotton, which was fast becoming Georgia's leading cash crop. By 1860, cotton was the number one export product for the entire United States, accounting for nearly half the total. Southern cotton output amounted to twice that of the rest of the world combined. Little wonder that the South was called the Cotton Kingdom.

The rise of King Cotton had been a relatively recent phenomenon. In 1791 the nation produced just 5,000 bales. Slaveholders devoted little of their labor force to cotton because it took too long to separate the seeds from the fibers by hand. Then came the cotton engine, commonly called the cotton gin, which did the job mechanically and much more quickly. Eli Whitney, a Connecticut man employed as a tutor on Catherine Greene's Georgia plantation, is usually credited with the cotton gin's invention. Though there were simpler versions of the cotton gin in use dating to as early as the fifth century in India, the gin Whitney patented in 1793, using a second cylinder to clean fibers off the first, was considerably more efficient.

There is some controversy over the origins of Whitney's gin. Whitney may have gotten the design, or at least the idea, from Catherine Greene. Or the idea may have come from conversations Whitney had with enslaved Africans on the Greene plantation. There is even some evidence that an Augusta mechanic named Hodgen Holmes had his own gin in the works at the same time Whitney was developing his. We do know that in 1796, Holmes patented an improved version that used saw teeth in place of Whitney's metal spikes on a rotating cylinder, making it easier for the cotton fibers to be removed by the second cylinder.

The gin's impact on cotton production was dramatic. By 1801 the nation's output was up to 100,000 bales. In 1833 it was ten times that amount at 1,099,500. And in 1859, production had ballooned to 5,868,000 bales. Georgia's yield was 780,750 bales that year, accounting for more than 15 percent of the US total. Only Alabama and Mississippi produced more cotton. That production reflected the good prices cotton growers were getting for their crop. Those prices encouraged producers to buy up as much good cotton land as they could, most of it in the Black Belt, a broad swath running from the Savannah River across central Georgia to the Chattahoochee and down into the state's southwest quadrant. What money did not go into land went mostly into slaves to work it.

Much less of Georgia's investment capital went toward industrialization, a trend reflected in the state's overwhelmingly rural population. In 1860 less than 10 percent of Georgia's people lived in towns of one thousand or more. Still, though Georgia had 3.4 percent of the nation's population that year, it produced just under one percent of value added by manufacturing. Georgia's industrial output totaled $17 million, about half the value of the

Holmes had   saw teeth, fast as gravel
Gin   steel wire, slow dumping

76

cotton crop, with most of that economic activity related to cotton in the form of ginning, pressing into bales, and textile manufacturing. Georgia led the South with thirty-three cotton textile factories employing 2,813 workers, 1,682 of them women. Virginia was a distant second with about half Georgia's textile workforce.

Savannah was Georgia's leading commercial and industrial center, with an 1860 population of just over twenty-two thousand. It manufactured goods worth almost $2 million annually and was Georgia's major port city. Augusta, Macon, and Columbus, all with about half Savannah's population, each produced more than $1 million worth of goods. Atlanta, with nearly ten thousand residents, produced about half that amount. But as a rapidly growing hub of rail transportation, Atlanta had one of the largest iron plants in the South, with a capacity to roll out 18,000 tons of rail a year.

Transportation, which was key to Georgia's cotton economy, initially centered on the state's rivers as much from necessity as convenience. The state's dirt roads, a few improved with wooden planks and all county maintained, were poorly kept. Some were impassable for much of the year. According to one account, Georgia's roadways were most often "indebted for their improvement to nothing but the wheels that run over them."

Though water transport was preferred, none of Georgia's rivers was navigable beyond the fall line shoals, where elevation changed rapidly. So the cities of Augusta, Macon, and Columbus, all located along the fall line, became major inland ports for steam-powered riverboats. Georgia's rivers were dangerous, and river pilots were always on the lookout for hidden boulders, sand bars, and downed trees. During dry spells when water levels were low, stranded boats were either dug out by hand or abandoned until there was enough water to float them again. Another danger was steam power itself. One of Georgia's worst riverboat accidents occurred on the Chattahoochee in 1840 when the *LeRoy*'s boiler exploded and engulfed the boat in flames. Within fifteen minutes it was little more than a pile of charred timbers. Such accidents were so common that insurance rates for river cargoes ran as high as 3 percent of the freight's value. By contrast, cargoes bound for any European port could be insured for half that rate.

High insurance rates and the dangers of navigation were major reasons that many cotton growers and merchants began to see railroads as a cheaper alternative, and construction began on several lines in the 1830s. The Panic of 1837 and resulting economic depression put so many Georgia banks out of business that capital was difficult to raise, but construction was going strong by the 1840s. By 1860 Georgia had 1,200 miles of track, mostly aimed at connecting the cotton lands of central and southwestern Georgia to the coastal ports of Savannah and Brunswick. There were lines linking Georgia to South Carolina, Tennessee, and Alabama as well.

Whether it was trade, manufacturing, or transportation, much of Georgia's economic activity was directly or indirectly driven by cotton. Towns depended on the plantations and served the needs of planters. Local cotton fed the cotton mills that were beginning to spring up in the state. Workers at train depots and river docks loaded cotton. Wagoners, steamer crews, and railroad workers hauled cotton. Carpenters and masons built cotton warehouses. Merchants and manufacturers sold their goods to the townspeople and to the plantations. Cotton brokers, for an average

2.5 percent commission, provided planters with access to the textile mills of the North and Europe.

The cotton market's stability in the 1850s made the dependence of so many people on cotton possible. Cotton prices remained relatively steady at ten to twelve cents a pound and were rising toward the end of the decade. By 1860 raw cotton brought twelve and a half cents a pound. With cotton leading the nation's exports, it is little wonder that so many planters thought of cotton as "king" and themselves as something of an aristocracy. One visitor to Georgia's cotton belt vividly described the planters' obsession with cotton: "People live in cotton houses and ride in cotton carriages. They buy cotton, sell cotton, think cotton, eat cotton, drink cotton, and dream cotton. They marry cotton wives, and unto them are born cotton children. In enumerating the charms of a fair widow, they begin by saying she makes so many bales of cotton." Cotton was, as this writer put it, "the great staple, sum and substance" of life for Georgia planters.

Planters and Plain Folk

Though cotton brought great wealth to Georgia, that wealth was concentrated in the hands of a very few. Only the planters traveled in "cotton carriages"—the ox cart was much more common. Horses and mules were usually too expensive for most people. Personal transportation was only one reflection of what had by 1860 become a rigid socioeconomic scale headed by planters, along with a few industrialists and financiers. At the bottom were poor whites and slaves.

Just over a third of Georgia whites were slaveholders. Planters, defined as those who owned twenty or more slaves, constituted a much smaller group. Ownership of at least twenty slaves was roughly the level at which a slaveholder could afford to hire an overseer to manage the plantation and its slave labor force. In 1860, in the South as a whole, planters and their families made up about 2.5 percent of the white population. That figure was slightly higher for Georgia at 3.2 percent, placing about 34,000 people in planter families. But planter holdings in land and slaves represented a much greater percentage of the state's wealth. There were 6,363 slaveholders who owned at least twenty slaves, putting planters at only 15.5 percent of the state's total slaveholders. Yet these few people held well over half of Georgia's slaves. Most planters, 5,049 of them, owned between 20 and 49 slaves; 1,102 held from 50 to 99. Only 212 planters owned more than 100 slaves. Of those, 181 owned from 100 to 199; 23 had between 200 and 299. Eight held between 300 and 500. The John Butler estate in McIntosh County headed the list at 505 slaves.

For sheer ostentation, big planters were hard to beat. The most affluent modeled themselves after the landed gentry of Britain. Many, like the Shacklefords of Early County, were renowned for the extravagance they displayed at every opportunity. One overnight guest at "The Pines," as the Shackleford plantation was called, arrived by horseback at dusk and was "ushered to a room where a body servant prepared his bath and laid out fresh linen. Downstairs, candles and an open fire illuminated a large room with French windows opening onto a veranda. There were comfortable chairs, tables for reading by lamplight, a secretary for writing, a piano piled high with music. A dinner table [was] laid with the finest silver, china and crystal." At "The Refuge" on the Flint River near Bainbridge, the Munnerlyns lived and entertained in similar high fashion at their "lovely mansion set in an English garden." Mrs. Munnerlyn was referred to by friends and family as "the Empress."

The vast majority of planters did not live in such lavish surroundings as the Shacklefords and Munnerlyns. Most lived not in opulent mansions but in eight- to ten-room homes made of clapboard planks, usually painted with whitewash. Some did not even reside on their plantations, preferring the comforts and conveniences of town life. Most were educated, but often lacked the social and cultural refinement so often associated in popular media with the planter class. The great majority, especially the smaller planters, viewed themselves mainly as businessmen whose wealth and status happened to confer upon them a degree of social prestige.

On the next rung down Georgia's social ladder stood a comfortably well-to-do class composed of prosperous slaveholding farmers owning between 5 and 19 slaves, together with a smattering of merchants and urban professionals. These slaveholders and their families totaled about 90,000 people, nearly a sixth of Georgia's white population of 591,550, or a little less than one-tenth the total of 1,057,248 by 1860 census figures. Their primary cash crop was cotton, but many also raised livestock and grew oats and corn for market. They lived in moderate homes of five or six rooms and were better fed, clothed, and usually better educated than the yeomen and poor whites.

Roughly 257,000 Georgia residents, nearly half the white population, comprised the state's yeoman class of small landholding farm families. Many of these folk, about 95,000, were members of small slaveholding households, owning fewer than five slaves. The other 162,000 belonged to families owning no slaves at all.

Yeomen generally lived in small two-to-four-room homes made of unpainted clapboard planks or squared, rough-hewn logs. Few had much formal education, and many were functionally illiterate. They usually grew some form of cash crop, but much of their acreage was devoted to subsistence farming. This was especially true for non-slaveholding yeomen. Many depended more on small herds of free roaming (or open range) livestock than produce, particularly in the mountains of northern Georgia and the pine barrens of Georgia's south-central and southeast regions. Whatever the family's economic focus, their main concern was having enough food on the table from day to day. For most non-slaveholding yeomen, cotton did not figure prominently in that effort. With few hands to work their land, cotton planting was a luxury they could not afford. It was unlikely that they ever would. There was only so much good farmland to go around, and by the 1840s most of it was already owned by planters and more affluent slaveholders. Land prices were so high that their chances of moving into the planter class or even reaching the ranks of the comfortably well off were not good, especially among lesser yeomen.

These lesser yeomen were sometimes only marginally better off than landless or near-landless poor whites, often called "white trash" by planters and more prosperous slaveholders. Poor whites made up close to a quarter of Georgia's white population. They included about 50,000 urban laborers and their families who one observer described as "in such a condition that, if temporarily thrown out of employment, great numbers of them are at once reduced to a state of destitution, and are dependent upon credit or charity for their daily food."

Just over 100,000 poor whites belonged to rural families of tenant farmers and sharecroppers who did not own enough land to support their families or owned no land at all. Some hired themselves out to landholders for meager wages. Others worked for a share of the crop. They lived mostly in plank or log structures with one or two rooms and plank or dirt floors. What vegetables they had were grown with their own hands in small gardens. What meat there was came from hunting or fishing. Illiteracy rates ran high among these people. Like most yeomen, few of Georgia's tenants and sharecroppers could ever hope to improve their condition.

Opportunities for upward mobility had been better only a generation before. Land prices earlier in the century had been relatively low as Indian land was becoming available. Wealthy men from increasingly crowded eastern Georgia bought much of the land, but small farmers had little trouble getting loans with which to purchase land and sometimes slaves. Cotton prices were on the rise, and there was every expectation that loans could be repaid. Farmers who had enough good land might even hope to become affluent slaveholders or even planters.

But a severe economic depression, the Panic of 1837, put an end to the hopes of thousands. Cotton prices fell dramatically and continued falling into the early 1840s. Aspiring yeomen found it impossible to keep up with loan payments. Their land and slaves were repossessed and sold at auction, usually to better-established slaveholders. Some farmers were able to keep a few acres and eked out a living as lesser yeomen. Many, however, lost everything and fell into tenancy and sharecropping. When the cotton market finally recovered in the 1840s, planters and the more affluent slaveholders held nearly all Georgia's better agricultural lands. By that time, most Georgia farmers found themselves trapped in a poverty from which few could ever escape.

The gap between rich and poor continued to grow through the 1850s not only in Georgia but throughout the South. Larger slaveholders bought up more and more land, forcing a rapid rise in land prices. This made it nearly impossible for smaller farmers to increase their holdings or for tenant farmers to buy any land at all. Wealth in terms of slaveholding was also becoming concentrated in fewer hands. During the 1850s, the proportion of slaveholders in the white population dropped by 20 percent. Georgia historian Numan Bartley noted that, "only the division of land and slaves of deceased planters among heirs prevented social mobility from being considerably more closed than it was."

By 1860 the wealthiest 5 percent of whites in the South owned 53 percent of the region's wealth. The bottom half owned only 1 percent. In Georgia's Early County alone, according to an antebellum resident, "there was a body of land east of Blakely … which made 216 square miles, and not one foot of it was owned by a poor man." Economic circumstances beyond their control were forcing so many yeomen into landless tenancy that the editor of one newspaper predicted the complete disappearance of small independent farmers from the South. By 1860 at least 25 percent of Southern farmers were tenants, and more were joining their landless ranks every day.

African Americans, Free and Enslaved

At the bottom of the social scale in a caste of their own, separate and distinct from the white class structure, were African Americans. Numbering 465,698, they made up nearly 45 percent of Georgia's population. Almost all were slaves. In the 1860 census, only 3,500 were listed as "free colored." Yet these people were not entirely free. They could not vote, testify against whites in court, or even hold property in their own names. Instead, the property of "free coloreds" was held by white people designated as their "guardians." To support the slaveholder argument that blacks could not take care of themselves, free blacks, even those who held no property, were required by state law to have white guardians.

Restrictions on blacks held as slaves were even tighter. In addition to those laws applying to free blacks, Georgia's slave code dictated that no slave could carry a gun, travel without a pass, or learn to read or write. Slave marriages had no legal standing, and slave gatherings, even for religious services, were forbidden without a white person present.

Such restrictions were born both of fear and a need for control. Despite slaveholder claims to the contrary, the "wise master," as historian Kenneth Stampp put it,

did not take seriously the belief that Negroes were natural-born slaves. He knew better. He knew that Negroes freshly imported from Africa had to be broken into bondage; that each succeeding generation had to be carefully trained. This was no easy task, for the bondsman rarely submitted willingly. Moreover, he rarely submitted completely. In most cases there was no end to the need for control—at least not until old age reduced the slave to a condition of helplessness.

Control of elderly slaves was hardly ever a concern in any case. Fewer than four in a hundred ever lived to see age sixty.

Slave resistance took a variety of forms ranging from work slowdowns to running away. Suicide was not unheard of. Some slaves were treated so badly that death was a welcomed relief. In

1856 a Cuthbert slave belonging to Lizzie McWilliams took her own life by swallowing strychnine. Sometimes slaves took their owners' lives as well. When the overseer on a Muscogee County plantation began beating a young slave girl with a sapling tree, one of the older slaves grabbed an axe and killed him.

More often slaves were on the receiving end of violence. They were defined as property both by slave-state courts and finally, in the Dred Scott case of 1857, by the United States Supreme Court. As personal property, slaves were subject to the absolute authority of their owners and to whatever controls they chose to employ. As one member of the Georgia Supreme Court said, "subordination can only be maintained by the right to give moderate correction—a right similar to that which exists in the father over his children." But that was little protection for slaves. The definition of "moderate correction" was left entirely to the owner. "Should death ensue by accident, while this slave is thus receiving moderate correction," recalled one observer, "the constitution of Georgia kindly denominates the offence justifiable homicide."

Because slaves had monetary value, death as a direct result of discipline was unusual. The objective of physical punishment was to inflict as much pain as possible without doing permanent damage. Scarring or mutilation might decrease the slave's resale value or ability to work. Owners or overseers frequently administered beatings in the "buck" or "rolling jim" positions. In each case the slave was stripped naked and bound tight. Rias Body, a former Harris County slave, remembered the buck as "making the Negro squat, running a stout stick under his bended knee, and then tying his hands firmly to the stick—between the knees. Then the lash was laid on his back parts."

Nat Turner - 1831

Another common method of punishment was to string slaves up by their thumbs with only their toes touching the ground and whip them. The slave might be "further tormented by having his wounds 'doctored' with salt and red pepper." Former slave Rhodus Walton of Stewart County belonged to an owner "whose favorite form of punishment was to take a man (or woman) to the edge of the plantation where a rail fence was located. His head was then placed between two rails so that escape was impossible and he was whipped until the overseer was exhausted. This was an almost daily occurrence, administered on the slightest provocation." After recalling the variety of tortures inflicted on slaves, one Columbus freedman told an interviewer in the 1930s, "Sir, you can never know what some slaves endured."

Little wonder that slaveholders lived in constant fear of slave rebellion. To mitigate that fear, they frequently hired poor whites to ride on slave patrols, designed to guard against the possibility of insurrection. Slaves found away from the owners' premises without written permission could be given up to twenty lashes or more on the spot.

Besides the constant threat of physical punishment, owners found that the most effective means of intimidating slaves was by threatening their families. Any slave might be pushed to the point of disregard for his or her own safety and attempt to fight back or escape. But when owners threatened to punish loved ones, slaves were more likely to hold their anger in check. Slave marriages were, therefore, encouraged even though they had no recognition in law. That would have established a state-sanctioned bond between members of the slave family, implicitly infringing on the "property" rights of the owner—specifically the right to deal with and dispose of his property as he saw fit.

To further stress their power, slaveholders used a variety of means to drive home the point that even within the slave family, the owner was still in control. Some personally presided over the marriage ceremony. Others, like Peter Heard in Troup County, did not even allow parents to name their own children. They reserved that privilege for themselves.

In naming the children of enslaved women, many owners were actually exercising their own parental rights. For a planter to have any number of mistresses among his slaves was not uncommon. Some slaveholders viewed rape as another method of enforcing psychological dominance. Others did it simply because they viewed slaves as property to be used at the owner's pleasure. Whatever the motive, slaves of light complexion were present on nearly every plantation. Fanny Kemble, the British wife of Georgia planter Pierce Butler, wrote that "Mr. [Butler], and many others, speak as if there were a natural repugnance in all whites to any alliance with the black race; and yet it is notorious that almost every Southern planter has a family more or less numerous of illegitimate colored children."

Some enslaved people used their light skin to good advantage. In 1833 the Columbus *Enquirer* ran an advertisement offering twenty dollars for the return of an escaped slave named Mabin. The paper described him as "a bright mulatto, with grey eyes— hair straight and sandy.... He will pass for a white man where he is not known." Ellen Craft, daughter of a slave mother and her white owner, also used her light complexion to escape. In December 1848, she and her husband William both escaped from slavery in Bibb County. With Ellen posing as a slaveholder and William as her slave, they boarded a train in Macon and headed for Savannah. Traveling several legs of their long and dangerous journey by steam ship and railroad, they reached freedom in Philadelphia on Christmas morning.

No matter how the children were sired, owners usually encouraged slave women to have as many as possible. More children, of course, meant more field hands, but they also gave the owner an effective tool of control. Not only did slaves fear punishment for family members, there was also the concern that they might be sold off at any time. As slaves well knew, an owner's threat to sell spouses or children was no idle one. One witness wrote that, "such separations as these are quite common, and appear to be no more thought of, by those who enforce them, than the separation of a calf from its brute parent."

A Georgia woman recalled slave traders driving groups of children to market "the same as they would a herd of cattle." Slaves constantly feared having their families put through such misery. They were also less likely to run away since that too would mean permanent separation from loved ones. Of the hundreds of thousands of slaves who did escape bondage in the early nineteenth century, most were young, unmarried, and childless.

The Solidification of Slavery

By the mid-nineteenth century, slavery was firmly established in Georgia and the South. But it had not always been so. The Presbyterians at Darien and the Lutherans at Ebenezer had argued against slavery. In the Western world generally, the eighteenth century was a time of rising arguments against slavery. The Scientific Revolution had shown that there were natural laws governing the physical world. Some reasoned that there were also natural laws governing human interaction. Perhaps people had natural rights. John Wesley, Anglican minister and a resident of colonial Savannah, was sure of it. "Liberty," he insisted, "is the right of every human creature ... and no human law can deprive him of that right which he derives from the law of nature."

Thomas Jefferson wrote in the Declaration of Independence, a document signed by three representatives from Georgia, that "life, liberty, and the pursuit of happiness" were "unalienable rights" endowed by the Creator. If true, was not slavery a violation of natural rights? The question troubled many slaveholders of Jefferson's generation, schooled as so many were in Enlightenment philosophy. Most were not willing to give up slavery, Jefferson included, but they did see it as an unnatural institution destined to end one day. Some, like George Washington, freed their slaves in their wills. Others freed their slaves long before their deaths. Georgia court records from the late eighteenth century are filled with manumission documents freeing hundreds of slaves.

Aside from the moral issues involved, many Americans of the Revolutionary era tended to view slavery as an economic dead end. The institution thrived only in the tobacco fields of the Chesapeake region and the rice country of coastal Carolina and Georgia. As the nation expanded, slavery would become proportionally less important to the nation's economy and would eventually die a natural death. But the cotton gin changed all that and became the vehicle by which slavery was carried westward across the Deep South. Not surprisingly, slaveholder attitudes changed with slavery's increasing profitability.

That change did not occur overnight. Antislavery sentiment in the South remained vigorous well into the nineteenth century. Several anti-slavery societies were active in the South, Georgia included. Robert Finley, president of the University of Georgia, was a founder of the American Colonization Society in 1816.

While some supported the society simply as a means of ridding the South of free blacks, many early members such as Finley had genuine anti-slavery motives. Even those who considered slavery at best a necessary evil were open about saying so. During debate on the Compromise of 1820, Congressman Robert Reid of Georgia, though he did not call for its immediate end, insisted that "slavery is an unnatural state; a dark cloud which obscures half the luster of our free institutions." The next year a leading state newspaper, the *Georgia Journal* of Milledgeville, wrote: "There is not a single editor in these States who dares advocate slavery as a principle."

But this was also the era of Indian Removal, which completed the transition in slaveholder attitudes begun a generation earlier by the cotton gin. Not only did they have the technology and labor force with which to make cotton king, they now had the land on which to do it. Slaveholders began to view slavery not as a temporary evil but as a positive good for both slaveholder and slave. Attitudes of the Founding Fathers toward slavery, they now argued, were erroneous. Benjamin Hill, one of Georgia's leading planter-politicians, wrote that "in our early history the Southern statesmen were antislavery in feeling ...Washington, Jefferson, Madison, Randolph, and many of that day who never studied the argument of the cotton gin, nor heard the eloquent productions of the great Mississippi Valley. Now our people not only see the justice of slavery, but its providence too."

But the slaveholders' new position presented them with a difficulty. Just a quarter of Southern whites owned slaves. Outside the southern United States chattel slavery survived only in Brazil, Cuba, Puerto Rico, Dutch Guiana, and parts of Africa. How were they to guarantee the survival of slavery in a society where most voters did not own slaves and in a world where slaveholders were a dying breed?

In the 1830s slaveholders launched a campaign designed to educate their fellow Southerners, and the world, on the virtues of slavery. In the first place the world could not do without Southern cotton. Textile mills in Britain and the North depended too much upon it. Benjamin Hill insisted that, "the world can never give up slavery until it is ready to give up clothing." Besides, slaveholders argued, people of African descent were content in slavery because it was, as Georgia planter-politician Alexander H. Stephens put it, their "natural and normal condition." Dr. Samuel A. Cartwright of New Orleans claimed that their supposed child-like state of mind was due to a disease he called *dysesthesia*, which Cartwright defined as "defective atmospherization of the blood conjoined with a deficiency of cerebral matter in the cranium." If slaves were content in slavery, why then did so many try to escape? Cartwright had an answer for that too—*drapetomania*, or simply an insane urge to run away.

There was also the Biblical defense. How could slavery be an evil institution when the patriarchs of the Old Testament had owned slaves? Was not slavery the result of Noah's curse on his younger son Ham and all his descendents, since dark complexion was assumed to be a result of the curse? Georgian Patrick Hues Mell, later president of the Southern Baptist Convention, stressed that point in an 1844 work entitled *Slavery. A Treatise, Showing that Slavery is Neither a Moral, Political, nor Social Evil.* "From Ham were descended the nations ... that now constitute the African or negro race. Their inheritance, according to prophecy, has and will *continue to be* slavery." Mell took it literally as gospel that "God, by the mouth of Noah ... instituted slavery ... it cannot be an immorality."

Mell's fellow Georgian, Augustus Baldwin Longstreet—a prominent apologist for slavery among Southern Methodists—agreed with Mell's conclusion. In 1845 Longstreet authored a leading pro-slavery tract, *Letters on the Epistle of Paul to Philemon: Or, the Connection of Apostolical Christianity with Slavery*. The Apostle Paul's instruction that servants should be obedient to their masters made clear that, in Longstreet's view, "there is no sin in holding slaves" and that "there is no *moral evil* in slavery." For those whose conscience might be bothered by slavery, Samuel Cassels of Georgia gave them comfort in an 1853 issue of the *Southern Presbyterian Review*: "God is our only true moral governor.... Our subjection, then, is not to be a subjection of conscience.... but a subjection to God." For Cassels, God clearly condoned slavery.

Throughout the South, clergymen emerged as some of the most eager and influential allies of slaveholders in defending slavery. Those ministers who held that scripture must be taken literally had been for some time disturbed by a strong opposing trend in Christianity. Science had shown that the Bible contained many factual errors and omissions. By the eighteenth century, influential clergymen and laity began to argue that the Bible must be understood symbolically, not literally. But if the Bible was to be interpreted symbolically, what might that mean for its treatment of slavery? Was that to be taken symbolically as well? Could Paul have been using the relationship of servant to master as a metaphor for the relationship of humanity to God? No, such symbolism would not do. If the scriptures were to be used effectively as a moral defense of slavery, they must be taken literally, and not just in part but in whole. As the slaveholding South in the early

LeConte Brothers

nineteenth century changed its attitude toward slavery's morality, it became increasingly tied to a literalist view of the Bible.

Perhaps the most effective tactic adopted by slaveholders was their encouragement of racist fears. By playing on such fears, slavery's defenders hoped to make all whites feel they had a stake in preserving the slave system whether they owned slaves or not. Poor whites were encouraged to think of what slavery's end might mean for them. No longer would they be in a position of social superiority to blacks, or anyone else for that matter. A writer in the *Columbus Times* stated the case clearly: "It is African slavery that makes every white man in some sense a lord.... Here the division is between white free men and black slaves, and every white is, and feels that he is a MAN." A correspondent of the *Southern Recorder* in Milledgeville agreed. It was slavery that gave "dignity to the poor man of the South." Without slavery, the rights guaranteed to whites would have to be shared with blacks, including perhaps even the right to vote.

Class and Political Culture

Though all adult white males could vote, and most did, there was little for them to decide in a general sense. Then, as now, any successful bid for high political office depended as much on wealth as votes, and planters held most of the wealth. In Southern state politics, both major parties, Whig and Democrat, centered as much on personalities as issues, and both represented slaveholding interests. Whigs tended to attract larger slaveholders whose wealth and wider investments gave them broader national concerns. Smaller slaveholders generally dominated the Democratic Party, which often differed with the Whigs on issue such as banking, infrastructure, and how best to use state revenues. But party leaders were united when it came to slavery. Promoting racist fear—that traditional staple of Georgia politics—was always a central campaign objective.

The influence of slaveholder wealth in politics was not lost on plain folk. As one farmer observed, the slaveholder, or slaveholder-backed candidate, "used money whenever he could. This fact usually elected him." The effect was easy to see. In the Georgia General Assembly's 1849–50 session, though only about one-third of voters owned slaves, 80 percent of senators and representatives were slaveholders. More than half owned at least ten slaves.

Legislative apportionment had much to do with slaveholder dominance in the Assembly. Each county elected one state senator and up to four House representatives depending on population, but blacks, who could not vote, were counted as three-fifths of a person in awarding state House representation, meaning that voters in high slaveholding counties carried much greater weight in the Assembly. For example, in 1840 coastal Glynn County and upcountry Campbell County (later part of Douglas and Fulton counties) had roughly the same total population and two representatives each. But Glynn's population was only 17 percent white while Campbell's was 84 percent white. The result was that Glynn's roughly 250 eligible voters had the same representation in the Assembly as Campbell's approximately 850.

The poll tax gave slaveholders an edge as well. Though the poll tax might keep poor men from voting, it could also be used as a tool of political control. Landless whites and even yeomen who depended on larger landholders either for credit or employment or both could usually be counted on for political support, sometimes with the big landholder paying their poll tax. It was also common for wealthy slaveholders to hold expensive barbeques at election time, when good food and fine liquor proved politically influential. A similar scheme operated in urban centers. In Columbus a practice known as "penning" was frequently used. Campaign workers would round up men off the streets, get them drunk, and then march them to the polls. The party with the largest "pen" usually won. In his extensive study of antebellum Georgia's political culture, Donald DeBats concluded that, "far from encouraging citizen participation in the party system, the leaders of both parties discouraged grassroots politics.... Beyond the simple casting of a ballot, the role of the citizen in the party system was passive by design."

Slaveholder control of Southern state politics was near absolute. One Southerner observed that although the majority of those eligible to vote owned no slaves, "they have never yet had any part or lot in framing the laws under which they live. There is no legislation except for the benefit of slavery and slaveholders." While it is true that some non-slaveholders held high public office, they were nearly always backed, directly or indirectly, by slaveholders. Some even married into planter families. During the 1850s, though the proportion of slaveholders in the general population was falling, their numbers in Southern state legislatures were on the rise. It seemed that slaveholder dominance of the South was secure and that slavery as an institution was secure as well. But even as slaveholders consolidated their political control, cracks began to appear at the base of the South's social pyramid. As wealth became concentrated in fewer hands and opportunities for economic advancement were increasingly closed to plain folk, those cracks began to grow.

Antislavery sentiment never completely died in the South despite efforts to wipe it out. Some continued to view slavery as a moral evil, while others opposed it on economic grounds. Still others opposed slavery simply because they were too poor ever to own slaves. One source of unease was the attitude of many slaveholders toward plain folk. As one farmer put it: "Slaveholders always acted as if they were of a better class and there was always an unpleasant feeling between slaveholders and those working themselves." In a private letter to a friend, one planter wrote of poor whites: "Not one in ten is ... superior to a negro."

Most planters tried to keep such opinions concealed lest their hypocrisy be exposed. Occasionally, though, suggestions of planter arrogance slipped into print. In his 1854 defense of slavery, *Sociology for the South, or The Failure of Free Society*, George Fitzhugh not only insisted that slavery was "the best form of society yet devised for the masses" but also "that slavery, *black or white*, was right and necessary." Could white slavery result should the slave system continue to grow? Some were beginning to think it might.

Whatever the reason, discomfort with the slave regime was on the rise among non-slaveholding whites in the late antebellum era. Some were even willing to speak out or take action. In 1849 a Georgia carpenter openly declared his opposition to slavery. Competition with slave labor, he believed, kept his wages low. In 1859 one poor Hancock County laborer confided to an acquaintance that if it came to a war over slavery, he was going to "black himself" and fight to end it. Without slavery, perhaps he could get better wages. That same year, a farmer in Taliaferro County was convicted of hiding a runaway slave for three months. William Allen of Troup County wrote fake passes for slaves. So did another white man in Greene County, who also taught slaves "to write and cipher."

The most outspoken Southern opponent of slavery was Hinton Rowan Helper. Born the son of a yeoman farmer in North Carolina, Helper wrote what one historian has called "the most important single book, in terms of its political impact, that has ever been published in the United States." In *The Impending Crisis of the South*, published in 1857, Helper argued vigorously that the "lords of the lash are not only absolute masters of the blacks ... but they are also the oracles and arbiters of all non-slaveholding whites, whose freedom is merely nominal, and whose unparalleled illiteracy and degradation is purposely and fiendishly perpetuated." Slavery, Helper pointed out, benefited few except slaveholders. Its very existence, funneling investment capital not into industrial development but into purchasing more land and slaves, kept most white Southerners in poverty. Slavery made the South little more than a colony of the North, providing raw materials and buying back manufactured goods.

Helper was hardly alone in pointing out the economic drawbacks of slavery. A British traveler named James Stirling, who passed through Georgia in the 1850s, wondered why the Southern states were lagging behind in "development and prosperity." He could find only one answer—slavery. "When Southern statesmen count up the gains of slavery," warned Stirling, "let them not forget also to count its cost. They may depend upon it, there is a heavy 'per contra' to the profits of niggerdom." Many Georgians, too, recognized slavery's retarding influence, though few spoke of it openly. One who did was Roswell King, Jr., for nineteen years an overseer on the Butler plantations near Darien. He confided to Pierce Butler's wife Fanny: "I hate slavery with all my heart; I consider it an absolute curse wherever it exists. It will keep those states where it does exist fifty years behind the others in improvement and prosperity."

Not only did slavery hinder economic growth, but the concentration of cotton and tobacco grown on the South's most productive lands forced it to import foodstuffs. Georgia's comptroller-general lamented in the late 1850s that, with regard to food, the state was "every day becoming more dependent upon those 'not of us.'" The state's livestock production was declining. The corn crop was stagnant. In just ten years the oat crop had dropped by almost three-fourths, a decline not offset by a two-fold increase in the state's relatively meager wheat production. One newspaper editor complained about huge shipments of high-priced foodstuffs from the Midwest coming up the Chattahoochee River. He blamed planters who, more concerned with cotton, preferred to import food rather than grow it. Other Georgia editors urged planters to grow more corn and less cotton. Such pleas accomplished little. By 1860 Georgia was importing around half a million bushels of corn annually.

Rising discontent within the Cotton Kingdom, of little concern to the planters only a decade earlier, was by the 1850s causing panic among many of them. One planter asked, "If the poor whites realized that slavery kept them poor, would they not vote it down?" Many were beginning to suspect it. How could support for slavery be maintained among plain folk if they owned no slaves and had no prospects of ever owning any? Some suggested state laws mandating that each white family be given at least one slave. Others recommended a slave for every white person. One editor suggested re-opening the slave trade from Africa, with or without the approval of Congress, to bring the price of slaves down.

Those who took a larger view realized that the problem was not just the expense of slaves but the lack of land as well. There was only so much good farmland to go around, and the more affluent slaveholders already had most of it. Such people saw the future security of slavery in terms of territorial expansion. To them it was clear—slavery must expand or die. The issue of slavery's expansion into the western territories would dominate national politics for more than a decade and finally lead to the Civil War.

Chapter 5

Secession and Civil War

Slavery's Expansion and the Georgia Platform

The issue of slavery's expansion, though pressed with new urgency by slaveholders, was not new. It was older than the nation itself. Shortly after Georgia's founding in 1732, the Trustees excluded a number of evils from their colony—among them hard liquor, lawyers, and slavery. But they did not remain outlawed for long as there was too much money to be made. Pressure in favor of slavery from Savannah merchants and South Carolina rice planters was constant, and slaves were smuggled into the colony in spite of the Trustees. They finally lifted the ban in 1750, and within twenty years nearly half of Georgia's people were enslaved.

At the same time, slavery as a viable economic institution was dying in the North. But in the South, the cotton gin gave slavery an economic vitality that grew in strength with each new slave state added to the Union. Congress reached a temporary settlement in 1820 with the Missouri Compromise. Missouri was admitted to the Union as a slave state and Maine as a free state, thus preserving the balance of free and slave states in the Senate. More significantly, a line extending from the southern border of Missouri to the Rocky Mountains (then the western boundary of the United States) established a line between slavery and freedom. All future states created north of the line would be free. Those south of the line would be slave.

When the United States took the upper half of Mexico in 1848, slavery was again thrust onto the nation's political stage.

Mexico had abolished slavery two decades earlier. Would it now be reintroduced in the new US territories? Many, like Alexander Stephens, who as a Whig Congressman from Georgia had opposed war with Mexico, hoped the divisive issue of slavery could be avoided. But in 1849 California requested admission to the Union as a free state and Congress was forced to act. The next year California entered the Union under the Compromise of 1850, giving the free states a two-seat advantage in the Senate. As compensation, slaveholders got a fugitive slave law mandating the return of slaves who escaped to the North. As for the remaining territories of the Mexican Cession, "popular sovereignty" would prevail. Voters in both the New Mexico and Utah territories would make the decision on slavery themselves.

Reaction to the Compromise of 1850 in politically active circles was mixed throughout the South. Slaveholders liked the fugitive slave law but were concerned that a loss of parity in the Senate would relegate them to second-class status in national politics. Using their opposition to the Compromise of 1850 as a pretext, pro-secessionists organized movements in Mississippi, Alabama, Georgia, and South Carolina. In all but South Carolina, Unionists quickly organized to oppose them. Georgia held a popular vote for delegates to a convention to consider the state's future in the Union, a vote that supporters of the Compromise won by a 46,000 to 24,000 margin. Even most of those who opposed the Compromise still supported keeping Georgia in the Union. Of the 264 delegates, 240 were Unionists.

When the delegates met in December 1850, all but 19 voted to accept the Compromise. Still, they warned that slavery took priority over the Union. In what came to be called the Georgia Platform, the convention declared Georgia ready to secede if Congress restricted the domestic slave trade, refused to admit new slave states to the Union, or interfered with slavery in the territories. Furthermore, the convention insisted that the Union's preservation depended on "the faithful execution of the Fugitive Slave Bill." Alabama and Mississippi supported the Georgia Platform, and newspapers across the country credited it with having saved the Union. But given its preeminence of slavery over the Union, the ambiguities of popular sovereignty, and the ambivalence of Northern law enforcement toward taking time to hunt down fugitive slaves, the Georgia Platform was a sure formula for the Union's impending collapse.

Popular sovereignty's inherent complications became clear soon after Congress passed the Kansas-Nebraska Act in 1854. In exchange for Southern congressional votes favoring organization of these territories through which Northerners hoped to build the first transcontinental railroad, both the Nebraska and Kansas territories were opened to the possibility of slavery under popular sovereignty. It seemed to most Northern Congressmen a small price to pay. They were certain there was no real danger of Kansas or Nebraska becoming slave states since their geography was not suitable for large-scale cotton or tobacco production. But Kansas was just west of Missouri, a slave state, and Northerners feared the consequences. Even so, few white Northerners called themselves abolitionists. Most were by no means opposed to slavery where it existed since it kept most African Americans confined to the South. Racism played a large role in forming Northern white attitudes, as did economic fears. Laborers worried that freedom for slaves would enable them to migrate north and compete for already low-paying jobs. Northern industrialists and financiers worried that the end of slavery would mean the end of cheap Southern cotton, which fueled textile manufacturing, the North's leading industry. What most Northerners opposed, and all they opposed, was slavery's extension into the western territories, land they wanted for themselves.

In the wake of Kansas-Nebraska, most Northern Whigs and many Democrats joined with Free Soilers and a smattering of abolitionists to form the Republican Party, dedicated to free land and free states in the West. They ran their first presidential candidate in 1856, John C. Fremont, calling for "free men, free land, and Fremont!" Ironically Fremont was a Southerner, born in Savannah and raised in Charleston, who as a young man had joined the army and made a name for himself as military governor of California and one of the state's first two senators. Fear of Fremont's anti-slavery leanings led Southern Whigs to join with Democrats, or with the short-lived nativist American or "Know Nothing" Party, to keep Fremont out of the White House. Pennsylvania Democrat James Buchanan, who was no threat to slavery's expansion, won the election.

Still, the Kansas question remained unsettled. Free Soil activists rushed to get settlers into Kansas. Proslavery men did the same. Few slaveholders themselves made the move, but they did finance proslavery expeditions of Southern poor whites to Kansas, providing them with wagons, horses, oxen, and, most importantly, land. The controversy turned violent when a proslavery raid on the town of Lawrence left one man dead. An antislavery band led by John Brown, later of Harpers Ferry fame, retaliated by killing five proslavery men along Pottawatomie Creek. By the end of 1856, more than two hundred settlers on both sides were dead.

The Supreme Court tried to settle the issue in 1857 with the Dred Scott case, calling enslaved blacks property that could be taken anywhere in the United States, including the territories. This decision pushed most Northerners into the Republican camp, practically ensuring that the next president would be a

Republican. Fearing the result, leading Southern secessionists, called Fire-Eaters for their extremist rhetoric, tried to build support for their cause by labeling all Northerners, Republicans in particular, abolitionists bent on fomenting slave rebellion. The Fire-Eaters got a boost in October 1859 when John Brown led an attempt to seize the federal arsenal at Harpers Ferry, Virginia, and arm the state's slaves. His effort failed, and a state court sentenced Brown to hang for treason. But Fire-Eaters now had an incident they could use to portray Northerners as abolition-supporting, rebellion-promoting, "Black Republicans."

Fire-eating Georgia papers carrying news of Harpers Ferry wrote that the raiders were blacks organized and led by "blatant 'freedom shriekers.'" Some warned that it was the start of a general slave uprising designed "for the extermination of the southern whites." Several fires in November 1859 were blamed on rebellious blacks and secreted abolitionists. One fire destroyed an estimated six thousand dollars worth of corn, fodder, and cotton on a Muscogee County plantation. Another swept through a gin house two miles from Columbus, taking more than two dozen cotton bales with it. One Columbus editor called it "Kansas work in Georgia."

The Crisis of Secession

This volatile atmosphere of panic and paranoia formed the backdrop of the presidential campaign in 1860. The Democrats split over slavery in the territories, with Northerners holding to popular sovereignty and Southerners clinging to the Dred Scott decision. Most Southern delegates left the convention and formed their own party, the Southern Rights Party, nominating John Breckinridge of Kentucky. Democrats nominated Stephen Douglas of Illinois, who selected former Georgia governor Herschel V. Johnson as his vice-presidential running mate.

Southern Whigs who refused to join the Southern Rights Party formed their own Constitutional Union Party, stressing their adherence to the Union, and nominated John Bell of Tennessee. Republicans, united on everything but a candidate, finally settled on a dark horse from Illinois named Abraham Lincoln. As nearly everyone expected, Lincoln carried the November election. In Georgia, Breckinridge polled slightly more than Bell, with Douglas running a distant third despite the efforts of Herschel V. Johnson and his old friend Alexander H. Stephens, an active supporter of the Douglas/Johnson ticket. Lincoln's name was not even on the ballot.

Nevertheless, Lincoln had strong support in Georgia and the South, albeit mostly among an enslaved people who could not vote. They attended so many public campaign rallies in Georgia that some whites became alarmed by their "unusual interest in politics, and the result of the Presidential election." What blacks repeatedly heard from Southern Rights men was that Lincoln, despite his repeated promises to the contrary, intended to invade the South and free the slaves. Some slaves apparently tried to start the war themselves. At 2:30 a.m. on the night before the election, much of Fort Gaines was consumed by fire. Not long after town residents brought the flames under control, two blacks were shot in the act of trying to re-start the blaze. It was but one example of the increasing resistance slaveholders would face with expectations for freedom running so high among their slaves.

With Lincoln poised to enter the White House, secessionists pushed hard for disunion. Most slaveholders would now almost certainly support such a move. If lesser yeomen and poor whites could be made to see Lincoln as a John Brown writ large, they too might support withdrawal from the Union. Secessionist leaders had to act quickly before Lincoln took office the next March or they might never have another chance.

Less than two weeks after Lincoln's election, the General Assembly passed, and Governor Joseph E. Brown signed, a bill calling for the election of two delegates from each county to a secession convention. Though the slaveholder-dominated Assembly had forced the question, it was hardly united behind secession. In what one contemporary called "a large meeting of the Members of the General Assembly" at the Georgia capitol, twenty-two men were appointed to draft a resolution urging Georgia voters not to support secessionists in the upcoming election. Secession would, they insisted, lead to "nothing but divisions among our people, confusion among the slaveholding States, strife around our firesides, and ultimate defeat to every movement for the effective redress of our grievances."

Benjamin Harvey Hill, a member of the committee, reminded Georgians that Lincoln was no threat to slavery where it existed. Lincoln himself had repeatedly made that point during the campaign. "The wisest policy," Hill maintained, "is to demand the unconditional observance of the Constitution." Hill knew that Southerners were divided on secession, and that a divided South could not survive a civil war. The Southern government would fall and slavery with it.

Alexander H. Stephens, ironically soon-to-be vice president of the Confederacy, agreed with Hill, saying: "The election of no man, constitutionally chosen to that high office, is sufficient cause to justify any state to separate from the Union…. to withdraw from it because any man has been elected, would put us in the wrong." Prophetically, Stephens also predicted an inner civil war among Southerners themselves. "The movement will before it ends I fear be beyond the control of those who started it," and Southerners would "at no distant day commence cutting one another's throats."

Secessionist leaders brushed such fears aside and urged voters to fear Lincoln instead. Though he knew better, Governor Brown repeated the secessionist drumbeat that Lincoln intended to free the slaves, and he encouraged plain folk to believe that both their pocket book and their pride would suffer for it. Blacks would, in Brown's words, "come into competition with [plain folk], associate with them and their children as equals—be allowed to testify in court against them—sit on juries with them, march to the ballot box by their sides, and participate in the choice of their rulers— claim social equality with them—and ask the hands of their children in marriage." Men like Brown hoped that playing on racist fears would swing the popular vote their way.

Robert Toombs, a leading secessionist, expressed his determination to see Georgia out of the Union regardless of the popular will. "We demand at your hands the sword," Toombs blustered. "If you will not give it to us, we will take it." Responding to Toombs's threat, an anti-secessionist editor in west Georgia's Upson County wrote, "Let him take it, and, by way of doing his country a great service, let him run about six inches of it into his left breast."

Among Georgians at large, it was clear that immediate secession was not a forgone conclusion. Those who opposed it, calling themselves Cooperationists, held rallies throughout the state urging restraint among their fellow Georgians. Citizens at a "large meeting" in Crawfordville resolved that "we do not consider the election of Lincoln ... as sufficient cause for Disunion or Secession." A mass meeting in Walker County expressed the same sentiment: "We are not of the opinion that the election of any man in accordance with the prescribed forms of the Constitution is sufficient cause to disrupt the ties which bind us to the Union." Rallies in Fayette, Gordon, Chattooga, Talbot, Meriwether and other Georgia counties declared the same.

Harris County's local newspaper editor firmly stated that "we are a Union loving people here, and will never forsake the old 'Star Spangled Banner.'" To stress his point, he printed the names of 175 local men, all pledging themselves to "preserve the honor and rights of the South *in the Union*." In Stewart County a similarly "large number of citizens" attended an anti-secession meeting. Union sentiment was so strong in neighboring Randolph County that secessionists were sure the tide was turning against them. In a letter to Howell Cobb, one of the state's leading secessionists, they asked, "Where are all our speakers? We have done what little we can here but there is great need for missionaries [of secession] in every part of the State." They urged Cobb to take a short tour through southwest Georgia to bolster the secession cause. By late December, it appeared that anti-secessionists might win the day. "All the masses of the people," wrote one Georgian from Milledgeville, "are for the Union."

The day balloting took place, 2 January 1861, was cold and stormy, making it difficult for poorer folk in isolated areas to get to the polls. Alexander Stephens estimated that the foul weather cost anti-secessionists at least 10,000 votes. Still the vote was very close. Historian Michael Johnson, whose detailed study of secession in Georgia remains the standard, concluded that opponents of immediate secession won the vote by a likely majority of 42,744 to 41,717.

When the secession convention met in Milledgeville, delegate Eugenius A. Nisbit proposed a pro-secession resolution to gauge the feeling of the delegates. Enough delegates who had been elected on a promise to vote against secession were enticed by the promise of a slaveholder republic to pass the resolution by a 166-to-130 vote. The next day, with more delegates switching sides in an attempted show of unity, the convention approved an ordinance of secession by a vote of 208 to 89. Even Benjamin Hill and Alexander Stephens finally voted for secession. The remaining anti-secession delegates urged that the ordinance be presented to Georgia's voters for ratification. Fearing the outcome of such a move, secessionists refused, and Georgia left the Union without submitting the ordinance to a direct popular vote.

News of secession touched off wild celebrations across Georgia and the South among supporters of disunion. But not everyone saw secession as a cause for celebration. As bells rang out in Milledgeville during the secession "jubilee," Judge Garnett Andrews, a long time Union man, said of the merrymakers: "Poor fools, they may ring their bells now, but they will wring their hands—yes, and their hearts, too, before they are done with it."

In February Georgia representatives, along with others from the Deep South, met in Montgomery, Alabama, to form the Confederate States of America. Two months later, on 12 April 1861, Confederate artillery opened fire on Fort Sumter in Charleston harbor, setting off the bloodiest conflict in American history.

Conscription and Cotton in a Rich Man's War

In the wake of Lincoln's subsequent call for volunteers to put down the rebellion, four of the remaining eight slave states left the Union. Confederate President Jefferson Davis called for volunteers as well, and so many men responded that the Confederacy could not arm them all. Georgia alone furnished more than eighteen thousand volunteers by May, second only to Virginia. The War Department quickly developed manufacturing facilities to address its lack of munitions, and Georgia was central to that effort. Iron was produced in Macon, arms in Columbus, and gunpowder in Augusta. Atlanta became a central rail hub for the distribution of military supplies. So well did the Confederacy arm itself that its forces never lost a major battle for lack of munitions.

Despite the mass volunteering, there were early signs that support for the war, and for the Confederacy itself, might not last. Some Georgians continued to support the Union openly. Anti-secessionists led by Harrison Riley threatened to seize the US mint in Dahlonega and hold it for the Union. Officials in Pickens County flew the US flag over the courthouse for weeks after secession. Private citizens did the same. Randolph Mott of Columbus kept the Stars and Stripes flying from the cupola of his home. Some accorded it the recognition of being the only place in Georgia that had never left the Union.

Expressing popular sentiment in Walker and Dade counties, James Aiken wrote to Governor Brown in February 1861 insisting that he and his neighbors would never submit to the secession convention's decision. It had taken Georgia out of the Union not for the good of its citizens, but for "those that owns lands and Negroes!" He begged the governor to allow Georgia voters to decide the issue directly, promising to abide by the outcome. But if Brown refused, there were 2,500 volunteers prepared to defend northwest Georgia's right to secede from the state and rejoin the Union. "If we cannot get it one way," he warned, "we know how we can get it at the point of the bayonet and the muzzle of the musket. We are just as willing as you ever seen mountain boys."

From Fannin County came word that "quite a number" there were prepared to defend the old flag and help "whip Georgia and the South back into the Union." The correspondent left no doubt what lay behind Fannin men's Unionism: "They are not interested in the nigger question." "This fuss," they believed, "was all for the benefit of the wealthy."

People across the South expressed doubts about the legitimacy of secession, so much so that an Augusta newspaper editor warned: "The greatest danger to the new Confederacy arises not from without, not from the North, but from our own people." Governor Brown so feared an anti-secession backlash that he did not announce the results of Georgia's vote for convention delegates until late April. Even then he gave false figures. Brown insisted that the secessionists had won by more than thirteen thousand votes when in fact they were likely defeated by a margin of just over a thousand.

With the Confederacy established, many Southerners were more concerned with how the war might affect the South in general, and themselves in particular, if it did not end quickly. The consequences of an extended conflict were evident enough to those on the front lines. When soldiers of the 15th Alabama Regiment, many of whom were from southwest Georgia, arrived in Virginia and visited Manassas a few weeks after the war's first major battle, they found hundreds of shallow graves scattered over the field. Skeletal remains protruded from the ground, and hogs were feeding on the dead. Some began to reexamine their motives for volunteering. Joel Crawford of Quitman County wrote to Governor Brown's office wanting to know "if after the signing of a written instrument binding the signer to go to the present war, if any signer thereof has the legal right to withdraw his name."

With or without permission, hundreds of men were leaving the ranks in late 1861, mostly on the pretext of helping their families with the fall harvest. There were few volunteers to take their places. In October word came from Greene County to the governor's office that "our people don't seem to be inclined to offer their services." That same month, Captain Edward Croft of the Columbus Artillery reported that it was almost impossible to find volunteers. In February 1862, W.H. Byrd of Augusta wrote to Governor Brown that he had been trying for two weeks to raise a company in what he called "this 'Yankee City,' but I regret to say every effort has failed." That failure did not result from a lack of potential recruits. The Augusta *Chronicle and Sentinel* noted a week earlier that "one who walks Broad street and sees the number of young men, would come to the conclusion that no war ... was now waging." Willing or not, as far as the government was concerned, more men had to come.

In April 1862, the Confederate Congress passed its first Enrollment Act giving Davis authority to force young men into the military with or without their consent. Under the terms of this act, commonly known as conscription or the draft, white males between the ages of eighteen and thirty-five became subject to involuntary military service. As an inducement to enlist before the draft went into effect, the government offered a $50 cash bonus to those who volunteered and allowed them to serve with units of their choice. Fearing that they would be drafted anyway, hundreds of reluctant men volunteered in March and early April. One was John Joseph Kirkland of Early County. A small farmer who owned no slaves, Kirkland had a wife and five children when he enlisted with the Early Volunteers. He was just short of thirty-three years old. Little more than a year later he lost a leg, and nearly his life, at the Battle of Chancellorsville.

Conscription was a controversial issue, even among Confederate officials. Alexander Stephens opposed it, citing states' rights principles. So did Governor Brown, though Georgia's Supreme Court upheld the draft's constitutionality. Because Jefferson Davis never called the Confederate Supreme Court into session, the question was never resolved. Bickering over state-versus-central authority regarding conscription and other issues continued for the rest of the war.

Among plain folk, the most offensive provisions of the draft were those allowing wealthy men to avoid service. Those with enough money could hire a substitute or pay an exemption fee. Few but the most affluent could afford either option. And then there was the infamous twenty-slave law, which exempted one white man of draft age for every twenty slaves owned. This meant that any planter could be excused from the draft. Though few seemed to realize it at the time, this law would come to define the war for the great mass of Southern plain folk. From 1862 until the conflict's end, it was for them a rich man's war.

When one Georgia farmer was drafted, he complained bitterly to a neighbor: "They've got me in this war at last. I didn't want to have any thing to do with it any how. I didn't vote for Secession— but them are the ones who have to go & fight now—and those who were so fast for war stay out." Planters justified being excused from the draft by pointing out that soldiers would need food and so would their families back home. Who better to provide that food than the planters? They had the best land on which to grow food and the slave labor force to produce it. Many planters agreed to what were called "bonding" contracts that obligated them to contribute food to soldiers' families. As soldiers left for the front, they were told to have no worries where food was concerned. They and their families would be well fed.

But common folk quickly learned that planter patriotism was more apparent than real. Food production never came close to meeting demand because planters devoted far too much acreage to cotton. In 1862 cotton production reached its second highest level on record to that time. Governor Brown received scores of letters

Fred Burke

complaining of planters growing too much cotton and imploring him to do something about it. A southwest Georgia man wrote to Brown: "I hope your Excellency will adopt some plan to stop those internal enemies of the country, for they will whip us sooner than all Lincolndom combined could do it."

The Confederacy never acted to restrict cotton production. Some states did, though with little success. In Georgia, Governor Brown proposed, and the Assembly passed, an act limiting cotton production, but it inspired little fear among planters. Enforcement was nearly non-existent. According to one source, "not one acre in fifty in the best corn district in Georgia was planted in corn."

An enraged Georgia trooper wrote to an Atlanta newspaper: "For God's sake don't tell the poor soldier who now shivers in a Northern wind while you snooze in a feather bed, that it is *just* and *right* that the men, who Congress has exempted, should enjoy ease at home, amassing untold riches, while *he* must fight, bleed, and even die." Another Georgia soldier called planters

> the most contemptible of all our public enemies.... These fellows talk loudly about *their* constitutional rights'—that no body has a right to say how much cotton they shall plant.... But listen again and you will hear them loud for the enforcement of the Conscript Law. Oh, yes! Their negroes must make cotton and whilst doing it the poor men must be taken from their families and put in the Army to protect their negroes. Was ever a greater wrong, or a more damning sin, perpetrated by men or devils?

In a September 1863 letter to the *Savannah Morning News*, one outraged Georgian asked, "What class has most interest in the war and has made the most money by it, *and sacrificed the least to maintain it?* ... It is the class known as the planters."

The dire food shortage brought on by cotton over-production marked the beginning of a spiraling inflationary cycle that rendered Confederate currency nearly worthless. The problem was made worse by speculators, who bought as much food as they could and hoarded it waiting for prices to rise. E.H. Grouby, editor of the *Early County News*, called speculators "far greater enemies to the South and do more to injure her cause than ten times their number of Yankees in the field." Such people, said Grouby, "carry their patriotism in the *pocketbook.*"

Rampant inflation made farmers less willing to exchange what food they had for Confederate currency. By 1863, the Richmond government determined that what it could not buy it would take by force. That summer it passed a 10 percent confiscation tax, called impressment, on farm produce and livestock. But there was a loophole. Impressment officials could take as much as they wanted beyond 10 percent as long as they paid for it in Confederate currency or promissory notes, neither of which carried much value.

Georgia's Inner Civil War

The home front situation was hardest on women laboring under the burdens of inflation, impressment, hungry children, and absent husbands. One Columbus man wrote to a local paper that many women could get offers of help only "at the sacrifice of their honor, and that by men who occupy high places in church and state." Thousands of letters from women themselves describing their desperate situation flooded into the governors' offices and to Richmond. Typical of these was a September 1863 letter from soldiers' wives and widows in Miller County describing their grim plight:

> Our crops is limited and so short ... cannot reach the first day of March next ... But little [food] of any sort to rescue us and our children from a unanimous starvation.... We can seldom find [bacon] for none has got but those that are exempt from service ... and they have no humane feeling nor patriotic principles.... without some great and speedy alerting in the conducting of affairs in this our little nation God will frown on it and that speedily.

Miller County women were in such dire straits that they were known to steal livestock on a regular basis. At one point, a group of about fifty soldier's wives raided the depot in Colquitt and took a hundred bushels of corn.

By 1863, food riots were breaking out in major cities all across the South, including the Confederate capital of Richmond. Georgia saw more than its share of riots. When an Atlanta merchant on White Hall Street told a group of women that bacon was more than a dollar a pound, they protested that they were soldiers' wives and could not afford such prices. One of the women drew a pistol and told the others to take what they needed. From there, they moved on to nearby stores, ransacking as they went. Similar riots broke out in Macon, Augusta, Marietta, Forsyth, Cartersville, Hartwell, Thomasville, and Blackshear. Dozens of starving women rioted in Savannah, looting several stores on Whitaker Street. In Valdosta a group of women broke into a warehouse and stole a wagonload of bacon. And a mob of about sixty-five Columbus women, some armed with pistols and knives, marched down Broad Street "to raid the stores of speculators."

Nelson Tift – speculator

Thom. Watson
left 4 Union

A few days later, Daniel Snell of Harris County wrote home to his wife Sarah: "You spoke of a riot in Columbus ... it is no more than I expected. I understand there was also one in Augusta.... What will become of the women and children with the food situation?" Indeed, thousands of soldiers wondered how their families would get along in their absence. With planters exempt from the draft and unwilling to help their families, many soldiers began to question whether their Confederacy was worth fighting for. As the war lumbered on and conditions worsened, more and more soldiers decided it was not.

A report from Franklin County made clear that the large numbers of deserters and draft evaders made conscription efforts too dangerous. At Fort Gaines, one conscript officer was nearly killed when he tried to enforce the draft. Threats to his life became so serious that he fled the state. Resistance to the draft was rampant all across the South. General Howell Cobb, commanding the military District of Georgia, thought it would take the whole Confederate army to enforce conscription.

Residents of Carroll County formed a home guard unit, as many communities did, just to keep their men at home. Its members did little more than meet at the courthouse in Carrollton once every few weeks for muster. One contemporary reported that, "persons wishing to get their friends home from the army write them that they can come home and by joining this command, remain at home." Some home guard units did not even bother with the occasional muster. A unit near Dahlonega composed entirely of draft dodgers and deserters never met at all. When a Confederate officer was sent to investigate, he found the command "scattered over the country as if quartered at home."

By October 1862 more than half the soldiers from northeast Georgia had "skedaddled" and were hiding out in the mountains.

At least a third of Lumpkin County's Blue Ridge Rifles deserted, and nearly half the county's Boyd Guards did the same. One Confederate officer reported to Secretary of War James Seddon that, "the conditions in the mountain districts of North Carolina, Georgia, and Alabama menaces the existence of the Confederacy as fatally as ... the armies of the United States."

Some of these deserters and other anti-Confederates formed a loosely organized movement, widely known as the Peace Society, to end the conflict with or without Southern independence. The Peace Society was perhaps the largest of many secret or semi-secret organizations that sprang up across the South to oppose the war. Little is known of the society's early days. It probably formed in north Alabama or east Tennessee during the spring of 1862 and later spread to Georgia.

From the war's outset anti-Confederate sentiment was surprisingly strong in the South. More than 300,000 slave-state whites served in Union armies, with more than 2,500 of them coming from Georgia—not counting those in irregular companies who numbered many more. Unionism found its greatest strength among whites in areas with few slaves such as Georgia's northern mountains and southeastern pine barrens. But even in Black Belt regions where slaves made up more than half the population there were significant numbers of anti-Confederates.

As early as March 1862, John O'Connor of Fort Gaines warned Governor Brown of "spies and traitors" operating along the lower Chattahoochee River. E.H. Grouby noted in the *Early County News* that there were deserters "in every direction." One officer called the wiregrass region "one of the greatest dens for Tories and deserters from our army in the world." A Lowndes County resident warned Governor Brown of local deserters and draft dodgers throughout the piney woods of south Georgia. In

October 1863, a Savannah man wrote that troops in southeast Georgia were demanding peace and would soon turn to mutiny or desertion if they did not get it. There were already well over a thousand deserters hiding in the Okefenokee Swamp. A few months later, troops at the Rose Dew Island batteries south of Savannah plotted mutiny. Encouraged by local citizens connected with the Peace Society, the soldiers took an oath never to fight against the Union, to desert at the earliest opportunity, and encourage others to follow their lead.

Popular support and innumerable hiding places made it difficult for Confederate forces to track down deserters and draft dodgers. The Bureau of Conscription's superintendent admitted that public opinion worked against draft enforcement. There was, he lamented, no disgrace attached to desertion or draft evasion. A Bibb County man wrote that the area around Macon was "full of deserters and almost every man in the community will feed them and keep them from being arrested." In Stewart County several men of the Third Georgia Infantry Regiment openly declared that they had no intention of returning to the army. Forty men in Marion County built a sizeable fortress to defend themselves against conscript companies. Well armed and provisioned, they offered sanctuary to anyone who sought their protection.

Despite empathy from local residents and their growing numbers, life for deserters hiding out in the mountains and bottomlands was often precarious. They were harassed by army patrols, and sympathizers had little food to give them. Some became so desperate that they fled to Union lines. After the Union army was driven out of northwest Georgia in September 1863 following the September 1863 Battle of Chickamauga, Chattanooga, Tennessee, became a haven for anti-Confederate refugees. When William T. Sherman's army entered north Georgia in the spring of 1864, hundreds of Confederate deserters greeted the Federals. Some were put to work as support troops for frontline Union soldiers. They even helped the Federals dig entrenchments in preparation for the assault on Rebel lines at Kennesaw Mountain in June 1864.

After Sherman captured Atlanta in September, hundreds of soldiers and civilians remained in the city and aided the Union army. Later that year during his famous March to the Sea, Confederate deserters and draft dodgers from Liberty and Tattnall counties sent Sherman a letter. In it they insisted that they opposed secession and offered him their services in whatever capacity he saw fit. Some went further than that. One band of Georgia ex-Confederates formed a battalion called the "Volunteer Force of the United States Army from Georgia," effectively joining the Union army.

As the ranks of deserters and draft evaders grew through 1863, some formed active anti-Confederate guerrilla bands. They raided plantations, attacked army supply depots, and drove off impressment and conscript companies. A Confederate loyalist in Fort Gaines begged Governor Brown to send a company of cavalry for protection against these raiders. So did pro-Confederates in Dade and Walker Counties. A band of local deserters had threatened to burn the crops of any farmer in the region who expressed Confederate loyalties.

In January 1863, Governor Brown sent the state militia to put down deserter gangs around Dahlonega; the effort had little effect. When authorities in Fannin County arrested members of one deserter gang, some of their comrades, along with local sympathizers, mounted a violent rescue. Several pro-Confederates were killed in the bloody gun battle, but only one deserter lost his life. So brutal had Georgia's inner civil war become by 1863 that the editor of a Milledgeville newspaper wrote: "We are fighting each other harder than we have ever fought the enemy."

The rise of deserter bands was only the most violent reflection of widespread discontent with the Confederacy and the war, and, as the war entered its final year, few expected the Confederacy to survive for very long. Some blamed an incompetent and corrupt Confederacy for that. In a March 1864 *Early County News* editorial, E.H. Grouby wrote: "We cannot help thinking this is the last year of the war.... we have now entirely too many little jackass upstarts filling positions in our government." Though some were willing to fight on, most Georgians were tired of the war and wanted to see it end with or without Confederate victory. In October of that year, Grouby wrote that the only people who still backed the war effort were those who held "fat Government contracts" and corrupt officials who were "not yet done fleecing the Government. Their voice," he said, "is still for war, war, war!"

The voice of the common folk was expressed in local meetings throughout Georgia that fall and winter where declarations were drawn up demanding an end to the war. The people of Wilcox County urged Governor Brown "to settle this Bloody conflict at once by negotiations." A few such declarations were sent to General Sherman insisting that the respective counties wished to rejoin the Union whether the state did or not. At one anti-war meeting in Thomas County, a fight broke out that the Unionists won. In Irwinville local Unionists adopted a number of resolutions, including one calling for the Confederacy's surrender. When a militia lieutenant tried to break up the meeting, long-time anti-Confederate Willis Bone knocked the officer down with his musket and led three cheers for Abraham Lincoln. The assembly then drove the lieutenant and every other pro-Confederate out of town.

With Confederate defeat all but inevitable, the army's desertion rate continued to rise. In September 1864, Jefferson Davis admitted that, "two-thirds of our men are absent ... most of them without leave." Among Georgia troops, as many as 60 percent or more had deserted. So many soldiers were leaving the ranks that the Confederacy's remaining supporters began to seriously consider what until then had been unthinkable—arming the slaves.

Enslaved Georgians Take Freedom for Themselves

As early as 1863, high-ranking Confederate officials had begun to advocate using slaves as soldiers. The Union had more than 200,000 blacks in uniform, 80 percent of them native Southerners. At least 3,500 were Georgians, though the actual number was probably far greater. And they were proving to be very effective troops. As prospects for Confederate victory became ever more dim, support for arming slaves began to grow.

Not surprisingly, most slaveholders fiercely resisted any suggestion that slaves be placed in the army. They feared not only the loss of their "property" but also what slave conscription would mean for slavery's future, dead though it nearly was in any case. Georgia's General Howell Cobb summed up the prevailing slaveholder view when he insisted that, "the day you make soldiers of them is the beginning of the end of the revolution. If slaves will make good soldiers, our whole theory of slavery is wrong."

There was also the question of whether giving guns to slaves would make them Confederates. It was an unlikely assumption. From the war's outset, most slaves thought that Lincoln intended to free them. How could they think otherwise with Southern Fire-Eaters insisting it was true? "The idea seems to have gotten out extensively among them [slaves] that they are soon all to be free," wrote William Harrison of Calhoun County in April 1861, "that Mr. Lincoln & his army are coming to set them free."

But enslaved blacks were not simply waiting to be given freedom; they were taking it for themselves. Though Lincoln's Emancipation Proclamation is often credited with having freed the slaves, it was little more than a practical recognition of what blacks themselves had forced on Lincoln's government. During the war's early months, Lincoln repeated that he had no intention of ending slavery. In July 1861, Congress backed him up with a resolution stating that this was a war to preserve the Union, not to free the slaves. Nevertheless, tens of thousands of escaping slaves took freedom for themselves and forced Lincoln to deal directly with the issue—a fact that many blacks well understood.

Late in the war, the Rev. Garrison Frazier, a black Savannah preacher, expressed his understanding of the war's relationship to slavery in these terms:

> The object of the war was not, at first, to give the slaves their freedom, but the sole object of the war was, at first, to bring the rebellious States back into the Union.... Afterward, knowing the value that was set on the slaves by the rebels, the President thought that his [emancipation] proclamation would stimulate them to lay down their arms, ... and their not doing so has now made the freedom of the slaves a part of the war.

Not all Southern blacks were so aware of the war's finer points, but they did have a keen sense that the Confederacy stood for slavery and that its fall would mean slavery's end.

Throughout the war, Georgia blacks resisted enslavement in increasingly overt ways, sometimes finding whites willing to help them. Willis Bone frequently hid both deserters and runaway slaves on his Irwin County farm. So did William Huskey of Clay County, Lindsey Durham of Lee County, and John Anderson of Lumpkin County. In spring 1862, Calhoun County authorities arrested three local whites for supplying area slaves with firearms in preparation for a rebellion. August of 1864 found slaves in Brooks County conspiring with John Vickery, a white community resident, to stage an uprising. Blacks frequently worked with deserter bands, supplying them with food, equipment, and information. And when Sherman's troops passed through Georgia in 1864, thousands of blacks escaping bondage followed after them. One column alone reported at least seventeen thousand black refugees trailing behind it.

Hundreds of thousands of slaves deserted their owners in what historian W.E.B. Du Bois called a general strike against the Confederacy. Every slave taken as a worker to the front by Georgia's Troup Artillery escaped Union lines. One southwest Georgia slave was hanged for attempting to organize a mass exodus of local blacks to Federals on the Florida coast. Many, like Susie King Taylor of Savannah, fled to Union forces operating along the Georgia coast. Taylor served one of the Union army's first black regiments, cooking for the men, doing their laundry, and acting as nurse. She also served as a teacher, having secretly learned to read and write while enslaved. She eventually married one of the soldiers and after the war opened a school for black children in Savannah.

Enslaved blacks in the interior for whom escape was more difficult nevertheless found various ways to resist. In areas of the Black Belt from which many of the white males had gone off to war, slaves were particularly defiant. In August 1862, slaveholder Laura Comer wrote in her diary: "The servants are so indolent and obstinate it is a trial to have anything to do with them." Slaves feigned ignorance or illness, sabotaged equipment, and roamed freely in defiance of laws requiring them to carry a pass.

What work slaves did, they did grudgingly. Some refused to work at all. Others used the threat of escape to force wage payments from their owners. Even if escape did not result, slaves could be difficult to deal with when suitable rewards were not forthcoming. A Georgia mistress wrote concerning one of her slaves: "Nancy has been very impertinent.... She said she would not be hired out by the month, neither would she go out to get work." Another woman wrote to her husband: "We are doing as best we know, or as good as we can get the Servants to do; they learn to feel very independent."

When independence led to escape and they could not make it to Union lines, runaway slaves often gathered in small, isolated communities. Sometimes these settlements were multiracial. They were so numerous in south Georgia's wiregrass country that one source called it "the common retreat of deserters from our army, tories, and runaway negroes." In northern Georgia, a number of escaped slaves hid out with Jeff Anderson's deserter band in the mountains around Dahlonega. Like their white counterparts, groups of runaway slaves sustained themselves by making raids on local towns and plantations. S.S. Massey of Chattahoochee County complained to Governor Brown that local slaves were "killing up the stock and stealing every thing they can put their hands on."

Trying to stem the rising tide of resistance among slaves, the General Assembly made several additions to the state penal code. In December 1861, it stipulated that any black person found guilty of arson would be put to death. A year later the Assembly reinforced laws forbidding slaves to travel without passes and canceled all exemptions from slave patrols. Such efforts did little to restrain slaves. They had long since begun to anticipate their coming freedom, even taking it for themselves, and were more and more ignoring the patrols. Some even fought back. They often tied ropes or vines neck-high across a dark stretch of road just before the patrollers rode by. According to a former slave, these traps were guaranteed to unhorse at least one rider. When patrollers raided a prayer meeting for freedom near Columbus, one slave stuck a shovel in the fireplace and threw hot coals all over them. Instantly the room "filled with smoke and the smell of burning clothes and white flesh." In the confusion, every slave got away.

Defeated by the People at Home

With resistance so widespread, it seems little wonder that slaveholders opposed placing firearms in the hands of slaves. Nevertheless, on 13 March 1865 the Confederate Congress finally passed legislation authorizing recruitment of up to three hundred thousand slaves. But there was no promise of freedom for those who agreed to serve. It hardly mattered in any case; by then the Confederacy was nearly spent.

In April the last major Confederate armies surrendered. On 16 April, in what became the last battle of the war, Union troopers under General James Wilson forced their way across the Chattahoochee River, captured Columbus, and burned its industries. From there they fanned out across central and southern Georgia. One detachment rode to Andersonville prison, where about thirteen thousand Union prisoners had died of exposure, disease, and starvation. That number totaled roughly a third of the prisoners held at Andersonville, giving it the highest mortality rate of any prison on either side. Confederates had already relocated the survivors when Wilson's men arrived, but they arrested the post commandant, Henry Wirz, a Swiss immigrant. In November

1865, Wirz became the only official executed for war crimes during the Civil War.

On 10 May, Wilson's men captured Jefferson Davis near Irwinville, Georgia, as he fled south trying to get out of the country and establish a Confederate government-in-exile. They arrested Georgia officials as well—Vice President Alexander Stephens, Governor Joseph Brown, and Senator Benjamin H. Hill among them. With its leaders in custody and its armies deserted and defeated, the Confederacy ceased to exist.

In a sense the Confederacy's existence as a national entity was questionable from the start. States' rights politicians like Stephens and Brown undermined Richmond's authority at nearly every turn. Plain folk increasingly abandoned the struggle, calling it a rich man's war. On 5 April 1865, only days before the Civil War's end, the *Early County News* expressed a resentment widespread in Georgia.

> This has been "a rich man's war and a poor man's fight." It is true there are a few wealthy men in the army, but nine tenths of them hold positions, always get out of the way when they think a fight is coming on, and treat the privates like dogs.... There seems to be no chance to get this class to carry muskets.

Even at its inception the Confederacy lacked unqualified support. Most white Southerners, and likely most Georgia voters, had opposed secession in the first place, and blacks could hardly be counted on to support a government dedicated to slavery. What support the Confederacy had begun to erode as the passions of 1861 faded under the realities of war. The conflict lasted as long as it did mainly because Lincoln had his own problems maintaining support for war in the North. Though Union armies consistently outnumbered those of the Confederacy by two-to-one, men from the slave states, black and white, totaled about one-fourth of the Union's armed forces. In other words, it was Southerners themselves who gave the Union its numerical advantage on the battlefield.

Even among Southerners who stuck with the Confederacy to its end, most had little affection for the Richmond government. What loyalty they still felt was more for their comrades in arms than anyone else. William Andrews of Clay County had joined the army in February 1861 and remained through the entire war. Few could match his record of service to the cause. Still, in May of 1865, just a few weeks after he surrendered with General Robert E. Lee at Appomattox, he wrote: "While it is a bitter pill to have to come back into the Union, don't think there is much regret for the loss of the Confederacy. The treatment the soldiers have received from the government in various ways put them against it." That was just as true of the civilian population, not only in Georgia but throughout the South as well. Such attitudes among Southern whites, together with resistance of Southern blacks, were a major factor contributing to the Confederacy's downfall. That came as no surprise to people of that time. As early as the fall of 1862, an Atlanta newspaper bluntly stated: "If we are defeated, it will be by the people at home."

Chapter 6

Post Civil War Georgia

Reconstruction, Political and Social

Following the Civil War, those Southern states that seceded had to be readmitted to the Union, which meant having their representation in Congress returned. The Reconstruction Era was one of the most complex, and at times confusing, chaotic, and violent, periods in American History, and in Georgia it was no different. The process of political Reconstruction in Georgia lasted from 1865 until 1871. During these years Georgia seemingly met the requirements of Reconstruction not once, not twice, but three times; rewrote its state constitution twice; ratified the Thirteenth Amendment; rejected then ratified the Fourteenth Amendment; rejected then ratified the Fifteenth Amendment; saw the emergence of the Ku Klux Klan with its racial violence; enacted Black Codes; elected black legislators to the General Assembly, expelled them, and reinstated them; moved the capital from Milledgeville to Atlanta; elected a Republican governor and a Republican-controlled General Assembly; had Reconstruction ended; and "redeemed" itself for the Democratic Party.

The politics of Reconstruction was complex. The first two plans for Reconstruction, Lincoln's Plan of Reconstruction and the Wade-Davis Bill, failed to be implemented for a number of reasons. The first plan to be enacted was put forth by President Andrew Johnson on 29 May 1865 and is commonly called Johnson's Plan of Reconstruction. Johnson's Plan called for pardons to former Confederates (with some exceptions), the rewriting of the state constitution, repudiation of the states' Confederate debt, and the nullification of the Ordinance of Secession. President Johnson would appoint a provisional governor to supervise the Reconstruction process. When Reconstruction had been completed and the state readmitted and represented in Congress, this provisional governor would step aside and a permanent governor, elected by the voters, would take office. On 17 June 1865 President Johnson appointed James Johnson (no relation to the president) to be Georgia's provisional governor. Governor Johnson attended the University of Georgia, practiced law in Columbus, served in the US House of Representatives from 1851 to 1853, opposed secession, and remained loyal to the Union during the Civil War. Johnson's primary responsibilities included the rewriting of the state's constitution, holding elections based upon the new document, repudiating the state's Confederate debt, and nullifying Georgia's Ordinance of Secession.

Governor Johnson began with the rewriting of the state's constitution, and called for a convention to meet in Milledgeville on the fourth Wednesday in October 1865. The resulting document was Georgia's Constitution of 1865. This constitution did not differ much from the 1861 constitution, so it can be called a conservative document. Notable changes included abolishing slavery, limiting the governor to two successive terms, and defining who could vote, namely "free white male citizens" who had paid all taxes required of them, although the term "poll tax" was not used. In addition, the convention repudiated Georgia's wartime debt (about $18 million) and repealed the state's Ordinance of Secession. Governor Johnson ordered statewide elections based upon the new constitution to be held 15 November 1865. Voters chose members of the General Assembly and a permanent governor, Charles J. Jenkins, who ran unopposed. Jenkins attended the University of Georgia, practiced law in Augusta, served in the Georgia House of Representatives in the 1830s and 1840s, was appointed to the Georgia Supreme Court in 1860 where he served throughout the Civil War, opposed secession but supported the Confederacy, and served as a delegate of the convention that wrote the Constitution of 1865. Governor Jenkins was sworn in on 14 December 1865, and James Johnson, having fulfilled his duties, relinquished the office.

Shortly before Governor Jenkins was sworn in, the newly elected General Assembly convened in Milledgeville (the session opened on 4 December 1865). This session of the legislature would try to complete the requirements for Reconstruction, so that the state could reclaim its representation in Congress. After some debate, the General Assembly ratified the Thirteenth Amendment to the US Constitution, which abolished slavery. The legislators then turned their attention to the status of freedmen and passed a series of bills generally called Black Codes. Georgia's Black Codes were not nearly as harsh as those in other Southern states; although Georgia did not have a comprehensive set of Black Codes there were restrictions on freedmen. Included in these restrictions were that blacks could not testify in court against whites, blacks could not serve on juries, and that blacks could not intermarry with whites. The legislature also elected the state's US senators and chose Alexander H. Stephens and Herschel V. Johnson. Although neither supported secession, both served in the Confederate government, Stephens as vice president and Johnson in the Confederate Senate. These choices were not likely to be well accepted by Northern senators, especially the Radical Republicans; however, Georgia had seemingly complied with President Johnson's requirements for representation in Congress.

The Republican-controlled Congress, however, did not seat any Southern senators and representatives and embarked on a course that led to new requirements for readmission into the Union. Control of Reconstruction was passing into the hands of Congress. The catalyst for Congressional control was the creation of the Joint Committee on Reconstruction in December 1865. Composed of fifteen members (nine from the House, six from the Senate), this committee was charged with investigating whether the Southern states and determining if they were entitled to representation in Congress. One result of the committee's work was the Fourteenth Amendment, which provided citizenship and equal protection rights. Passed in April 1866, the Fourteenth Amendment was sent to the states for ratification. Georgia, like all Southern states except Tennessee, rejected the amendment in November 1866. In the meantime, the Radical Republicans in Congress were formulating a new set of Reconstruction requirements. These new requirements were outlined in the First Reconstruction Act, which passed Congress over President Johnson's veto in March 1867 and included ratification of the Fourteenth Amendment, the registration of voters, and the rewriting of the state constitution yet again. In addition, the South was divided into five military districts with a Northern general in command of each district. This general supervised the Reconstruction process in the Southern states, and the state governments then in existence became "provisional." Army troops were also placed throughout the South, and the Southern states suffered through martial law. This Reconstruction plan was often called Radical Reconstruction, as it was put forth by Radical Republicans in Congress.

Georgia was placed in the Third Military District along with Florida and Alabama, and General John Pope commanded the district from his headquarters in Atlanta. Pope was appointed on 1 April 1867 and Governor Jenkins became "provisional," a status that he did not accept. Jenkins opposed the new Reconstruction requirements, filed suits to have military rule overturned and to block implementation of the Reconstruction Acts, and even went to Washington, DC, to appear before the US Supreme Court seeking an injunction against implementation of the Reconstruction Acts. All of Jenkins' actions were futile, and he was forced to accept that General Pope was his superior.

Pope's first order of business was to register voters in Georgia. Forty-nine registration boards consisting of three men each were formed to register the state's voters in the summer of 1867. The outstanding feature of the registration boards was that they were biracial—one of the three members of each board was an African-American man. These were Georgia's first biracial government bodies. Between June and September 1867 these forty-nine boards registered Georgia's voters, and during this period 102,411 whites and 98,507 blacks registered.

Following the registration of voters, General Pope ordered elections in late October 1867 for a new constitutional convention, the first elections in Georgia in which African Americans participated. Georgia Democrats tended to boycott this election, so the convention was strongly Republican in sentiment. The delegates to this convention, which included thirty-seven African Americans, were set to convene in Milledgeville in December 1867. Innkeepers in the capital city, however, refused to rent rooms to the black delegates, and General Pope moved the convention to Atlanta. This was the first step in Atlanta becoming Georgia's capital. The convention met from December 1867 to March 1868 and drafted the Constitution of 1868, which included several significant changes. The voting provision was revised to read "male persons born in the United States," the capital was moved to Atlanta, a poll tax was included as a prerequisite to voting, and the constitution assured citizenship and equal protection of the law for blacks. The document did not, however, include a specific statement about the right of African Americans to hold office.

The rewriting of the constitution fulfilled one of the requirements for Reconstruction. Next, General George Meade, who took over command of the Third Military District in December 1867, ordered elections for state offices based on the new constitution. In April 1868, voters elected a new governor, members of the General Assembly, and accepted the new constitution. The Democratic candidate for governor was Civil War hero John B. Gordon, an outspoken opponent of Radical Reconstruction and the alleged leader of the Ku Klux Klan in Georgia. The Republican candidate was Rufus Bullock, who opposed secession but served in the Confederate Quartermaster Corps in a civilian capacity and was a delegate to the convention that wrote the 1868 constitution. Bullock was elected by a majority of about 7,000 out of 160,000 votes and became the first Republican elected governor in Georgia. In the legislative elections Republicans won small majorities in both House and Senate. The House was comprised of 93 Republicans and 80 Democrats, while the composition of the Senate was 27 Republicans and 17 Democrats. One other important result was that 32 African American men were elected to the General Assembly (29 in the House and 3 in the Senate), something that will later spark controversy. In July 1868, Governor Bullock took office and the new General Assembly met. It ratified the Fourteenth Amendment, completing the requirements of Reconstruction. On 25 July 1868, Congress approved the state's readmission to the

Union and Georgia was once again a member of the Union in good standing. The federal government no longer supervised the state, General Meade left Georgia, and the troops were removed.

However, Union membership in good standing did not last. Two events took place in September 1868 that earned Georgia the distinction of being kicked out of the Union: The first was the expulsion of the black legislators from the General Assembly. Once the state was readmitted to the Union and did not have the federal government supervising its activities, the white conservative members of the General Assembly began discussing the expulsion of the black legislators. Since there was no provision in the Constitution of 1868 guaranteeing blacks the right to hold office, there was nothing preventing their expulsion. For that reason, 28 of the 32 African American legislators were expelled in early September 1868 (4 who were considered mulattoes were permitted to keep their seats). They were replaced by the runners-up in the elections, men who were conservative Democrats. The second event was perhaps the worst act of racial violence in Georgia during Reconstruction—the Camilla Massacre. On 19 September 1868, a Republican political rally/meeting was scheduled for Camilla, located about twenty-five miles south of Albany in Mitchell County. Numerous black Republicans traveled from Albany to Camilla, but as they reached the town limits they were ambushed by some fifty armed, white residents of Camilla, leaving about twelve killed.

As a result of these two events Governor Bullock requested the reinstatement of military rule in Georgia; he testified before Congress that the state had not complied with federal laws. Later, in March 1869, the state legislature rejected the Fifteenth Amendment, which provided voting privileges for citizens. In the same month Georgia's members of Congress were not permitted to take their seats even though the state had been readmitted to the Union (in July 1868). Georgia was truly in Reconstruction limbo and remained that way until December 1869 when military rule was reinstituted; the state was essentially kicked out of the Union. A new military commander, General Alfred Terry, assumed authority over the state, Governor Bullock became "provisional," and a new set of requirements was established for Georgia's readmission to the Union. General Terry moved to reinstate the expelled black legislators, which he accomplished in January 1870 in an event known as "Terry's Purge." Congress also required Georgia to ratify the Fifteenth Amendment, which the legislature did in February 1870. With these acts Georgia had, for a third time, met the requirements of Reconstruction, and, on 15 July 1870 Congress passed legislation readmitting the state. In February 1871, Georgia was fully represented in Congress for the first time since before the Civil War. Georgia was once again, and for the last time, a member of the Union in good standing.

The final part of the politics of the Reconstruction Era, known as Redemption, took place in 1871. Redemption was the process of the Democratic Party taking control of the state government, and with the removal of federal supervision this was not difficult to accomplish. A Democratic-controlled General Assembly was elected in December 1870, and a Democratic governor, James M. Smith, was elected in December 1871. Georgia had been "redeemed" for the Democratic Party. Following Redemption, the Democratic Party controlled Georgia politics for more than a hundred years, and the state became part of the Solid Democratic South.

The social aspects of the Reconstruction years were perhaps less dramatic, but no less important. The most important theme in social Reconstruction was the transition of the former slaves to freedom and the exercise of the rights and privileges that go with this new freedom. To assist in this transition, Congress created the Bureau of Refugees, Freedmen, and Abandoned Lands—more commonly known as the Freedmen's Bureau. President Lincoln signed this legislation in March 1865, and General Oliver O. Howard became the agency's commissioner. The Bureau's charge was to oversee all subjects related to freedmen, in essence the country's first social welfare agency. More specifically, the Freedmen's Bureau provided freedmen and refugees with food rations and medical care, helped reunite families displaced by the war, relocated former slaves onto abandoned lands, negotiated labor contracts, and provided education opportunities.

Heading the Bureau in each state was an assistant commissioner, and General Rufus Saxton was Georgia's first assistant commissioner. Saxton, a native of Massachusetts and winner of the Congressional Medal of Honor during the Civil War, served as assistant commissioner from May to September 1865 and was primarily concerned with distributing abandoned lands to freedmen. He spent much of his tenure carrying out General William T. Sherman's Special Field Order No. 15, which set aside abandoned land along Georgia's coast to be distributed to former slaves. Called Sherman's Reservation, this land included the sea islands from Charleston to the St. Johns River in Florida and that part of the low country thirty miles inland from the coast. Within months Saxton claimed to have settled forty thousand freedmen on four hundred thousand acres within Sherman's Reservation. Unfortunately for the freedmen, by the fall of 1865 President Johnson ordered the land restored to its original owners, and in September 1865, General Saxton was removed as assistant commissioner for failing to establish the Bureau's presence in Georgia.

Saxton's successor was Davis Tillson, also a Union general during the Civil War, who was charged with establishing the Bureau's presence. During his tenure, which lasted from September 1865 to January 1867, Tillson quickly expanded the Bureau's size and presence in Georgia. With an appropriations bill having passed Congress in July 1866, Tillson had the resources to hire agents to carry out his mission, and by the end of his tenure he had hired more than 250 Freedmen's Bureau agents. Many of Tillson's agents were controversial because they were local Georgia residents, many former wealthy slave owners, who may not have freedmen's best interests at heart while carrying out their duties. For this reason and others Tillson was removed as assistant commissioner in January 1867. His successor was Caleb Sibley, who served until October 1868. Sibley significantly reduced the number of agents in the state, and he tended to appoint Georgia unionists to those posts, avoiding former slave owners. In the summer of 1868, the Bureau's effectiveness declined dramatically after Georgia met the requirements of Reconstruction, as Bureau agents could no longer directly intervene on behalf of the freedpeople. The Bureau lingered in Georgia until the summer of 1870 but functioned only as an educational support agency. Ultimately, the Freedmen's Bureau has to be evaluated as having only a limited impact on freedmen's welfare in Georgia.

Among the new rights Georgia freedmen exercised after the Civil War were voting and holding office; black politics and black politicians became a new issue in the state. The beginning of black politics can be traced to two organizations, the Union League and African Methodist Episcopal (AME) Church. The Union League spread into north Georgia just after the war ended and provided much of the structural foundation for the Republican Party in the state. The AME Church was an influential black institution and became the focal point of postwar black politics in Georgia. The church mobilized voters, supported campaigns, hosted political rallies, and produced most of Georgia's black political leaders. AME preachers became the unchallenged political leaders of black Georgia.

Who were Georgia's black politicians? The most powerful black politician in postwar Georgia was Henry M. Turner. Born to free parents in 1834, Turner was educated, joined the Methodist Church, and became a licensed preacher in 1853. President Lincoln appointed Turner to the First USCT (United States Colored Troops) in 1863, making him the country's first black chaplain. After the war, Turner helped organize the AME Church in Georgia and began to focus his energies on politics. He was one of the 37 black delegates to the convention that wrote the 1868 constitution and won election to the General Assembly later in 1868. Expelled from the legislature in September 1868, Turner was reinstated during "Terry's Purge" in January 1870 and defeated for reelection later that year. Aaron Bradley was another important black politician in Georgia after the Civil War, noted as the most outspoken black politician in the state. Born a slave around the turn of the century, young Bradley successfully ran away to New York City and moved to Boston where he later practiced law. After the Civil War he launched a campaign for black political and social rights. Like Turner, Bradley was a delegate to the constitutional convention (1867–68) and elected to the General Assembly in April 1868. Bradley was likewise expelled, reinstated, and defeated for reelection in 1870. Lastly, Tunis Campbell was another significant postwar black politician. Born in New Jersey, Campbell was a trained missionary and a minister in the African Methodist Episcopal Zion Church. Campbell's political experiences were similar to those of Turner and Bradley—a delegate to the constitutional convention, elected to the legislature in 1868, he was expelled, reseated, and defeated for reelection in 1870. Campbell then built a political machine in Darien in the 1870s where he was elected justice of the peace in McIntosh County. Turner, Bradley, and Campbell were Georgia's most visible black politicians, but numerous African Americans served in public office on the local, state, and national level. Between 1867 and 1872, sixty-nine African Americans served in the General Assembly or as delegates to constitutional conventions, sixty-five served in local offices, and one man, Jefferson Long, served in the US House of Representatives.

Another theme in post-Civil War Georgia, as in most other former Confederate states, was the attempt to maintain white supremacy. The abolition of slavery forced the white South to find alternate methods of oppressing freedpeople, and in Georgia those included the Black Codes, the Camilla Race Riot, the expulsion of black legislators, and general intimidation and violence. The primary agent for intimidation and violence against African Americans (and Republicans) was the Ku Klux Klan, formed in Pulaski, Tennessee, in 1866, seemingly for the amusement of a few former Confederate veterans. The goals and objectives of the organization changed, however, with the passage of the Reconstruction Acts in the spring of 1867. Following the implementation of Radical Reconstruction, the Klan's goals were to deprive freedmen of their citizenship rights, oppress all freedpeople, keeping them at the bottom of the social and economic hierarchy, and to oppose (violently if necessary) the Republican Party in the South. The Klan has been described as the terrorist arm of the Democratic Party.

The Ku Klux Klan arrived in Georgia in early 1868. In March of that year Nathan B. Forrest, the alleged national leader of the Klan, visited Atlanta on business and shortly thereafter notices appeared in Atlanta newspapers announcing the existence of the organization. The head of the Klan in Georgia was John B. Gordon, former Confederate general and failed 1868 gubernatorial candidate, although he never admitted to leading the organization. The Georgia Klan was responsible for countless crimes between 1868 and 1871, with most action designed to intimidate black and Republican voters. Activities increased as elections neared: Republican leaders and candidates were threatened, voters were intimidated and violently attacked at the polls, and Klan members rode at night intimidating African Americans in the state.

The Klan in Georgia was most active in 1868; from 1 January through 15 November Freedmen's Bureau agents reported 336 cases of assault or murder on freedmen. Almost half of these took place between August and October, as the national election approached. The Freedmen's Bureau reported 142 "outrages," which consisted of 31 killings, 43 shootings, 5 stabbings, 55 beatings, and 8 whippings of 300–500 lashes. The first major outrage reported in Georgia was the murder of George Ashburn, a white Republican organizer, in Columbus on 31 March 1868. One of the places where the Klan was most active was Warren County, located just west of Augusta. Violence began in the summer of 1868 and night riding, beatings, whippings, and shootings became nightly occurrences; in October a freedman died after receiving 900 lashes with saddle stirrups. The most prominent Klan victim in Warren County was state senator Joseph Adkins, who was murdered in May 1869. Systematic violence was probably worse in Warren County than any other place in Georgia.

Political terrorism was effective, and a comparison of the elections held in Georgia in April and November 1868 bear out this fact. In April the Republican candidate for governor, Rufus

Bullock, received 83,527 votes to win the election. In contrast, in November, Ulysses S. Grant, the Republican candidate for president, received just 57,109 votes. The number of votes cast for Democrats increased from 76,356 for John Gordon, the gubernatorial candidate in April, to 102,707 for Horatio Seymour, the Democratic candidate for president. A greater contrast is evident when looking at results at the county level. In Oglethorpe County, the number of votes cast for Republicans decreased from 1,144 in April to 116 in November; in neighboring Columbia County the number of Republican votes dropped from 1,222 to 1. A number of Georgia counties reported no Republican votes cast in November.

Klan activity continued in Georgia throughout 1869 and into 1870, but decreased shortly thereafter. The redemption of Georgia for the Democratic Party in 1871 meant that political terrorism was less necessary. Also, the federal government took action to thwart the activities of the Klan, specifically the passage of the Enforcement Act in 1870 and the Ku Klux Klan Act in 1871 by Congress. Klan terror probably accomplished as much in Georgia as in any Southern state to subvert and undermine the Republican Party and Radical Reconstruction, and little was done to stop Klan activity.

Another method of maintaining white supremacy in Georgia was the convict-lease system. The state attempted to implement this prior to the conflict, but the legislature refused to pass the legislation. During the war the penitentiary building was burned and there was no place to house state prisoners. In December 1866, the General Assembly established a convict-lease system in Georgia. The law authorized the governor to accept proposals to "farm out" the state's prisoners. Bids would be accepted and contracts drawn up; leases would last no more than five years;

those leasing prisoners would have to provide for them. The first lease was negotiated in May 1868 when 100 prisoners were leased to work on the Georgia & Alabama Railroad. By 1875 926 were leased out. An examination of the convict-lease system suggests that it was used discriminately against African Americans. Of those 926 prisoners, 835 were black, while 91 were white; 90.1 percent of those in Georgia's convict-lease system were African American. Because the system was run by the state, this was a state-operated method of maintaining white supremacy.

Postwar Economics

The Civil War wrought great destruction and devastation to Georgia's economy. The Thirteenth Amendment destroyed the principal labor system, as three-fourths of Georgia's wealth—approximately $272 million—vanished. Georgia's railroads also suffered great damage. In 1860 Georgia had 1,420 miles of railroads, second only to Virginia in the South, and Union Generals Sherman and Wilson took dead aim at that track. Sherman's campaign and Wilson's raid also caused considerable physical destruction to the state's agricultural resources and industry. The state had accumulated an $18 million debt during the war, but fortunately for Georgia that debt was repudiated. It would not be far off to say that Georgia, like most of the rest of the South, was an economic desert in 1865.

Georgia's economy had long been largely agricultural, based upon the production of staple or cash crops, and at the time of the Civil War, there was little industry in the state. This economic pattern would persist in the immediate postwar period—the state remained primarily agricultural and industrialization came to Georgia only slowly. One of the most pressing concerns in the state's postwar economy, as it was throughout the agricultural

South, was a labor issue. With the abolition of slavery the labor system had become unstable, and farmers with large landholdings had to find an alternative to slave labor. Attempts were made to replace slave labor with wage laborers, immigrants, and machinery, but all failed, and large farmers were forced to rely on the former slaves as sharecroppers and tenant farmers.

Sharecropping and tenant farming solved two labor problems that were closely intertwined: Who was going to work the farmlands and what work would the former slaves do? Thus, a system by which the former slaves worked the farmland would solve both issues, and in the years after the Civil War sharecropping and tenant farming became the prominent labor system in Georgia. Initial variations, such as the contract wage and share wage systems, did not take hold in the state. Under these systems the laborers, who were former slaves, worked the large farms under the watchful eye of white supervisors, but many workers believed this was simply a modified form of slavery. A more acceptable arrangement evolved whereby former slaves worked for themselves and handed over part of their crop to the landowner.

There were several variations in Georgia, but simply it was a system by which the farmer (sharecropper/tenant) rented the land he worked and paid the rent with the crops he grew. It was a largely black institution, although whites became sharecroppers and tenant farmers as well. The owner of the land negotiated a contract with the tenant that stated what work the tenant would perform, what crops he would grow, and how the harvest would be divided. The agreement also identified what the owner provided, such as housing, farm implements, tools, and seeds. Contracts were negotiated on an annual basis, and in the immediate postwar years Freedmen's Bureau agents helped negotiate some agreements.

Tenants preferred these arrangements, as they felt they had more control over their work.

Georgia's banking structure collapsed after the Civil War, and both landlord and tenant needed credit for the necessities of life, so a system of credit was devised for the state's farmers—the crop-lien system. This gave merchants and store owners considerable power over tenant farmers. The General Assembly passed the Georgia's first crop-lien law in December 1866, formalizing and legalizing this financial arrangement. The law gave merchants liens upon the tenant's crops, but merchants took advantage of their authority and charged higher prices to those buying on credit; sometimes the markup was astronomical. The crop-lien system had the potential to be financially disastrous for tenants because the only way for the tenants to meet their obligations was to have a good harvest and for their crop to "pay out." If the tenant's crop did not pay all of the debt, the unpaid portion was added to the following year's crop. Thus, tenants and sharecroppers had the potential to get deeper and deeper into debt every year with little chance of getting out.

The tenant/sharecropping system was intended to be a temporary solution to the labor problems in the South (and Georgia) after the war but unfortunately was not. By 1890 the tenancy rate in Georgia was 53 percent, increased to 65 percent by 1910, and by 1930 reached 68 percent. Tenancy/sharecropping became a permanent institution in Georgia, and rather than solving problems became a problem in its own right by creating a permanent, debt-ridden laboring class that had no way to escape. In that sense, tenant farming/sharecropping was an economic form of slavery.

What crops did Georgia farmers grow after the Civil War? Many were traditional crops that had been grown in the state for years, and in the immediate postwar years cotton remained king.

For a decade after the war, demand for cotton remained high. Textile manufacturers were willing to pay higher prices for the commodity as mills were starved for raw cotton. For twenty-five years after the Civil War, Georgia farmers increased production from 246,000 bales in 1866 to 1.05 million bales in 1880 to 1.2 million bales in 1890. Some farmers tried to diversify, but they were in the minority; those farmers experimented with livestock, grains, fruit orchards, and by the turn of the century, tobacco. Diversification of Georgia's agriculture was not terribly successful during the nineteenth century, and cotton remained the state's staple.

To improve farming in Georgia after the Civil War, research was conducted on farming methods, agricultural education was encouraged, and scientific methods were applied to farming. There was a concerted effort to combat declining soil fertility, smaller yields per acre, increased labor costs, and depressed prices. One example was the idea of applying fertilizer in the form of manure to Georgia farmlands, something that has been called the "guano craze." To many it appeared to be a great scientific discovery, and was nothing short of a mania in Georgia. By the late 1870s Georgia farmers were spending $4 million annually on fertilizer, double the amount of any other state, and by the turn of the century Georgians used 400,000 tons of fertilizer per year, roughly one-fourth of all the fertilizer in the country. Many farmers believed fertilizer was a cure-all and tended to ignore other practices such as rotation, cover crops, and proper tillage. It succeeded only in glutting the market with crops, particularly cotton.

Another way to promote agricultural education was the creation of societies, clubs, agencies, and publications to improve farming techniques. The Georgia State Agricultural Society, formed before the Civil War and revived shortly after the conflict, sent agents throughout the state to help educate farmers on new methods and techniques. A prewar farming journal that was likewise revitalized after the Civil War was the *Southern Cultivator*. Originating in Georgia, it was one of the two or three leading agricultural journals in the country and arguably the most respected farm journal in the South. In 1874 Georgia became the first state in the country with an agricultural department. This agency promoted agricultural improvements, inspected fertilizer, and gathered and dispensed a wide range of farming information. Georgia also benefited from the Morrill Land Grant Act, which the US Congress passed in 1862 to support agricultural education. The state built several agricultural programs with the proceeds from this federal legislation. The first was in Athens, which eventually became affiliated with the University of Georgia, and opened in 1873; subsequent schools were later opened in Dahlonega, Milledgeville, Thomasville, Cuthbert, and Savannah. Georgia farmers had many opportunities to learn about the latest crops, methods, and techniques.

Georgia's economy was predominantly agricultural in the years after the Civil War, but industrialization did begin to play a small role. The person most outspoken in favor of industrialization in Georgia and the South was Henry W. Grady, a newspaperman who eventually became part owner and editor of the *Atlanta Constitution*. His most notable editorial on the subject appeared on 14 March 1874 and was titled "The New South," in which he advocated for an increase in manufacturing. He claimed that the southern economy had survived relying on farming, but that it was time to change. Grady pleaded for industry and manufacturing to complement agriculture if the region and state were to progress economically. If not, he warned that the South would remain economically inferior to other regions of the country. Grady spent the rest of his career preaching this New South gospel of industrialization because he recognized that industry equaled economic progress. In 1881 Grady wrote that the Southern cotton crop was valued at $300 million when harvested, but $900 million after it was manufactured, mostly outside of the South; he wanted this transformation to take place in the South.

If Georgia were going to industrialize at all, then the state would have to have an efficient transportation system, which meant rebuilding the railroads. At the beginning of the Civil War Georgia had 1,420 miles of railroad, many of which were destroyed during the conflict. The state began rebuilding destroyed track and laid hundreds of miles of new track, some of which was financed by state bonds. By the turn of the century Georgia had 5,730 miles of track—a viable transportation system.

One of the most important industries in postwar Georgia was textiles. At the time of the Civil War, Georgia had 33 textile mills, but many were destroyed during the war, particularly during General Wilson's raid in 1865. Rebuilding took some time, but by 1870 Georgia had 34 mills, in 1890 the state had 53, and by the turn of the century 75 mills operated in Georgia. Other industries also thrived in Georgia after the war, particularly the lumber and naval stores industries. Lumber had been a traditional Georgia industry since the colonial era and regained its strength after the Civil War. Perhaps the fastest growing industry in the state was fertilizer: Georgia farmers used more of it than any other state, so it made sense to manufacture it. Much of the growth in the fertilizer industry was during the 1880s, and by 1890 Georgia had 44 factories that produced $5 million worth of fertilizer. One of the unintended results of greater industrialization was the increased urbanization of the state. Atlanta was becoming the most spectacular city in the New South, largely because it was a rail center, and its population grew rapidly by the turn of the century. Other Georgia cities with an industrial presence, such as Columbus, Macon, Augusta, and Savannah, also experienced significant growth.

In summary, Georgia's economy was largely agricultural, but industry grew in the postwar period. In 1870, 76 percent of Georgia's workforce was engaged in agriculture, while only 6 percent was engaged in manufacturing, and 18 percent in trade, professional occupations, and domestic service. US Census Bureau statistics noted Georgia's slowly growing industrialization: in 1870 the state had 3,836 manufacturing establishments employing 17,871 persons; by 1890 those numbers had increased to 4,285 establishments employing 52,298 Georgians.

Post Redemption Politics

Following Redemption in 1871, the Democratic Party had control of state government and maintained that control for a long period of time. Once Reconstruction ended, the Republican Party faded away and provided virtually no opposition to Georgia Democrats. In many elections during the next fifty to seventy-five years, there was no Republican opponent to contest state, gubernatorial, legislative or local elections. There was not total harmony in the Democratic Party, however, and factions developed. By the late 1870s the faction that came to dominate Georgia politics was known as the Bourbons. The term "Bourbon" is somewhat vague, but it was the name commonly applied to the faction more accurately referred to as New Departure Democrats (the two names will be used interchangeably).

The Bourbon philosophy emphasized reconciliation with the North, a willingness to put the issues of Reconstruction behind them, and a more pro-business economic outlook. Bourbons realized that the war was over, and they were willing to move past the divisive issues of Reconstruction. New Departure Democrats accepted the New South economic creed that Henry Grady was preaching. Their leaders were men like Benjamin H. Hill, Joseph E. Brown, John B. Gordon, and Alfred H. Colquitt. Gordon and Colquitt, both Confederate generals, could symbolize and glorify the old ways but look forward to a more progressive Georgia. Another faction in the Democratic Party was the traditional Southern Democrats. They held Southern conservative views, opposed Radical Reconstruction, wanted to eliminate any remnants of Reconstruction, and tended to look backward to the Old South. The leaders of this faction were Robert Toombs and Alexander H. Stephens. A third faction called themselves Independent Democrats. Independents earned the enmity of others in the party by garnering the support of the remaining Republicans in the state. William H. Felton was the Independent standard-bearer, and Tom Watson started his political career as an Independent.

By the late 1870s the New Departure Democrats gained control of the government, but before they asserted their authority there was a move to revise the state constitution. Robert Toombs was the unquestioned leader of the movement; he believed the 1868 document was the work of traitors (Republicans, carpetbaggers, scalawags, African Americans). In early 1877, the General Assembly passed legislation authorizing a new constitution. The convention, which worked from 11 July to 25 August 1877, was thoroughly dominated by Robert Toombs, and when the state ran out of money for the convention he advanced enough money to complete the work (about $20,000, which the state later repaid).

The Constitution of 1877 was by far the most conservative constitution the state had ever written. It prevented Georgia from implementing the New South economic creed that Henry Grady and the Bourbons supported, and it hindered industrialization. The state was not permitted to offer tax exemptions to encourage industrial development and could not invest state funds in private corporations. The requirements for voting did not change, except that a poll tax was included, however, the way in which the state apportioned seats in the House of Representatives was modified. The 6 largest counties received three representatives each, the next 26 counties had two representatives each, and the remaining 105 counties received one representative each. This apportionment system laid the foundation for the county unit system at a later time. In December 1877, Georgia voters approved the new constitution. There was not another revision of the state constitution until 1945.

Once the New Departure Democrats took control of the state government in the late 1870s there was a small clique within the faction, the Bourbon Triumvirate, that dominated Georgia politics. The trio included Joseph E. Brown, John B. Gordon, and Alfred H. Colquitt, with Henry Grady encouraging them. In the 1870s, 1880s, and 1890s these three men rotated in and out of the offices of Governor and US Senator and exercised considerable control over politics in Georgia. At times two of these men occupied both of Georgia's US Senate seats simultaneously, and from 1886 to 1890 they served as the state's US Senators and Governor (Gordon as Governor and Brown and Colquitt in the Senate). All three had served in some capacity during the Civil War—Gordon and Colquitt as Confederate generals and Brown as Georgia's governor—and all three had come to believe in the Bourbon/New Departure philosophy. (Brown even joined the Republican Party for a short time during Reconstruction.) Although the Triumvirate accepted the New South economic creed that their friend Henry Grady was pushing, they still held many traditional Southern beliefs, such as states' rights, the Democratic Party, and white supremacy (Gordon was the alleged leader of the Ku Klux Klan in Georgia).

The Bourbon Triumvirate was involved in a controversy in 1880 that merits mention. In that year, Colquitt was governor and Gordon had just been reelected to his seat in the US Senate. Shortly after being reelected, Gordon resigned and Colquitt, as governor, had to appoint somebody to fill the unexpired term. Colquitt appointed Brown. While that may not seem unusual as all three shared similar political beliefs, there was collusion, and the appointment of Brown was prearranged. All three denied collusion in 1880, but their correspondence bears out that they and Henry Grady arranged the appointment of Brown beforehand. The fact that the three of them exchanged coded letters on the matter suggests that they knew they were involved in something questionable. Despite the obvious collusion, which was not public knowledge until years later, none of them suffered any damage to their political careers or reputations.

The Farmers' Revolt

Although the Bourbons/New Departure Democrats were in power, there were challenges to their political supremacy, the most significant of which came from farmers. Georgia's farmers were faring poorly in the years after the Civil War; they were suffering economically, and nobody seemed able to help them. Distressed and distraught, farmers organized a revolt that seriously challenged the Bourbons. This revolt occurred in stages, with the Grangers the first organization to work for farmers. The Farmers Alliance then built upon the groundwork the Grangers had laid, and the Populists emerged as a true political party.

The Grangers (National Grange of the Patrons of Husbandry) was formed in 1867 as an organization to assist farmers. They lobbied Congress for farm-friendly legislation, operated crop-reporting services, organized social activities, and tried to create cooperative exchanges. The first local Grange in Georgia was formed in 1872, and by the following year there was a state organization. At its peak in 1874, Georgia Grangers boasted 684 local organizations with a membership of about twenty thousand. Unfortunately their influence was not great, and the organization began to decline. There was internal dissention, cooperative exchanges never materialized, and perhaps, most importantly, non-farmers were permitted significant influence in the organization (the non-farmers often held occupations that clashed with farmers: lawyers, merchants, and bankers). The decline continued through the 1870s and into the 1880s. In 1890, in an attempt to revitalize the organization in Georgia, the national convention was held in Atlanta, but this failed to save the Grangers in the state. Shortly thereafter, the US Department of Agriculture listed no Grange chapters in Georgia.

The Granger movement was the first stage in the farmers' revolt and led to the creation of the Farmers Alliance. The Alliance, founded in Texas in 1887, became the largest farm organization in the South during the nineteenth century; by 1890 it counted 1.2 million members. The first Alliance organization in Georgia appeared in Greene County in the summer of 1888, and a state Alliance was formed later that summer. By the following year there were Alliance lodges in 134 of Georgia's 137 counties, with a membership of about one hundred thousand. The Farmers Alliance learned from the Grangers and limited membership to farmers while expressly prohibiting those whose occupations clashed with farmers. In keeping with Southern society, the Alliance was segregated, so African American farmers formed the Colored Farmers Alliance, which first appeared in Georgia in 1890. The general goal of the Alliance was to improve the plight of the farmers through education (the spread of new farming practices), the formation of cooperative exchanges, and through lobbying Congress and state legislatures for farm legislation.

One of the Alliance programs that met with some success in Georgia involved cooperative arrangements with local merchants. Alliance farmers negotiated agreements with local merchants by which farmers would agree to buy from a single merchant and in return the merchant would sell goods to the farmers at reduced prices. Some Alliances, like the one in Putnam County, opened their own stores for Alliance members. They chose a board of directors, sold stock in the store, and a hired store manager. The Georgia Alliance also organized a state exchange, which sold the farmers' goods directly to markets (or in the case of cotton farmers, sold directly to the textile mills), eliminating the need for a middleman.

In 1888 and 1889 an opportunity arose for Georgia farmers and the Alliance to unite in a common cause. In 1888 jute manufacturers announced an increase in the price of jute, which was a burlap-type material used to wrap cotton bales. The announcement came too late for action in 1888, but the following year the state Alliance announced a boycott on jute, and cotton farmers wrapped their bales in other materials. The boycott succeeded on several levels: the price of jute was reduced, the issue united all Georgia farmers, and the boycott helped the Alliance grow.

The Farmers Alliance became a powerful political force in Georgia and the state Democratic Party, and its influence in state politics peaked in 1890. Farmers' issues were popular with politicians, and many ran on a platform that included helping the farmers. In 1890 politicians associated with the Alliance dominated the legislative and gubernatorial election. Both candidates for Governor, William J. Northen and Leonidas F. Livingston, were Alliance men; Northen won the election, so an Alliance politician was now Governor. A majority of those elected to the General Assembly were also associated with the Alliance, and the Assembly became known as the Farmers Legislature. Great reforms to help farmers were expected from this legislature and governor, but they did not happen; instead, laws that seemed to work against farmers—such as strengthening the crop-lien laws—were passed. Thus began the demise of the Farmers Alliance, as it was unable to maintain its political influence, and it soon gave way to another reform-minded group, the Populists.

The Populists, also known as the People's Party, continued the farmers' revolt and became perhaps the most serious challenge to the Bourbons. Populists in Georgia supported all of the Alliance issues, but also broadened their platform to be a national political party. Georgia Populism included reform of the convict-lease system, implementation of an income tax, low-interest loans for farmers, and the direct election of senators, along with other national reform issues. Without doubt, the most influential Georgia Populist was Tom Watson. Watson began his political career as a Democrat but became disillusioned with how little the party cared for farmers. He became a leader and spokesman for the Farmers Alliance, even though he never joined. Elected to the US House of Representatives in 1890, Watson joined the Populists the following year in a move that antagonized Georgia's Democratic

Party. With the Democratic Party lined up against him, Watson was defeated for reelection in 1892 and lost again in 1894 in elections marred by voting irregularities. The zenith of the Populist Party in Georgia came in 1894 when the party occupied fifty-two seats in the General Assembly. In 1896 the national Populist Party named Watson its vice presidential candidate, certainly the high point in Watson's association with Populism. Following the election, Populist fervor receded and the farmers' revolt effectively came to an end. A new reform movement was beginning in America and Georgia: Progressivism.

Chapter 7

The Progressive Era and Jim Crow

The Progressive Era (1890–1920) was a period of reform in
the United States. By 1890, many Americans perceived that the
country had problems, and the Progressive Era was a movement to
find solutions to problems associated with the rapid
industrialization and urbanization of America. This was also a
period when race relations in the South were at their worst; this
was the era of Jim Crow.

Progressive Era

Nationally, the goals of the Progressives included government
regulation, democratization of government, and social justice. In
many instances, reforms such as prohibition and women's suffrage
were enacted on a state level prior to becoming national reform
movements. In Georgia, Progressive goals included prohibition,
regulation of the railroads, education reform, and penal reform, but
Progressives in the state did not unite on a single issue. Georgia
Progressives should not be confused with the Populists as there
were marked differences between the two. Populists tended to
work for the interests of small farmers and tried, on occasion, to
unite white and black farmers (notably the efforts of Tom Watson).
Progressives, on the other hand, worked for more moderate reforms
and focused more on regulating business and professional interests.

In identifying the most progressive politicians in Georgia
during this period, two stand out—Joseph Terrell and Hoke

Smith. Joseph Terrell served two terms as governor, first elected in 1902 and then reelected in 1904. Typically regarded as a conservative, Terrell oversaw the passage of significant progressive legislation in the General Assembly. His major achievement was in education, where he won pay increases for teachers and increased appropriations for higher education. The state legislature also passed a bill regulating child labor, a state pure food and drug bill was enacted, while agricultural schools were established in each congressional district. The legislature also passed a bill making the buying and selling of votes in a primary election a misdemeanor. Joseph Terrell established a reputation as a progressive reformer, but his accomplishments have been overshadowed by his successor, Hoke Smith.

Generally regarded as Georgia's most progressive governor, Hoke Smith had, prior to his election, campaigned for Grover Cleveland in the 1892 presidential election and had been rewarded with appointment as Secretary of the Interior, a cabinet post he held from 1893 to 1896. Smith ran for governor in 1906 on a platform of progressive reform and won. During his term the state passed a prohibition bill, abolished the convict-lease system, increased appropriations for schools, strengthened the state railroad commission, and established fixed locations and times for primary elections. However, as an example of taking steps backwards in race relations, Smith also oversaw the passage of a constitutional amendment to disfranchise black voters. Denied reelection in 1908, Smith returned to the governor's office in the 1910 election and continued passing reform measures. His second term was short because he was elected to the US Senate, but Smith was able to establish a state board of education, a state department of labor, and have a bill to regulate lobbyists passed.

One issue that Georgia Progressives addressed was penal reform. In 1866 the state had created a convict-lease system, and since its inception there had been numerous attempts to reform or abolish it. Legislation to abolish the system failed to pass in 1877, and it was not until 1891 that the House Committee on the Penitentiary would condemn the system. Four years later, that same committee reported that all of the convict camps were in bad condition. After the turn of the century, opposition to the convict-lease system had become intense. In 1908 the state Democratic convention announced that it was against the system, and in the same year, the *Atlanta Georgian* began a crusade against leasing convicts.

It seemed the General Assembly would have to address the convict-lease system during its 1908 session, but astoundingly, the legislature adjourned without acting. Governor Hoke Smith then called a special session for August 1908 specifically to address the convict-lease problem. The General Assembly heard testimony from more than one hundred witnesses, and several proposals were submitted for plans to deal with the state's prisoners. One plan called for the convicts to be distributed among the counties, while another proposed the current leases be extended for two years and revenue from the leases be used to construct penitentiary buildings. In September the legislature settled on a plan by which existing leases expired on 1 April 1909 and thereafter, the state's convicts were worked on public roads. Georgia's infamous chain gang had been created. In terms of progressive reform, this development was clearly an example of Georgia taking one step forward by ending convict-lease, then taking two steps backward by creating the chain gang.

Another national reform movement in America was Prohibition: the movement to outlaw alcohol. Prohibition fit into the progressive goal of social justice; temperance reformers believed alcohol destroyed families and brought about crime, poverty, and general disorder in society. Georgia has a long history of opposing alcohol, dating back to the Trustee period in which strong drink was prohibited. Although the colonial restriction was lifted, Prohibition societies were formed in the state as early as the 1820s. In the late nineteenth and early twentieth centuries, other temperance societies appeared in Georgia, including chapters of the Women's Christian Temperance Union and the Anti-Saloon League. The first local chapter of the WCTU was formed in Georgia in 1880, while a state chapter opened in 1883. The Georgia chapter of the Anti-Saloon League was formed in 1906.

Attempts to outlaw alcohol in specific areas of the state ("making them dry") had to be accomplished through petitions to the General Assembly. Some of the first petitions went to the legislature in the 1870s and 1880s and were used to prohibit alcohol around schools and churches. The General Assembly then started drying up entire counties, and by 1881 forty-eight Georgia counties had outlawed alcohol. Four years later, in 1885, the legislature passed a local option bill that permitted each county to pass Prohibition legislation without going through the General Assembly. By the early part of the twentieth century, most Georgia counties were dry. In August 1907, while Hoke Smith was governor, the General Assembly passed a bill that prohibited the manufacture and sale of intoxicating beverages; it did not outlaw the importation and possession of such beverages. It was an imperfect act, if the goal was to make the state completely dry—a shortcoming that was fixed when a Prohibition bill passed in 1916 and Georgia became a bone-dry state. When the Eighteenth Amendment to the US Constitution came to Georgia for ratification, the General Assembly did not hesitate, and on 26 June 1918, the legislature ratified the Eighteenth Amendment, the eighth state to do so. Georgia was in step with the rest of the country on the issue of Prohibition.

One progressive issue in which Georgia was not in line with the rest of the country was women's suffrage. While many other states accorded women voting privileges, Georgia—and the South in general—hesitated to take that step. Suffrage and women's rights movements in the North built upon the antislavery and temperance movements that began in the years prior to the Civil War. In the immediate postwar years, a women's suffrage amendment was proposed to Congress in 1869, but no action was taken. Western states were the first to grant women the right to vote in the last half of the nineteenth century, but that sentiment made little headway in Georgia.

Numerous national organizations were founded to support women's suffrage, and most had chapters in Georgia. The Georgia Woman Suffrage Association (GWSA), formed in Columbus in 1890, was the state branch of the National American Woman Suffrage Association (NAWSA). Progress in Georgia was slow, and by 1893 the GWSA reported members in only five counties in the state. In an attempt to make further inroads, the NAWSA held its annual meeting in Atlanta in 1895, and 93 delegates, including Susan B. Anthony, attended. Four years later, the GWSA also held its first convention in Atlanta. Mary Latimer McLendon was chosen president of the convention, and the delegates passed a number of resolutions, none of which were enacted. One of the resolutions requested that the University of Georgia be opened to women, while another suggested that women should not pay taxes as long as they could not vote.

Although real accomplishments for women's rights and suffrage were nonexistent in Georgia, numerous organizations were formed to support those issues. In 1913 the Georgia Woman Equal Suffrage League was created, as well as the Georgia Men's League for Woman Suffrage, which was a largely symbolic organization with little to no influence. The following year, the Equal Suffrage Party of Georgia was formed, and by 1915 claimed members in thirteen counties. All of these organizations and parties competed with each other for membership and consequently accomplished little. Additionally, women's rights advocates faced opposition groups that were far more popular in Georgia. The National Association Opposed to Woman Suffrage opened a chapter in the state in 1914 and claimed to have two thousand members later that same year. Opponents of women's rights and suffrage far outnumbered supporters in Georgia.

By the mid-1910s, numerous states had granted women the right to vote, and in 1914 the General Assembly held hearings on the issue. The House Committee on Suffrage heard testimony in support of suffrage from women such as Mary Latimer McLendon and her sister Rebecca Latimer Felton. Others, including Mildred Rutherford, testified against suffrage for women. The House committee voted against a resolution for women's suffrage in a 5–2 vote. The following year, 1915, both House and Senate committees held hearings on suffrage and both voted against it. Two years later, New York granted women the right to vote in state elections, a significant and influential development in the eyes of many, particularly for suffragists in Georgia. The Georgia Senate committee held suffrage hearings again in 1917, and this time the committee approved a resolution for suffrage by an 8–4 vote. The General Assembly adjourned, however, before taking action on the resolution. One other development in 1917 was significant: it was the year that Waycross permitted women to vote in municipal elections, the first time women could vote anywhere in Georgia. Two years later, in 1919, Atlanta passed a similar ordinance permitting women the right to vote in municipal elections.

Nationally, New York granting suffrage was an important step for the campaign. With New York in the fold, women's suffrage could now claim to be a valid national movement (such was the influence of New York). A women's suffrage amendment was proposed in Congress, and in June 1919 it passed with the support of only one Southern senator—Georgia's William J. Harris; all other Southern senators opposed it. The amendment was then sent to the states for ratification, and Georgia acted quickly. On 24 July 1919 both houses of the General Assembly overwhelmingly passed resolutions against the amendment; Georgia was the first state to reject the Nineteenth Amendment. The vote in the Senate was 39–10, and in the House it was 118–29. Despite Georgia's actions, the amendment was ratified in August 1920, and women across the country had won the right to vote. Georgia, however, still dragged its feet. The state required that voters be registered for six months prior to an election before casting a vote. The legislature refused to pass a bill to permit women to vote in the November 1920 elections, so Georgia women had to wait until 1922 to cast their first vote in state and national elections. As a symbolic gesture the Georgia General Assembly later ratified the Nineteenth Amendment—in 1970 (the last state to do so).

Without doubt, the most influential woman in Georgia in the late nineteenth and early twentieth centuries was Rebecca

Latimer Felton. Although most closely associated with the women's suffrage movement, Felton was active in politics, spoke for other reform issues, and was a prolific writer. Her marriage to William Felton in 1853 was her conduit into state politics. William Felton, a Whig prior to the Civil War, aligned with the Independent Democrats, having rejected the ideals of the Bourbon/New Departure Democrats. Between 1874 and 1890 Felton served three terms in the US House of Representatives and three terms in the Georgia General Assembly. Rebecca Felton served as his campaign manager and closest advisor during his political career. The Felton constituency believed that they got two representatives when they elected William Felton. The pair constituted a team, and Rebecca Felton wrote many of her husband's speeches and drafted much of the legislation he proposed. Even so, she developed a political and public identity separate from that of William Felton.

Rebecca Felton emerged from William Felton's shadows after he retired from public service in the 1890s. She immersed herself in reform-type movements, such as Prohibition, abolition of the convict-lease system, and women's suffrage. In the late 1890s she began writing a column in the *Atlanta Journal* called "The Country Home," a column that was in print for two decades. Although she fought for progressive reform, Felton held many opinions that were typical of white Georgians; she had conservative racial views and at one point supported the lynching of black men. What Felton is best known for is being the first woman to serve in the US Senate, in 1922. It is ironic that the first state to reject the Nineteenth Amendment also had the first woman in the Senate. When Senator Tom Watson died in 1922, Governor Thomas Hardwick appointed Felton to serve until a special election was held to choose a permanent replacement. She was sworn in on 21 November 1922 and gave a speech in which she called the Senate's attention to the ten million women voters who were observing the event. The following day her successor, Walter George, took his place in the Senate. Rebecca L. Felton died in 1930 and is one of the most significant women in Georgia's history.

One of the national goals of Progressivism was the democratization of government, and Georgia joined the rest of the country by implementing primary elections in 1898. With this political development, party officials no longer had control over who ran for public offices in Georgia (such as governor, state legislature, and local offices). Primary elections would be held, and the voters of the state would choose the candidates who ran in the general elections. Primary elections were often held in the summer of an election year with the general elections in November. In 1912 Georgia extended the primary system to the presidential election and held presidential primary elections. This was political progress, but it should be noted that the parties conducted the primary elections and could implement their own rules on how the elections were run. In this era the Democratic Party controlled Georgia politics; the Republican Party often did not field candidates and therefore did not conduct primary elections. In 1912, for example, the Democratic Party in Georgia held a presidential primary but the Republican Party did not.

Another political development in Georgia during this era was the implementation in 1917 of the county unit system for statewide elections. A county unit system of representation in the General Assembly had been written into the state's constitution in 1877. This formula called for the 6 largest counties to receive three representatives each, the next 26 counties had two representatives each, and the remaining 105 counties received one representative each. In 1917, with the passage of the Neill Primary Act, this formula was applied to determine the outcomes of statewide elections, such as governor's elections; the candidate who received the most county unit votes won the election. Under this system, the larger, urban counties such as Fulton, Chatham, and Richmond were not nearly as significant as the smaller, rural counties like Echols and Chattahoochee. All votes did not count equally as votes in the smaller, rural counties counted a great deal more than votes in larger, urban ones. The county unit system determined how gubernatorial candidates campaigned—in order to win, more emphasis was placed on the small, rural counties. Candidates could skip or ignore the large, urban counties and still win the election, a lesson well-learned by politicians such as Eugene Talmadge. The county unit system was decidedly unfair, but was used until the US Supreme Court declared it unconstitutional in the 1960s.

Jim Crow Era

The reform sentiment did not extend to African Americans in Georgia; this era was arguably the worst in race relations in the state's history. It is fair to portray the Progressive Era as "for whites only" as white oppression of black Georgians continued unabated between 1890 and 1920, and beyond. The state legislature passed Jim Crow laws, the economic exploitation of African Americans continued, race riots took place, the Ku Klux Klan was revitalized, mob violence and lynchings were commonplace, and African Americans were disfranchised. It was simply a bad time to be a person of color in Georgia.

One of the goals of Georgia Progressives was to maintain white supremacy, and Georgia joined the rest of the South in accomplishing this by passing Jim Crow laws. These laws legalized and institutionalized segregation, but they could also be implemented locally through ordinances or practices and customs without legislation. Jim Crow succeeded in segregating virtually all aspects of Georgia society, including all public accommodations. Georgia's General Assembly passed the state's first Jim Crow law in 1891, which segregated public transportation. This law required that separate railway cars be provided for white and black passengers and empowered the conductor to "eject" from the cars any person who sat in the wrong place. The law also made it illegal for any railway employee to permit white and black passengers to ride in the same car. The separate cars were, however, required to be equal. The US Supreme Court upheld segregation in transportation in the *Plessy v. Ferguson* case in 1896, which made "separate but equal" accommodations legal and constitutional.

Separation of the races was also achieved through city ordinances and local practices and customs. In 1913 Atlanta established segregated residential patterns when it issued an ordinance segregating white and black neighborhoods. Residents could legally object if a family of a different race moved into the neighborhood. Ironically, the first case tried under this ordinance involved a white family that moved into a black neighborhood; the white family was forced to move out. The Georgia Supreme Court struck down this ordinance in 1915, so the Atlanta city council rewrote the ordinance to make it more acceptable. What makes the segregation of neighborhoods stand out is that although the US Supreme Court outlawed this practice in its 1917 *Buchanan v.*

Warley case, cities simply ignored the court's decision and passed new ordinances anyway.

Another way of oppressing African Americans in Georgia was through peonage—the act of keeping them as peons for the commission of a crime, or involuntary servitude. When an individual was convicted of a crime (frequently a misdemeanor) there were limited punishment options: pay a fine or serve on the notorious chain gang. Most blacks in Georgia could not pay the fine, which left them vulnerable to those who needed laborers. A businessman (or large farmer, lumberman, or mine owner) could pay the fine and the convict would work for the businessman until the amount of the fine was satisfied. It was an informal and extralegal system, organized and controlled by law enforcement officials and often described as the "new slavery." In this new slavery, African Americans were specifically targeted, and the county sheriff can be described as a slave trader. Sheriffs often colluded with local businessmen to arrest black men, whose labor the businessmen then purchased.

Crimes for which African Americans were arrested were often flimsy and trumped up, or were laws that were passed specifically to target black men. By the beginning of the twentieth century, laws had been passed that criminalized many aspects of black life, and the violation of these laws were used to keep thousands of African Americans in a state of peonage in Georgia. Vagrancy laws, for example, were deliberately vague and therefore useful to sheriffs in maintaining peonage. Other "crimes" for which African Americans were sold into peonage included bigamy, miscegenation, illegal voting, homosexuality, using obscene language, gambling, carrying a concealed weapon, bastardy, and false pretense, among others.

A variation of peonage was created in Georgia in 1903 when the General Assembly passed a contract labor law. The law was ostensibly written to prevent laborers (such as tenant farmers, lumbermen, turpentine workers) from breaking their contracts; failure to fulfill a contract was seen as intent to defraud. Tenant farmers, for example, might be advanced a sum of money or amount of supplies and then disappear. This law was created to prevent that from happening, but ultimately was used to force blacks into peonage.

One of the worst abusers of peonage in Georgia was Edward McRee, a member of the state legislature. McRee and his brothers owned twenty-two thousand acres in Lowndes County, south Georgia, that included a plantation named Kinderlou, sawmill, cotton gin, crate factory, dairy, cigar factory, and naval stores operation. The McRees initially leased prisoners from the penitentiary, but after the turn of the century began trolling the county courthouse for laborers. When that provided insufficient numbers they arranged with sheriffs of local counties to have African Americans arrested. The McRees would pay the fines, and in this way obtain thousands of laborers in an arrangement that may be described as human trafficking. In 1903 Edward McRee and his brothers were indicted in federal court on thirteen counts of holding African American men and women against their will. Claiming ignorance, McRee pled guilty and was given a symbolic and token fine of a thousand dollars. McRee's indictment was unusual because those who held men and women as peons were almost never prosecuted.

While peonage and contract labor laws were illegal in the United States, it did not stop Georgia from maintaining them for many decades. In 1867 Congress passed the Peonage Abolition

A Brief History

Act, which enforced the Thirteenth Amendment ban on involuntary servitude. The act did not, however, apply to persons convicted of a crime so did not prevent peonage from continuing in Georgia. In 1905 the US Supreme Court upheld the Peonage Abolition Act in *Clyatt v. United States*, but defined peonage so narrowly that the federal government could not stop the practice. Contract labor laws were, likewise, invalidated in the 1912 Supreme Court case *Bailey v. Alabama*, but Georgia successfully circumvented this decision for thirty years. Finally, in 1942, the US Supreme Court struck down contract labor laws in *Taylor v. Georgia*. Peonage and contract labor laws were finally outlawed.

During the Jim Crow era, black voters in the state continued to be disfranchised through intimidation and violence even though the Fifteenth Amendment had been ratified in 1870. At the turn of the century, voting rights began to be denied to African Americans through legislation and party rules. The first such attempt in Georgia came in 1900 when the Democratic Party changed its rules for voting in primary elections, ruling that only white voters could participate and limiting black voters to voting only in the general election. Because the Republican Party essentially did not exist in Georgia during the early twentieth century, this move placed serious limitations on African American voters. Since this was a party rule and not a state law, it did not conflict with the provisions of the Fifteenth Amendment.

The General Assembly also passed disfranchisement legislation. Georgia had adopted a poll tax in its 1877 constitution, and ten years later the legislature made poll taxes cumulative. Major disfranchisement legislation was passed in 1907, ironically during the administration of Georgia's most progressive governor,

Hoke Smith. This bill established guidelines for who could vote in Georgia:

- Persons who served in US military during wartime;
- All persons descended from those who served during wartime (known as the grandfather clause);
- Persons who were of good character;
- Those who could read, write, and interpret a paragraph of the constitution;
- Those persons who owned 40 acres of land or taxable property of at least $500.

The bill was added to the state constitution in 1908, and effectively ended black voting; by 1910 the percentage of eligible black voters who were registered to vote had decreased to 4 percent.

African Americans were also oppressed through violence, such as that which ensued during the Atlanta Race Riot of 1906. The gubernatorial election of the same year paved the way for the riot, with Hoke Smith running a race-baiting campaign and the Atlanta newspapers carrying stories about African American men who assaulted white women; in most cases the stories were greatly exaggerated and in some cases fabricated entirely. The *Atlanta Constitution*, for example, ran a headline on 23 September 1906 that read "4 Attempts At Assault In One Day." These types of stories, along with the recent political campaign, led to three days of rioting in September 1906.

The previous day, Saturday, 22 September, the newspapers had run a series of stories along the same lines, and the pent-up anger of white Atlantans exploded. On that evening, thousands of whites roamed the city streets searching for African Americans to attack; by 10 p.m. the size of this mob was estimated at ten thousand. Many whites were buying guns, and one hardware store sold $16,000 worth of guns and ammunition in an hour and a half. The Fulton County sheriff banned gun sales, but arrested only one store owner, who had been selling guns to blacks. The Atlanta police sympathized with the mob and did nothing to stop the riot. The mob interpreted police non-involvement as approval, and assaults and beatings gave way to murders. Black businesses were also attacked. Unfortunately for Atlanta's black community Governor Terrell did not declare martial law.

The rioting continued for three days, from 22–24 September 1906. Official reports stated that 25 African Americans were killed and 150 wounded or injured, but W.E.B. Du Bois estimated that at least 100 had been killed. Additionally, one white police officer was killed in the riot. The Atlanta Race Riot was one of the most serious instances of race violence in Georgia history.

Another common way of oppressing African Americans was through intimidation, leading to the revival of the Ku Klux Klan in Georgia in 1915. The Reconstruction era Klan disappeared in the early 1870s and remained largely invisible until the Jim Crow era. The person most responsible for bringing the Klan back to public life was William J. Simmons. Simmons's father had been a member of the Klan in the 1860s and 1870s, and Simmons grew up hearing stories of their activities during Reconstruction. In 1900 Simmons claimed to have had a vision of white-robed horsemen riding across the wall of his bedroom, and he vowed to form an organization that would memorialize the Ku Klux Klan of old. Simmons may also have been influenced by D.W. Griffith's 1915 movie *The Birth of a Nation*, which portrayed the Reconstruction era Klansmen as heroes. In 1915 Simmons led a group of men to

Stone Mountain on Thanksgiving night, burned a cross, and the new Ku Klux Klan was formed.

This new Ku Klux Klan in Georgia did not limit its intimidation and violence only to African Americans, but expanded its list of undesirables to include Catholics, Jews, immigrants, radicals, organized labor, and any other segment of the population that might pose a threat (either real or imagined) to its view of Americanism. Klan members attempted to uphold their idea of traditional moral values, tried to have Catholic teachers removed, and targeted those suspected of violating their "moral code," including people suspected of adultery, bootlegging, drunkenness, and prostitution, among others. Membership in the Georgia Klan was slow to rise, but peaked at about 156,000 in 1925 then dropped to approximately 1,400 in 1930.

As an organization, the Ku Klux Klan exerted it most powerful political influence during the 1920s. In 1922 the Klansmen supported the gubernatorial campaign of Clifford Walker, who was also a member of the organization. Walker was elected governor and spoke at a national Klan meeting in Kansas City in 1924 while he was in office. Other prominent Georgia politicians were members, suspected of being members, sympathized with, or attended Klan functions. These included US Senators Tom Watson and William J. Harris, Georgia Supreme Court Chief Justice Richard Russell, Secretary of Agriculture J.J. Brown, and Atlanta Mayor Walter Sims. Those who spoke out against the Klan experienced the wrath of the organization. Governor Thomas Hardwick, elected in 1920, requested that the General Assembly pass a bill to unmask the Klan; the organization campaigned against Hardwick in the 1922 election, and he was ousted from office. Georgia Supreme Court Justice James Hines likewise attacked the Klan, and the organization worked against his reelection. The early to mid-1920s was the height of the Klan's political influence in Georgia, but this influence waned as the decade came to a close.

Perhaps the most vicious and systemic method of oppressing African Americans in Georgia was through mob violence and lynching. Lynching became commonplace in the South during Jim Crow; it was a semi-official institution and became a part of Southern culture. It was so prevalent that one historian called lynching a national pastime. Nowhere was mob violence more common than in Georgia. The number of victims is difficult to determine exactly, and the numbers vary. Historian Fitzhugh Brundage counted 460 lynching victims in Georgia between 1880 and 1930; the NAACP counted 386 between 1889 and 1918; and the Tuskegee Institute tallied 531 in the state between 1882 and 1968. The vast majority of the victims were African American: 441 of Brundage's 460; 492 of Tuskegee's 531; and 360 of the NAACP's 386 victims were black.

The causes of mob violence and lynchings varied—from the commission of a crime to a perceived slight (real or imagined)—but whatever the cause, it was certain that, in Georgia, an African American man or woman was more likely to become a victim than a white person. Women were not spared from lynching, and ten Georgia women ended up as victims. Most of these lynchings were carried out despite the presence of a state law passed in 1893 prohibiting them. Unfortunately, anti-lynching laws were routinely ignored, and those who carried out mob violence against blacks were not likely to be prosecuted or punished for their actions.

There were hundreds of lynchings in Georgia, including those of Sam Hose in 1899, Mary Turner in 1918, and Leo Frank in

1915. There were also cases of attempted lynchings such as that of Henry Delgale in 1899. Sam Hose was a farm laborer in Coweta County. During an argument with Alfred Cranford, his employer, Cranford allegedly threatened Hose and pointed a gun at him. In self-defense Hose hurled an axe at Cranford, hitting him in the head and killing him. Hose then allegedly raped Cranford's wife and left the premises. The manhunt was on, with at least $1,600 in rewards available for Hose's capture. Hose was soon captured and taken to Newnan to be identified by Mrs. Cranford (one of the rituals of lynching being identification by the victim). Word of Hose's capture spread, and special trains were organized from Atlanta to Newnan so spectators could witness the execution. Hose was sadistically tortured, dismembered (ears, fingers, and penis were cut off), and finally burned to death.

Another brutal lynching was that of Mary Turner, one of ten women in Georgia to be victims of mob violence. Mary Turner and her husband, Hayes Turner, worked on a farm in Brooks County in a state of peonage. Their employer Hampton Smith often beat his workers, including both Hayes and Mary Turner. Smith's employees planned to murder Smith, which they did in May 1918, and what followed was a lynching spree second-to-none in Georgia. Mobs in Brooks County lynched at least thirteen people, and an NAACP investigation afterwards suggested the number was higher. After Hayes Turner was killed during this lynching rampage, Mary Turner apparently stated that if she learned who killed her husband she would swear out warrants against them. This threat to the mob made her the next victim. Mary Turner, eight months pregnant at the time, was captured shortly thereafter and killed in a most brutal manner. Her feet were tied together and she was hung upside down from a tree while her clothes were burned off of her body. A member of the mob then cut her unborn baby from her stomach and she was riddled with hundreds of bullets. Mary Turner was proof that even women and unborn children were not spared the wrath of a Georgia lynch mob.

The case of Leo Frank stands out because Frank was a white man. In 1913 Leo Frank, the supervisor at a pencil factory in Atlanta, was accused and tried for murdering one of his employees, thirteen-year-old Mary Phagan. Though Frank was white, he was also Jewish, which is why he was tried for the crime. One of the remarkable developments in Frank's trial was that the jury was willing to believe the testimony of black factory workers over the testimony of Leo Frank himself. Frank was convicted and sentenced to death; after exhausting his appeals his execution was set for June 1915, but Georgia's governor, John Slaton, reviewed the case file and commuted Frank's sentence to life imprisonment. In Mary Phagan's hometown of Marietta, a lynch mob formed to dispense its own brand of justice. The mob plucked Leo Frank from the state penitentiary in Milledgeville, drove him two hundred miles to the outskirts of Marietta and hanged him.

Although hundreds of African Americans were killed, not every lynch mob got its victim. Such was the case with Henry Delgale. In 1899, in McIntosh County, Delgale was accused of raping a white woman, an accusation that was likely to lead to the formation of a mob. The accused man surrendered to the sheriff, who wanted to move Delgale to Savannah for his safety. Moving an African American man to another location provided an opportunity for a mob to take a prisoner from law enforcement officials, and the black community in Darien believed that this would be the case with Delgale. Black residents gathered around the prison to ensure that a mob did not take him, and they succeeded in protecting him. Delgale was put on trial and acquitted.

By the 1930s lynchings in Georgia decreased, but did not completely disappear. Reasons for the decline included a newly invigorated NAACP that often conducted investigations of mob violence, local law enforcement officials working to stop the practice, an expansion of federal authority, and the migration of African Americans out of the state.

So how did African Americans and other activists respond to the prejudice against blacks? One way was through the formation of the National Association for the Advancement of Colored People (NAACP). Initially created in 1909 with a statement opposing the lawlessness against African Americans, the NAACP officially adopted its name the following year. It wasn't until 1917 that branches were organized in Georgia, and early members tended to be in the professional classes, such as doctors, lawyers, businessmen, teachers, and ministers. The NAACP published a journal, *The Crisis*, which branded Georgia the "Empire State of Lynching." Georgia chapters could not count many civil rights victories, but the organization survived through World War II and expanded its influence. Georgian Walter White became the executive secretary of the national organization in 1930.

Another response to the dismal race relations in Georgia and the South was Booker T. Washington's "Atlanta Compromise Speech" in 1895. It was delivered at the Cotton States Exposition in Atlanta and outlined Washington's "accommodationist" view of relations between the races. The speech was directed to white Southerners, and it expressed a view that white Southerners would accept. Washington's idea was for gradualism in civil rights, for African Americans to gradually become part of white society;

blacks should work in agriculture, mechanics, and domestic service. The speech was well received in white Southern circles, but did generate some opposition, primarily from W.E.B. Du Bois. Du Bois, who joined the faculty of Atlanta University in 1897, believed Washington's speech represented black submission to white society. Despite opposition from Du Bois, Washington's speech is regarded as one of the most important in African American history.

A decade after Washington's speech some five hundred African American men and women gathered in Macon for the Equal Rights Convention. The statement they released was largely the work of W.E.B. Du Bois, proclaiming their fitness to vote and requesting enforcement of the Fourteenth and Fifteenth Amendments. The delegates also asked for an end to Jim Crow laws, particularly on railroad cars, and protested lynchings, especially those who had been murdered without a trial. The convention simply asked for equality under the law.

In 1921, Governor Hugh Dorsey published a pamphlet that described the living conditions of African Americans in Georgia. Dorsey chronicled 135 examples of general mistreatment of black Georgians in the previous two years. He listed four categories of mistreatment: lynching, peonage, organized lawlessness, and individual acts of cruelty. Dorsey suggested several remedies for the deplorable situation, such as generating publicity about the treatment of blacks, compulsory education, the creation of a state committee on race relations, investigation of lynchings, and a fine on all counties in which a lynching occurred. This was the first time in Georgia's history that a governor had taken up the cause of African American men and women in the state.

Ultimately, living conditions for African Americans were so deplorable in Georgia that many opted to leave the state during the Great Migration of the 1910s. Blacks migrated from all parts of the state, but the greatest exodus was from the South, as the black population in north Georgia was fairly small, and those in middle Georgia (the Black Belt) were tied to the land by contract or indebtedness. Savannah was probably the South's leading migration center, as it had good port and rail facilities. The Great Migration in Georgia surged during World War I (1914–18) when there were jobs available producing war materials in Northern factories. During the war years alone more than fifty thousand African Americans left the state.

The Progressive Era in Georgia had mixed characteristics: On one hand, some progressive reform was made, such as eliminating the convict-lease system, passing Prohibition, and fighting for women's suffrage. But as the state made some forward progress, so, too did it take steps backward: convict-lease was abolished and women gained the right to vote, but African Americans were disfranchised and the chain-gang was created. In fact, being such a low point in race-relations, the Progressive Era can be best be described as "for whites only."

Chapter 8

The Depression, New Deal, and World War II

The era between World War I and World War II was one of the most turbulent in Georgia's history. The state's agricultural economy was hit with a series of crises that began a decline from which it took years to recover. It was also during this era that Georgians got to know New Yorker Franklin D. Roosevelt, who discovered the therapeutic and recuperative value of Warm Springs (located sixty miles south of Atlanta in Meriwether County) and who became a regular visitor to Georgia. The Great Depression hit Georgia early, as it did in most Southern states, and the state did not emerge from this economic downturn until President Roosevelt's New Deal helped jump-start the economy. World War II had a major impact on the state as Georgians worked in the factories to manufacture war materials, trained at Georgia military bases, fought and died on the battlefields, and guarded enemy prisoners of war.

Economic Developments

Georgia's economy in the early twentieth century was mainly agricultural, as it had been since colonial times. Georgia's farmers were still largely tenants, and tenancy was on the rise, reaching almost 70 percent by 1930. Cotton was still king in Georgia, and the focus on cotton helped prevent many farmers from diversifying. Other obstacles to diversification included an inadequate banking structure and a lack of good roads; by 1930 only 6 percent of Georgia's farmers lived near paved roads. Industrialization continued its halting move into rural Georgia in the early twentieth century, which led to slow urban growth in the state. Industry grew more rapidly in Atlanta than other parts of the state, so naturally the city experienced the largest urban growth also.

Cotton was the most abundant cash crop in Georgia. The total acreage and proportion of the state's farmland devoted to cotton increased through the first two decades of the twentieth century. Cotton production increased, reaching a peak of 2.76 million bales (500-pound bales) in 1911; Georgia farmers never produced this much again (the closest was 2.22 million bales in 2001). Two problems beset cotton farmers at this time—low prices and the boll weevil. The drop in cotton prices was precipitous, from 35 cents per pound in 1919 to 17 cents in 1920 and 7 cents in 1932. A more serious problem for cotton farmers, however, was the boll weevil. Moving eastward from Texas at a rate of about seventy-five miles a year, this "winged demon" arrived in Georgia in 1913, leaving a path of devoured cotton in its wake. Initial losses in Georgia were not heavy, but by 1919 the damage was serious, and by 1923 the boll weevil became a disaster as Georgia's entire cotton production that year amounted to a mere 588,000 bales. The only consolation for cotton farmers was that some had diversified their crops, and these crops were more profitable. Cotton farmers recovered from this calamity, and by the beginning of the twenty-first century Georgia was the third-leading cotton-producing state in the union (with 1.5 million bales produced in 2002).

Some of the new crops Georgia farmers grew included tobacco and peanuts. Tobacco was not a traditional crop in Georgia and did not gain a foothold until the 1890s, but it soon became a suitable replacement for cotton as a cash crop. As the boll weevil wrought its destruction on cotton, tobacco became more attractive and production increased dramatically in Georgia from 4.2 million pounds in 1917 to 50 million pounds in 1927 and 104 million pounds in 1930. By the end of the 1920s, tobacco had become the state's second most important cash crop, and entering the twenty-first century, Georgia became the sixth-leading tobacco-producing state in the country (with 55 million pounds produced in 2002). Perhaps more spectacular even than tobacco was the rise of peanuts as a cash crop in Georgia. Until World War I there was only minimal interest in peanuts, and they were grown for grazing purposes only, but during the war years the demand for vegetable oil increased, as did interest in growing peanuts. Peanut production exploded in Georgia during World War I, increasing from 79 million pounds in 1916 to 244 million pounds in 1918. A similar increase occurred during World War II, as demand for vegetable oils again increased; in 1939, Georgia produced 368 million pounds of peanuts, and by 1943 the state's peanut farmers produced 788 million pounds. By mid-century peanuts had replaced tobacco as Georgia's second most important cash crop. In 1995 the General Assembly passed a resolution making peanuts the official crop of Georgia, and entering the twenty-first century, Georgia was the nation's leading peanut-producing state (with 1.8 billion pounds produced in 2003).

Industrialization in Georgia was slow to develop. In 1910 only 9 percent of Georgia's workforce was engaged in manu-facturing, and this number increased to only 15 percent by 1930. In 1910 Georgia produced only 1 percent of the nation's manufactured goods. The state's leading industry during the first half of the twentieth century was textiles. There were numerous advantages for the textile industry in Georgia, such as proximity to raw materials, an abundance of cheap power, low wages, long working hours, and an absence of labor unions. These advantages drew numerous textile mills from the Northeast to Georgia and the South, where they dominated towns in which they were located. The companies frequently owned most of the houses, churches, schools, and stores, and became paternalistic. In some respects a mill family lived much like a tenant family—the mill store provided supplies that would be charged to a worker's future earnings, and workers were often paid in mill scrip, which was redeemable only at the mill store. As harsh as this lifestyle might sound, it was better than being a tenant farmer. By 1940 conditions had improved for textile workers largely a result of a series of strikes by textile workers in the 1930s. Their workweek was reduced to forty hours, the number of company-owned stores declined, and the use of company scrip had largely disappeared. Wages were still low in 1940, and 60 percent of mill families still lived in company-owned houses, but most of these housing units had electricity and running water. Textile mills also provided one of the few opportunities for women to work outside the home.

One of the significant industries in Georgia in the early twentieth century was the naval stores industry. Naval stores came from the process of extracting the resin from pine trees, which were abundant, particularly in south Georgia. The resin was then used to produce turpentine, tar, and pitch, but the method of collecting the resin badly damaged the trees and often killed them. In 1901 University of Georgia chemist Charles H. Herty developed a new method to collect the pine resin that did not damage the tree. His cup-and-gutter system, for which he received a patent in 1903, revolutionized the naval stores industry and was the standard collection method for seventy-five years. By the 1920s Georgia led the nation in naval stores production.

The most famous industry in the state in the early twentieth century (and beyond) was undoubtedly Coca-Cola. Atlanta pharmacist John S. Pemberton created the concoction, which consisted of extracts of coca leaf and kola nuts, in 1886. Pemberton sold the fountain drink, which promised health benefits, out of an Atlanta drug store for several years before selling the rights to the drink to Asa Griggs Candler. Candler then formed the Coca-Cola Company in 1892, which went on to become the most successful soft drink company in the world. In the twenty-first century Coca-Cola is distributed in more than two hundred countries.

Political Developments in 1920s Georgia

Between World War I and World War II Georgians elected three largely undistinguished governors, Thomas Hardwick, Clifford Walker, and Lamartine Hardman, followed by two who stood out, Richard Russell and Eugene Talmadge. Prior to his election in 1920, Thomas Hardwick served in the Georgia House of Representatives and in both houses of Congress, where he earned a reputation as a racist. In Congress he sought to repeal the Fourteenth and Fifteenth Amendments and spoke in support of disfranchising African Americans. Once governor, however, Hardwick pursued a fairly progressive agenda, but the General Assembly did not cooperate with him and little of his legislative program passed. What did pass included the state's first tax on gasoline, which brought in a significant amount of revenue, and a secret ballot law. Hardwick proposed more progressive legislation that did not pass, such as a reorganization of the state government, which was badly needed, the creation of a Board of Regents for state colleges and universities, and a state income tax. Probably his most notable action was his appointment of Rebecca L. Felton to the US Senate in 1922 to fill the unexpired term of Tom Watson.

In an era when most Georgians did not approve of women's suffrage and Georgia was the first state to reject the Nineteenth Amendment, his appointment of Felton was notable.

Throughout his governorship, Hardwick clashed with the Ku Klux Klan; this clash seems to indicate a turnaround from his years in Congress. In the 1920s few public officials spoke out against the Klan, but Hardwick was probably the first Georgia politician to denounce Klan violence. The governor wanted the Klan to unmask and if it did not do so voluntarily Hardwick planned to work for legislation to accomplish that goal. Hardwick also wanted legislation to permit the governor to declare martial law in areas where the Klan was active, similar to the 1871 federal Ku Klux Klan Act. None of these proposals became law, and in 1922 the Klan campaigned vigorously against Hardwick and threw its support behind Clifford Walker.

With Klan support Clifford Walker was elected governor in 1922 and reelected in 1924. A graduate of the University of Georgia, Walker first served Georgia as the state attorney from 1915 to 1920. As governor, Walker had an undistinguished legislative record, but where he stood out was through his close association with the Ku Klux Klan. After his election, Walker announced that he would neither report Klan activity nor prosecute Klan members. In fact, he consulted with Klan leaders before making appointments and in formulating government policy. In 1924 Walker traveled to Kansas City and delivered an address at a national Klan meeting then consulted with the Imperial Wizard. The governor initially denied reports of his speech but later admitted they were true. Walker's two terms mark the high point of Klan influence in Georgia's state government.

The third in this trio of largely forgotten governors was Lamartine Hardman, who was elected in 1926 and reelected in 1928. Hardman had previously served in both the Georgia House and Senate, where he coauthored the state's Prohibition law. His most significant accomplishment was the appointment of a committee, the Ivan Allen Committee, in 1926 to make recommendations for streamlining state government. The committee reported that the structure of the state government was antiquated and lacked central oversight. Although Hardman did not act on the committee's report, reorganization of state government became a central issue in the next governor's election.

In the 1930 gubernatorial election Democrat Richard Russell, Jr. made state government reorganization the focus of his campaign. After serving ten years in the Georgia House, the last four as Speaker, Russell ran for governor in a campaign that emphasized the need for greater efficiency in state government. Russell was duly elected, and in his inaugural address called for the General Assembly to pass a reorganization bill. The legislature seemed receptive, perhaps because the body was familiar with Russell. The General Assembly promptly passed the Reorganization Act of 1931, which was the most important piece of legislation during Russell's administration. The bill overhauled government agencies, reducing their number from 102 to 17. It also created a Board of Regents that had authority over the state's colleges and universities. The Russell administration passed other reform bills, including a constitutional amendment that moved the gubernatorial inauguration from June to January. In 1932 Russell declined to run for reelection and instead sought election to the US Senate, where he became a fixture for almost forty years serving until he died in 1971.

Great Depression

By the mid-1920s, economic indicators were beginning to decline in the United States even though most Americans did not recognize the trend. A major exception was the stock market, which continued to grow throughout most of the decade. When stocks began to decline in the fall of 1929, America quickly entered a recession. Because of its primarily agricultural nature, Georgia's economy (and the rest of the South's) began to decline as early as 1920, however, before the national economic downturn started. American agriculture had boomed in the 1910s, a result of increased demand for American farm products during World War I, but when the conflict ended, demand for US agricultural products also ended; those states whose economy was largely agricultural, began to experience a decline.

Cotton was the state's most important crop, and the decline of cotton in the early 1920s was attributed to several factors: First was the arrival of the boll weevil, which wrought a path of destruction through Georgia that peaked in 1923 when only 588,000 bales were harvested. Second was the drop in cotton prices: from 1919 to 1920 cotton prices dipped from 36 cents per pound to 17 cents, and then continued to drop throughout the decade, hitting 7 cents by 1932. Between 1919 and 1920 the value of Georgia's cotton crop decreased by $176 million. The third factor in the decline of the state's cotton production was competition from states in the Southwest, particularly Texas and Oklahoma. Georgia's cotton farmers did not recover from the decline and never again reached 1919 income levels. Other agricultural commodities did not suffer to the extent of cotton, but they did not thrive either.

Other sectors of Georgia's economy also declined, but not to the extent of agriculture. Because industry did not make up as much of the state's economy in the 1920s, it served to limit the effects of the Depression, and Georgia's national rank in industrial output did not change as a result of the economic downturn. One sector of the state's economy that was hit hard, however was the banking system, which went into decline when the Florida land boom of the mid-1920s collapsed. Many Georgia banks had made loans to persons who bought land in Florida, and many of those loans could not be repaid when the land prices collapsed. The banking decline continued into the 1930s and did not recover until the New Deal was implemented. Additionally, during the Great Depression, Georgia lost Milton County and Campbell County, which could not survive the economic slide and which, in 1932, merged with Fulton County; Georgia thereafter had 159 counties. One sector of the state's economy that fared better comparatively was employment, or rather unemployment rates. In 1930 Georgia's unemployment rate was 11 percent and increased to only 15 percent by early 1933, whereas the national unemployment rate in early 1933 was 25 percent. Georgia had the best unemployment rate in the country during the winter of 1932–33.

Georgia, like the rest of the nation, survived the early years of the Great Depression as best it could with little to no assistance from the federal government. Georgians tried to occupy themselves while waiting for recovery, and silly events such as goldfish swallowing and flagpole sitting became popular as a way of keeping people's minds off of the economy. Residents of the state eagerly awaited the inauguration of Franklin D. Roosevelt in March 1933. Roosevelt had started visiting Georgia after learning about Warm Springs in 1924. Located just south of Atlanta, Warm Springs was known for its spring water that poured into a pool at a constant 88 degrees. Having contracted polio in 1921, Roosevelt needed warm water to soothe his aching legs. In 1927 he created the Warm Springs Foundation, eventually spending two-thirds of his personal wealth on the foundation. After being elected President in 1932, Roosevelt's residence at Warm Springs was called the "Little White House," and he spent a considerable amount of time there, visiting 41 times for a total of 797 days. President Roosevelt later died there on 12 April 1945. However, in 1933, Roosevelt's inauguration coincided with the inauguration of one of Georgia's most controversial governors, Eugene Talmadge.

Eugene Talmadge

This era also witnessed the emergence of Eugene Talmadge, arguably Georgia's most colorful and controversial governor. Talmadge was not terribly successful as a lawyer and fared only marginally better as a farmer, but politics mesmerized him. His first attempts at statewide public office, running for the General Assembly in 1920 and 1922, were not successful, but Talmadge finally broke through in 1926 when he won election as Agriculture Commissioner, a post to which he was reelected in 1928 and 1930. As Agriculture Commissioner, Talmadge established himself as a political force in Georgia. He was elected initially as a reform candidate and quickly made his mark. Talmadge cleaned up the department, eliminating the remnants of his predecessor's political machine. In the department newspaper, *The Market Bulletin*, Talmadge espoused his economic philosophy; he preached diversification and suggested that the solution to low prices for agricultural commodities was for farmers to keep their products off the market. There were criticisms of the Agriculture Commissioner, including that he hired too many relatives and his habit of extensive traveling to "observe agriculture in other states."

Still, Talmadge won reelection in 1928 and 1930, establishing himself as a politician with great potential.

After three terms as Agriculture Commissioner, Talmadge was elected Governor in 1932 and 1934. He was a master campaigner. He was a showman and has been described as "a prancing, dancing, arm-waving, holy-roller, circus barker, medicine man." Although highly educated (Talmadge had both a bachelor's degree and law degree from the University of Georgia), he tailored his speeches and language to the small dirt farmer, something that brought back memories of Tom Watson. His campaigns always began with a giant barbecue at the city park in the middle of McRae, Telfair County, Talmadge's home. A local man cooked massive amounts of food, and candidate Talmadge provided the entertainment with his campaign speech. One of the factors that made Talmadge a successful politician was that he understood how to campaign within the county unit system. He knew to campaign in the more rural counties and not expend time, energy, and resources in the highly urban parts of the state. His campaign, moreover, appealed to Georgia's small farmers.

His gubernatorial administration was controversial, though, and his actions as governor included the suspension of all state taxes in 1933, the declaration of martial law in 1934 to break a textile strike, outspoken opposition to President Roosevelt's New Deal, and, after the General Assembly failed to pass an appropriations bill in 1935, his discovery of an old law that permitted the governor to make appropriations if the General Assembly failed to act. As governor, Talmadge tried to pass legislation that appealed to his primary constituency—small farmers. His signature issue in the 1932 election, which was something of a gimmick, was to reduce the cost of automobile registration, which would help the state's poor farmers. The "three dollar tag" had a certain ring to it and was popular throughout the state. When the General Assembly refused to pass legislation reducing automobile tags to three dollars, Governor Talmadge implemented it after the legislative session ended. Talmadge became more popular around the state, and the legislature looked bad for not passing the bill; it was a double victory for the governor. Though the governor circumvented the legislature to implement parts of his agenda most Georgia residents approved.

One other action of note during Talmadge's administration was how he dealt with the textile strike in 1934. In the early 1930s the United Textile Workers started to organize in Georgia with some success. By the summer of 1934 textile workers in the South were planning a strike, which began in Alabama in August of that year. It soon spread across the Chattahoochee River into Columbus, a major textile center, and by September the textile union declared a general strike. About 75 percent of textile workers in Georgia joined the strike. Governor Talmadge, in the middle of a reelection campaign, announced in August that he would not use troops to break a strike. By September he had changed his mind and declared martial law in all areas around textile factories in the state, calling out some four thousand National Guardsmen to break the strike. Grass fields around the textile mills were strung with barbed wire to contain the strikers, and militiamen beat a striker to death in front of his family. The governor was immediately labeled as anti-labor, but he broke the strike. Significantly, Talmadge did not suffer from the negative publicity, as his primary constituents were farmers and not industrial workers.

The New Deal in Georgia

By the fall of 1932 many Americans were ready for a president who would use the resources of the federal government to provide relief to help overcome the Great Depression. Franklin D. Roosevelt, who spent a considerable amount of time at Warm Springs, Georgia, was that man. Almost immediately upon being inaugurated in March 1933, President Roosevelt began to implement his New Deal to combat the economic downturn. At the same time, Eugene Talmadge took the oath of office as governor of Georgia. Publicly Governor Talmadge supported the New Deal, but privately he was critical of Roosevelt's program and actively worked against its implementation in Georgia. Talmadge was a fiscal conservative and therefore opposed Roosevelt's deficit spending and the unbalanced budgets the New Deal produced. In addition, the governor did not appreciate the federal government's increased presence in state affairs and the government regulation that Roosevelt's program provided. Governor Talmadge once described the New Deal as "a combination of wet-nursing, frenzied finance, downright communism, and plain damned foolishness."

As such, Governor Talmadge became a serious obstacle to New Deal measures helping Georgia residents. When the Federal Emergency Relief Administration (FERA) was created in 1933, Talmadge meddled in the distribution of this assistance. The director of the FERA, Harry Hopkins, appointed Gay Bolling Shepperson to head the agency in Georgia. Shepperson had a background in social services, having worked in the field in Louisiana, Virginia, New York, and Missouri before moving to Atlanta in the late 1920s. She served as Georgia's New Deal relief chief until her retirement in 1939. Talmadge did all he could to obstruct Shepperson, demanding to review and sign all relief and

G

Georgia

salary checks before distribution, questioning the selection of relief clients, and even appointing an "adviser" to assist Shepperson. This "adviser" had no background in social services and was appointed simply to slow down the distribution of New Deal relief in the state. Talmadge also vetoed legislation in 1935 that would have permitted Georgia residents to participate in the new Social Security Administration.

Governor Talmadge's opposition to the New Deal was the most important issue in the 1936 gubernatorial election, and fortunately for those Georgians who needed assistance, Talmadge was not eligible for reelection. Eurith D. Rivers, unsuccessful in twice running for governor, was the anti-Talmadge candidate and defeated Talmadge's handpicked successor, Charles Redwine. Rivers, who had served in both bodies of the state legislature, ran on a platform of bringing the New Deal to the state; he promised a "Little New Deal" for Georgians. Once in office, Rivers helped the General Assembly pass numerous bills that allowed Georgia full participation in the New Deal. Social Security was available to Georgians, and the state benefited from many other programs, such as aid to dependent children, unemployment compensation, and aid for the disabled, among others. One agency that had a great impact on the state was the Rural Electrification Administration (REA), a program created to bring electricity to rural America. This was badly needed in Georgia, as 97 percent of farmers in the state did not have electricity in 1935; by the end of Rivers's administration Georgia led the nation in REA cooperatives.

The New Deal had a tremendous impact on Georgia, with numerous agencies providing significant relief to the state's residents, despite Governor Talmadge's opposition. The FERA provided $5.6 million in assistance to Georgians in 1933 alone,

194

and that number increased to $18.8 million in 1934 and $20.3 million in 1935. The Civil Works Administration (CWA), a temporary agency that existed only from November 1933 to March 1934, provided an additional $14 million in assistance to the state. Arguably the agency with the greatest influence on the state was the Agricultural Adjustment Act (AAA), which was Roosevelt's farm relief. In an effort to restore farm prices, the AAA advocated voluntary cutbacks in production to aid Georgia's farmers. By 1934, one million acres of cotton in Georgia had been diverted, and the price of cotton rose to 12 cents a pound. In return for reducing production Georgia farmers received benefit payments, which amounted to $7.9 million in 1933, $14.2 million in 1934, and $12.6 million in 1935. By the late 1930s, federal assistance to Georgia farmers reached over $20 million. Another New Deal agency, the Works Progress Administration (WPA), put Americans to work on public works projects and employed sixty-seven thousand Georgians at its peak in December 1938, while the Civilian Conservation Corps (CCC) employed men between the ages of 18 and 25 on conservation-type projects. One of the New Deal's most popular agencies, the CCC was also the most blatantly racist. Whites in need of assistance easily enrolled in the CCC while black Georgians found it nearly impossible. This problem was addressed in 1935 when a system of quotas was put in place. President Roosevelt's New Deal, once implemented in Georgia, had a tremendous impact on the state's economy. It did not pull Georgia (or America) out of the Great Depression, but the program provided much needed economic assistance to state residents.

The Return of Eugene Talmadge

The Georgia Constitution permitted governors to serve two consecutive two-year terms, but the governor then had to wait four years before running for office again. Eugene Talmadge served two terms as governor (1932 and 1934) and then sat out for four years, so he was eligible to run again in 1940. Talmadge's platform in 1940 was the strongest and most far-sighted of his political career: He promised to enforce economy in government, keep taxes down, encourage the development of the state's natural resources, and to cooperate with President Roosevelt as war approached. Talmadge's victory in the Democratic primary was so assured and so boring, that fistfights at his campaign appearances received more press coverage than the speech itself. He easily won the election, dominating both the popular vote and county unit vote. After the election, Talmadge sent his son Herman to meet with President Roosevelt and promised full cooperation from the governor.

The controversy that dominated Governor Talmadge's third term in office was one that Talmadge himself initiated—an attack on higher education. State colleges and universities were under the authority of the Board of Regents, but members of the board were appointed by the governor, and the governor sat on the board as an *ex-officio* member. The potential for political influence and control over the state university system by the governor's office was clear. A particularly unfortunate incident occurred involving Walter Cocking, dean of the College of Education at the University of Georgia, and Marvin Pittman, president of Georgia Southern University. They antagonized Governor Talmadge, and he decided the pair should be removed. During a July 1941 meeting of the Board of Regents, the governor announced the firing of Cocking and Pittman, and members of the Board, who Talmadge had appointed, voted to support the governor against the advice of Georgia's attorney general, Ellis Arnall.

There were immediate ramifications, the most significant of which came from the South's regional accrediting agency, the Southern Association of Colleges and Schools (SACS). In September 1941, SACS suspended the state university system's accreditation because of political interference. Though Georgia appealed the suspension, SACS ended accreditation for all colleges and universities in the state university system in December 1941. Losing accreditation had serious implications for institutions in the system as well as for the students. Education immediately became the most important issue in the upcoming 1942 gubernatorial election.

World War II Era

While SACS was ending accreditation for Georgia's colleges and universities, the United States was entering World War II. As America mobilized for war, Eugene Talmadge prepared for his 1942 reelection bid against perhaps his most serious challenge yet. Opposing Talmadge was his attorney general, Ellis Arnall, who broke with the governor over the Cocking and Pittman affair. Education was clearly the most important issue, and Arnall's campaign strategy was to portray Talmadge as anti-education, something that was not terribly difficult to accomplish. Talmadge, as usual, focused his campaign on small farmers, clearly demonstrating that he was out of touch with key issues of the day. Arnall promised to take politics out of education and to make progressive reform. Playing on the international climate of 1942, Arnall also made some headway by depicting Talmadge as a dictator. By focusing on education, Arnall was able to defeat

Talmadge easily in both the popular vote and county unit vote. The 1942 election was the only gubernatorial election Talmadge ever lost, and the only one Arnall ever won.

Ellis Arnall promised many reforms during the campaign and once in office he made good on those promises. Almost immediately upon being elected Arnall worked closely with SACS to have accreditation restored to the state's university system, which was done by the end of January 1943. To limit the potential for future political interference in education in the future, Arnall also removed the governor from the Board of Regents. Other progressive reforms followed quickly, more than any governor since the Hoke Smith administration. One important issue that Arnall addressed was prison reform. The chain gang that replaced the convict-lease system at the beginning of the twentieth century was in need of reform. Arnall abolished the state's chain gang, and the entire penal system was modernized. Arnall also pardoned Georgia's most famous chain gang prisoner, Robert Burns who had twice escaped and wrote a book about his experience. The state also undertook voting reform, and the General Assembly passed bills permitting 18-year-old citizens to vote and to allow soldiers who were away from home to vote.

Governor Arnall proved to be a forward-thinking chief executive by supporting civil rights reform during his administration; one issue that the governor took up was Georgia's poll tax. Arnall wanted the General Assembly to abolish it by legislation, but threatened to do so by executive order if the legislature failed to act. In March 1945, Georgia became the fourth Southern state (after Florida, Louisiana, and North Carolina) to abolish its poll tax. Another civil rights issue that Governor Arnall addressed was the white primary. In a 1944 Texas case, *Smith v. Allwright*, the US Supreme Court invalidated

Texas's white primary, effectively abolishing the practice everywhere in the South. Arnall received widespread recognition, especially in the North, when he publicly accepted and defended the Supreme Court's decision (his popularity among Georgia whites declined, however). These developments, drastically increased voter participation in Georgia; in the 1942 Democratic primary 303,000 votes were cast, while in 1946 691,000 votes were cast.

Governor Arnall also hoped to revise the state's constitution. The most recent revision was in 1877, and by 1943 it had been amended more than three hundred times. In March 1943, the General Assembly passed a resolution calling for revision. Rather than holding a convention to which delegates would be elected, this revision was done by a committee appointed and chaired by Governor Arnall, making the completed document largely his work. There were some significant changes in the new constitution, which was completed in 1945. In the executive branch of the state government, the governor's term was set at four years, and after one term the governor had to wait four years before running again. Also, the office of lieutenant governor was created and filled for the first time in the 1946 election. The Constitution of 1945 included provisions for 18-year-old citizens to vote, the poll tax written out (having already been eliminated by the state legislature), and the grandfather clause was likewise eliminated. Unfortunately, the constitution still included provisions for a literacy test as a requirement to vote. With a few glaring exceptions, Georgia's Constitution of 1945 was a bit more progressive than the previous document.

Governor Arnall was interested in helping Georgia and its citizens in other ways, too. Since the end of the Civil War, Georgia and the rest of the South had suffered from discriminatory freight rates charged by railroad companies. Railroads fixed arbitrary and noncompetitive rates that generally were 39 percent higher in the South than in the North. Arnall addressed this issue by suing twenty railroad companies for conspiracy against the state of Georgia in violation of the Sherman Antitrust Act. In January 1945, the governor appeared personally before the US Supreme Court and argued that freight rate differentials denied Georgia's products equal access to national markets. The Supreme Court accepted jurisdiction in this case, styled *Georgia v. Pennsylvania Railroad Company*, which amounted to a victory. As a result of Arnall's suit, the Interstate Commerce Commission began an investigation and soon implemented a uniform classification of rates.

While Governor Arnall was making progressive reforms, the state of Georgia was working to help the country win World War II. Because Georgia was located in the South, it was an ideal place for military training installations. The largest infantry-training center in the country was Fort Benning in Columbus, and thousands of GIs received their training there. Likewise, Camp Gordon, later Fort Gordon, in Augusta trained thousands of soldiers for military service. Robins Field in Macon and Hunter Field in Savannah were other important training facilities; at its peak Robins also employed 13,000 civilians. As for servicemen and women, 320,000 Georgians served in the armed forces with 6,754 making the ultimate sacrifice for their country.

Georgia also made significant contributions to the war effort by building machines and weapons of war. One of the most important wartime industries in the state was the Bell Bomber plant in Marietta. In February 1942 Marietta was selected as the site for the plant, and the federal government spent $73 million building and operating it. The facilities encompassed some 4.2

million square feet, and at its peak Bell employed 28,000 workers, 37 percent of whom were women and 8 percent of whom were African American. Bell Bomber built B-29 bombers for the Army Air Forces, and by the end of the war 663 had rolled off the assembly lines in Marietta. On the coast, in Savannah and Brunswick, Liberty Ships were constructed. Liberty Ships were cargo vessels that transported war materials, supplies, and weapons to various theaters of operation. The Savannah shipyard, run by Southeastern Shipbuilding, built 88 vessels, among them the SS *James Oglethorpe* and the SS *Juliette Low*. Over the course of the war, more than 46,000 Georgians were employed in the Savannah shipyard, including 3,500 women. In Brunswick, J.A. Jones Construction operated the shipyard, which built 85 vessels, including the SS *Henry Grady* and the SS *John B. Gordon*. At its peak the Brunswick shipyard employed 16,000 Georgians.

One unusual aspect of Georgia and World War II was that Axis prisoners of war were incarcerated in the state. When the North African Campaign ended in May 1943, Allied troops captured several hundred thousand Axis prisoners who were sent to the United States. By the end of the conflict, some 400,000 prisoners of war were held in more than 500 prison camps in the US. Forty of those camps, located in Georgia, held 11,800 prisoners, most of whom were German soldiers. Prisoners did forced labor, which in Georgia meant agricultural and lumbering work. In many places their labor was important as many Georgians were serving in the Armed Forces or had found higher-paying employment in the wartime industries. When the war ended most prisoners of war were returned to their homes, but many chose to stay in Georgia or returned shortly after being repatriated.

The World War II Era ended, with an election controversy that involved Eugene Talmadge, who ran for governor in 1946.

Georgia was also electing its first lieutenant governor. Talmadge's toughest challenge was in the Democratic primary, as the Republican Party still was not strong enough to mount significant opposition. James Carmichael challenged Talmadge in the Democratic primary, and won the popular vote. Talmadge, however, won the county unit vote and therefore won the election, which was tantamount to winning the governorship. Melvin Thompson defeated Marvin Griffin in the Democratic primary to win election as Georgia's first lieutenant governor.

Between the June Democratic primary and the November general election Eugene Talmadge's health quickly deteriorated to the point that some were not sure he would survive until the inauguration. For this reason a write-in campaign was organized for Talmadge's son, Herman. As expected, Eugene Talmadge won the governorship for a fourth time; Melvin Thompson was elected lieutenant governor. Concerns about Talmadge's health were well founded, and he passed away on 21 December 1946, just a few weeks short of inauguration. Who, then, would be Georgia's next governor since Talmadge did not live to be inaugurated? Three men claimed the governorship, and this bizarre (and embarrassing) episode became known as the Three Governors Controversy.

The three men who claimed the governorship were: 1) Melvin Thompson, who won election to the office of lieutenant governor; 2) Herman Talmadge, who claimed to have the most write-in votes; and 3) Ellis Arnall, the sitting governor who would not vacate the office until the issue was settled. The problem was that the state constitution was not clear on who became governor if the governor-elect died between election and inauguration. When the General Assembly convened in January 1947 it elected Herman Talmadge governor based upon Talmadge having received the highest write-in count (even though several dozen of those votes were cast by the deceased from Telfair County, Talmadge's home). Talmadge forcibly occupied the governor's office and changed the locks so only he could enter, Ellis Arnall set up an office in another part of the capitol, and Melvin Thompson, after being inaugurated as lieutenant governor, sued to be governor. The Georgia Supreme Court finally decided the issue when on 19 March 1947 it ruled that Melvin Thompson was the rightful governor. The court also ordered a special election for governor in 1948, an election that Herman Talmadge won.

Chapter 9

The Civil Rights Era

Segregation, the Brown Decision, Massive Resistance.

Segregation and the oppression of African Americans have had a long history in Georgia, dating back to the founding of the colony. The state's society had a rigid class structure even after the abolition of slavery was accomplished with the Thirteenth Amendment in 1865. During Reconstruction, Georgia's freedpeople were victims of bias and prejudice that took many forms, including violence, intimidation, economic repression, and political marginalization. Later, as Jim Crow sentiment dominated the state and the South in general, segregation became entrenched in law as a result of the *Plessy v. Ferguson* case (the legal doctrine became "separate but equal"). Georgia enacted legislation embodying that Supreme Court ruling, providing for legally separate public accommodations and facilities. Voting restrictions were put in place, and violence against the state's African American population reached its peak during the Jim Crow era. By mid-twentieth century, Georgia was not an ideal location for persons of color to live.

Fortunately, by the 1940s there had been numerous challenges to this social structure. During World War II many Northern black soldiers posted to Georgia for training demonstrated their dissatisfaction with the state of race relations. These men did not accept the seating arrangements in public transportation and refused to sit in the back of public buses. In 1944 students at Savannah State College occupied all of the seats on a city bus and refused to give them up to white passengers, leading to the arrest of two of the protesters. In March 1945, the state legislature passed a bill that eliminated the poll tax.

The next challenge was to the state's white primary. Primus E. King, a black registered voter in Columbus, attempted to vote in the Democratic primary in July 1944. After being roughly turned away, King went immediately to his attorney's office and prepared a legal challenge to the white primary. In the resulting court case, *King v. Chapman* (1946), King argued that his right to vote under the Fourteenth, Fifteenth, and Seventeenth Amendments had been violated. The federal courts ruled in King's favor, much as they had in the 1944 Texas challenge to the white primary, *Smith v. Allwright*. After a two-year legal battle, the white primary in Georgia was invalidated. The registration of black voters in the state immediately increased, and within a few months 125,000 African Americans had registered to vote.

Governor Herman Talmadge led Georgia's campaign to resist desegregation in the late 1940s and early 1950s. The son of former Georgia Governor Eugene Talmadge, Herman Talmadge attended the University of Georgia and served in the Navy during World War II. One of three claimants to the governor's office as a result of the 1946 election (commonly called the Three Governors Controversy), he lost when the Georgia Supreme Court ruled in favor of Melvin E. Thompson. Talmadge then won the 1948 special election for governor and was reelected in 1950 for a full term. As governor, Talmadge asserted that the mixing of the races would not happen in Georgia; he was determined that schools in the state would not be desegregated while he was in office. Public facilities likewise would remain segregated. In fact, he even published a book in 1955 entitled *You and Segregation* in which he warned of the dangers of desegregation. Surprisingly enough, in his

1987 autobiography Talmadge claimed that since 1955 he had changed his mind on segregated education. Regardless of his later change of heart, Talmadge led the early effort to keep Georgia society segregated.

The catalyst for the battle over civil rights was the US Supreme Court's decision in the 1954 case *Brown v. Board of Education*. The Court ruled that "separate but equal" accommodations had no place in public education. A year after its *Brown* decision, the Supreme Court issued what is generally referred to as *Brown II*, ordering that compliance with the *Brown* decision had to be done "with all deliberate speed." Though the *Brown* decision addressed education solely and specifically, it became a clarion call to Georgia, and the South, to oppose desegregation in all public accommodations and facilities. In Georgia and the rest of the South, the response to *Brown* and *Brown II* was to resist the decisions. Massive resistance became the doctrine of most white Georgians (and white Southerners generally) to impede compliance with *Brown* and to prevent any progress in civil rights.

After Governor Herman Talmadge left office in 1955, the unquestioned leader in resisting *Brown*, desegregation, and civil rights progress was his successor Governor Marvin Griffin. A graduate of The Citadel, Griffin ran his family's Bainbridge newspaper and had served in an antiaircraft battalion in the Pacific during World War II. In politics Griffin served one term in the General Assembly in the 1930s, but was defeated in his bid to win a seat in Congress. After World War II, Griffin won election as Georgia's lieutenant governor, in 1948 and 1950, serving six years in that office. In running for governor in 1954, Griffin announced that he stood for what he called Georgia's two greatest traditions, segregation and the county unit system. During the campaign Griffin promised to protect segregated schools, "come hell or high water." In his inaugural address in January 1955, the new governor stated that as long as he was governor there would be no race-mixing in Georgia's schools and colleges. Griffin kept his word—no schools were desegregated during his administration. No civil rights progress was made under Griffin, and the governor led the massive resistance campaign in Georgia. The General Assembly in fact passed legislation to block progress. Griffin established a good working relationship with the legislature while serving as lieutenant governor for six years, and he was able to get legislation passed to block implementation of *Brown*.

One method of carrying out massive resistance on the part of the governor and legislature was through the doctrine of interposition. Interposition became Georgia's basic response to the *Brown* decision; it was used to oppose desegregation on all levels. Interposition was the act of interposing a state's authority or sovereignty between the federal government and the citizens of that state. Generally, this was 1950s version of states' rights, and the state used its power to block federal action, such as Supreme Court orders to desegregate schools. Georgia's General Assembly passed an array of legislation to prevent desegregation.

The culmination of interposition in Georgia was the legislature's passage of the Interposition Resolution in 1956. This resolution claimed that the US Supreme Court did not possess the authority to issue its *Brown* decision, as it infringed on the rights of the states. It likewise suggested that the federal government had exercised powers not granted to it by the states. The resolution then flatly stated that the Supreme Court's rulings in *Brown* and *Brown II* were "null, void and of no force or effect" in Georgia. The resolution was symbolic of white Georgia's response to the *Brown* decision. Most, if not all, of this interposition legislation was actually unconstitutional and, according to Georgia Attorney General Eugene Cook, would be struck down if challenged.

In addition to opposing school desegregation, massive resistance was carried out in other ways; there were numerous examples of white backlash in Georgia, and no part of society was immune to this backlash—including college athletics. In the South, college football was one of the most popular sports, and this held true in Georgia, too. The most prominent college football teams were the Bulldogs of the University of Georgia and the Georgia Tech Yellow Jackets. During this era college athletics was segregated just like society. In football, this meant that since the early twentieth century the University of Georgia and Georgia Tech teams had practiced racial exclusion—they did not play against teams that had African American players. This practice and the desire for the teams to play in the most prominent games often conflicted. The most serious example of this conflict came in 1955 when Georgia Tech qualified to play in the Sugar Bowl, scheduled for 1 January 1956. The opposition was the University of Pittsburgh, whose roster included one African American player. Governor Griffin announced that he would not permit the Yellow Jackets to play simply because they would have to share the field with a black player. A storm of protest ensued, which culminated in two thousand students marching on the capitol and the governor being hanged in effigy. Griffin relented, and Georgia Tech played in the bowl game (and won 7–0). In 1957 the General Assembly even considered a sports segregation bill, but the legislature adjourned before it came up for a vote.

More white backlash and resistance came in 1956 when the legislature officially changed the state flag, and Governor Griffin was once again at the center of the controversy. The new flag included the most recognizable symbol of the Confederacy—the

St. Andrews cross—which adorned the Confederate battle flag. Placing it on the state flag sent a clear message of defiance of the US Supreme Court's *Brown* decision. Governor Griffin said the change represented his campaign promise to uphold segregation and the county unit system.

Protests, Sit-Ins, the Albany Movement

Despite the organized massive resistance campaign, progress was made in civil rights in the state. A serious challenge to Georgia's segregated society occurred in 1957 when a group of Atlanta ministers led by the Reverend William H. Borders hoped to desegregate public transportation. To achieve that goal, Borders launched the Triple-L Movement (Love, Law, and Liberation). On 8 January, Borders announced that he planned to ride a bus and sit in the white seats, to challenge the segregation of the buses. The next day, 9 January 1957, Borders and his fellow ministers boarded a bus and sat all over, including the front seats, which were reserved for white passengers. They were arrested the next day and promptly filed suit. In the resulting case, *Williams v. GPSC* (1959), the federal district court ruled in favor of Borders and the ministers, and public transportation in Georgia was desegregated.

Governor Griffin served his term and kept his promise that no public schools would be desegregated while he was in office. His successor, Ernest Vandiver, made similar promises, but he could not keep them; Vandiver was not nearly as obstructionist as Griffin. Within a year of taking office Vandiver was faced with the sit-in movement, specifically targeting department store lunch counters. The sit-ins began in Greensboro, NC in February 1960 and quickly spread to other Southern cities. The first Atlanta sit-ins were organized by student leaders Lonnie King and Julian

Bond, students at Morehouse College. On 15 March 1960 almost 200 students conducted sit-ins at several lunch counters throughout the city, and 77 were arrested for trespassing. The business community indicated it was willing to negotiate with the student leaders, but nothing was accomplished. Further protests were suspended until students returned to school in the fall.

In the fall of 1960 a new series of sit-in protests was planned, and this time student leaders convinced Martin L. King, Jr., to participate. Earlier in 1960 King had returned to Atlanta (to Ebenezer Baptist Church) from Alabama where he had earned a reputation as a civil rights leader. The lunch counter sit-ins were scheduled for 19 October 1960, and one of the stores targeted was Rich's Department Store, the largest department store in the city. King and more than fifty others were arrested for trespassing, as was expected. Perhaps as a result of the publicity from King's arrest, more than two thousand protesters came out the next day. Over the next several days, tensions were high, with counter-demonstrations held by Ku Klux Klan members. Merchants experienced serious decreases in sales as the demonstrations continued, and by the end of November every downtown lunch counter was closed. By early 1961 Atlanta business leaders were willing to open negotiations with the student leaders, which culminated in a March 1961 deal to desegregate the city's lunch counters. Actual desegregation would take place later in the fall, to coincide with the desegregation of the city's schools. The desegregation of the downtown lunch counters was a significant victory in the civil rights movement in Georgia.

Two organizations that worked for civil rights progress in Georgia were the NAACP (National Association for the Advancement of Colored People) and SNCC (Student Nonviolent Coordinating Committee). The NAACP first appeared in the state in 1917, and over the next few years local chapters were organized throughout Georgia, mostly in urban areas. Branches could be found in Albany, Atlanta, Augusta, Columbus, Macon, Savannah, and Valdosta. In these early years members tended to be professional men such as attorneys, physicians, businessmen, ministers, and teachers. Only five new branches were formed in the 1920s, and the organization was largely dormant for the next twenty to thirty years. The NAACP responded ineffectively to the *Brown* and *Brown II* decisions, and experienced little growth through much of the 1960s. SNCC was formed to launch nonviolent, direct-action protests against segregation and racism. Largely led by college students, SNCC objectives frequently clashed with the NAACP, the best example of which occurred in Albany.

In the fall of 1961 SNCC workers conducted a voter registration drive in Albany, and their work led to the creation of an organization called the Albany Movement in November of that year. Led by a local African American osteopath, Dr. William Anderson, the group held mass meetings and organized protests in the city. The protesters, mostly local students, demanded desegregation of Albany's public facilities, particularly the bus station. Protesters were arrested, as expected, and by December 1961 more than five hundred had been jailed with little to show for their work. The protesters lived in horrible conditions in the jail, conditions that were described as "hellish." At that point Dr. Anderson and other leaders asked Martin L. King, Jr., to help in Albany, hoping to generate some momentum and possibly gain some exposure for their work. SNCC leaders opposed King's appearance in Albany, however, as they wished to keep the movement local.

King and his SCLC colleague, the Rev. Ralph Abernathy arrived in Albany on 15 December 1961 and spoke at a rally that evening, spearheading a protest march to the bus station the following day. King, Abernathy, and the demonstrators were arrested; in a short time King and Abernathy permitted their bond to be posted. In February 1962, both were convicted of the charges from the march and returned to Albany in July 1962 for sentencing. They were fined $178 or 45 days in jail; both chose jail. While serving his sentence, King wrote a column for the *New York Amsterdam News* (King wrote a regular column for the newspaper) in which he outlined his reasons for choosing to serve his jail sentence. This column, or letter to his constituents, was a predecessor to his more famous *Letter From A Birmingham Jail*. King and Abernathy planned to serve the entire sentence as a symbolic act of protest, but their fines were paid anonymously and they were released. King protested, to no avail, and Abernathy remarked that they had been thrown out of many places, but this was the first time they had been thrown out of jail.

Although defeated in Albany, King was not deterred and determined to stay and continue fighting. His presence created some friction as SNCC leaders opposed King's presence. More protests were held in the summer of 1962 and made little headway, largely a result of the actions of Police Chief Laurie Pritchett. He had done his homework on King and did not use violence against the protesters as others had done in places like Birmingham and Montgomery. Pritchett met nonviolent protest with nonviolent law enforcement. When the demonstrators knelt down and prayed Pritchett and his officers prayed with them then arrested them. Pritchett also put King on 'round-the-clock police protection, which really annoyed King. When the police chief filled up his own jails, he sent the arrested demonstrators to jails in surrounding counties. King, Abernathy, Dr. Anderson, and the Albany Movement were making no progress in desegregating the city.

The final chapter of the Albany Movement came in July 1962 when King led another march (on 27 July) and was again arrested. He refused bail and intended to stay in jail until city leaders agreed to negotiate. At his trial the following month, he and Abernathy were duly convicted, but their sentences were suspended and the pair was released. They were kicked out of jail again. King returned to Atlanta, and the Albany Movement was essentially over. After all of the protests and arrests, the only public facility desegregated was the library. This was a staggering defeat for King and a setback for the black community in Albany.

School Desegregation

One of the major objectives of the civil rights movement was school desegregation. The US Supreme Court had sanctioned "separate but equal" in its 1896 *Plessy v. Ferguson* ruling. But in Georgia, and the South generally, educational facilities were more separate than equal. In 1930, the state spent $43 on every white student and $10 on every black student, and in 1953 the disparity was $190 per white student and $132 per black student. Likewise, the salaries for teachers were unequal, as white teachers earned $97 per month in 1929 while black teachers earned just $38. By the early 1950s there were numerous legal challenges to the "separate but equal" doctrine in educational facilities. In 1954 the Court handed down its decision in *Brown v. Board of Education*, ruling that separate educational facilities were inherently unequal. The Court, however, did not set a timetable for the desegregation of schools, and most Southern school districts did not willingly comply. In 1955 the Supreme Court issued another order in this case, which is commonly called *Brown II*. In this ruling the Court stated that compliance had to be done "with all deliberate speed." Like the original *Brown* decision, *Brown II* did not set timetables for compliance or state how school districts carried out the order. The Court offered no guidance on how or when this was to be done.

An early attempt to desegregate the state's public schools came with Horace Ward's application to attend the University of Georgia's law school in 1950. Ward was denied admission, but his effort put the state's politicians on notice that they would have to work hard to keep Georgia's schools segregated. As early as 1951 the General Assembly, following the leadership of Governor Herman Talmadge, considered several proposals to maintain segregation. One was an appropriations bill that prohibited the expenditure of public funds on desegregated schools. Another proposal, which the General Assembly passed in 1953, was a constitutional amendment to abolish the state's public schools in favor of a system of private schools. The Private School Amendment, as it was called, authorized payment of tuition grants directly to parents, who would then use the funds to send their children to a private school. In this way the state could not be accused of denying its citizens equal protection. Georgia's legislators apparently did not recognize, or ignored, the simple fact that tuition grants from the state would make the school a public institution, not a private school. The General Assembly passed this bill, and Georgia's voters approved it in November 1954, six months *after* the US Supreme Court's *Brown* decision.

The black response in Georgia to the *Brown* decision was issued in 1955, after the Court's *Brown II* order. NAACP leaders met in Atlanta to discuss how to respond to *Brown*, and issued the Atlanta Declaration. This document called on local NAACP chapters to petition their local school boards to comply with *Brown*. Sample petitions were supplied to local chapters along with a warning that petitioners should not include their home addresses on the documents. Throughout the state only eight local NAACP organizations filed petitions; seven of those eight were in urban areas (Atlanta, Augusta, Columbus, Macon, Savannah, Valdosta, and Waycross), while one was rural (Liberty County). No action was taken on the petitions.

The state's intransigence in complying with the Supreme Court's orders meant that black students and their parents had to take legal action if schools were to be desegregated. They filed desegregation suits in federal court, meaning federal courts oversaw school desegregation in Georgia and the South. As desegregation suits were filed, boards of education created "freedom of choice" plans in order to comply with *Brown*. These plans, which permitted families to choose which school their children attended, allowed local school board officials to control (and minimize) the level of desegregation. "Freedom of choice" was a common method used to avoid compliance with *Brown* throughout Georgia until the late 1960s.

At the time of the *Brown* decision there were 180 public school districts in Georgia, and every one operated a segregated school system. Of those 180 school districts, 71 voluntarily complied with the requirements of *Brown* and the US Department of Education. The remaining 109 school districts were sued in federal court to eliminate their segregated system; one suit was filed in the 1950s, 99 were filed in the 1960s, and nine in the 1970s. The vast majority of the desegregation suits, 85 of the 109, were filed in 1969.

Perhaps the most important of these desegregation suits was the one filed in 1958, as it led to a potential school crisis in

Georgia. In a case known as *Calhoun v. Latimer*, twenty-eight parents sued the Atlanta School Board to desegregate its schools. In the summer of 1959, a federal judge ordered the school board to present a desegregation plan by December of that year. What the board presented was a complex freedom of choice plan that would desegregate schools in the district over a twelve-year period. The judge accepted the plan, but delayed implementation until after the General Assembly met in January 1960. This gave the legislature time to review the law passed in the early 1950s that mandated school closures if schools were desegregated. The judge also reminded Georgians that the choice was desegregation or school closures.

In an effort to keep the state's schools open, parents in Atlanta formed the group called Help Our Public Education (HOPE) in December 1958, shortly after the *Calhoun v. Latimer* case was filed. HOPE's goal was simply to keep schools open, and the organization was officially neutral on the question of segregation or desegregation. Starting in Atlanta, HOPE spread to other parts of the state. It worked through 1959 and 1960 to educate Georgia's public about the gravity of the looming school crisis, and when the legislature convened in January 1960, HOPE presented a petition bearing ten thousand signatures to keep the schools open. In its goal of educating the public about the school crisis HOPE was successful.

Another effort to address the school crisis came with the Georgia General Assembly Committee on Schools, better known as the Sibley Commission. Created by the General Assembly in February 1960 and chaired by Atlanta businessman John Sibley, it was to hold public meetings in each congressional district to determine the public's preference on school desegregation and report back to the legislature by May 1960. The public meetings were conducted through March, and the committee heard testimony from more than 1,800 witnesses and received more than six hundred letters and petitions. Based on the testimony, by a ratio of 3:2 Georgians favored segregated schools, even if it meant eliminating public education. The committee's report, which was submitted on 28 April, concluded that public education in the state must be maintained. For the first time since the *Brown* decision in 1954 a Georgia state government agency recommended abandoning massive resistance.

Developments over the next year resolved the school crisis and led to the desegregation of Atlanta's schools in the fall of 1961. First, the federal judge presiding over the *Calhoun v. Latimer* case delayed implementing the desegregation plan, again giving the General Assembly an opportunity to repeal the school closure laws. Second, in January 1961 Governor Vandiver, who in 1958 campaigned on a platform of maintaining segregation, announced that he could not recommend the closure of Georgia's schools. Vandiver believed that keeping the massive resistance laws would ultimately lead to federal intervention. Third, the General Assembly repealed the massive resistance laws, paving the way for desegregation to be carried out. In the summer of 1961 the Atlanta School Board finalized its desegregation plan and Governor Vandiver announced that he would put down any violent responses to desegregation. Finally, that fall the Atlanta schools were peacefully desegregated.

Following the desegregation of Atlanta's schools in 1961 a few more school districts followed suit, including Savannah, Athens, and Brunswick. It was the Civil Rights Act of 1964, however, that led to significant desegregation of Georgia's schools. This legislation included provisions that withheld federal funding from those school districts that were still segregated. In addition, the US Supreme

Court's ruling in *Green v. School Board of New Kent County* in 1968 spurred more school districts to move toward desegregation. In the *Green* case the court ruled "freedom of choice" plans did not meet the court's standards in desegregating schools. Significantly more districts made the move to desegregate after the Civil Rights Act of 1964 and the Supreme Court's *Green* decision.

Like the state's public schools, Georgia's colleges and universities faced the issue of desegregation. The first attempt to desegregate higher education in Georgia was Horace Ward's application to the University of Georgia's law school in 1950. He was denied admission, the university added new admissions requirements, and Ward filed suit. Numerous interruptions, including service in the Army prevented the suit from going forward, and Ward eventually entered law school at Northwestern University. His enrollment at Northwestern invalidated his application at the University of Georgia, and the judge dismissed his suit in 1956.

The next attempt to desegregate higher education came in 1956 at what is now Georgia State University. Three middle-aged women sued the university after their applications for admission were denied. In 1959 a federal judge ruled that the admissions requirements created an unlawful burden on black applicants. Applicants were required to supply letters of reference from alumni, a virtual impossibility for blacks, as white alumni were not likely to write these references. The judge did not, however, order their admission because opposing attorneys had successfully discredited the women on moral grounds. Georgia State, like the University of Georgia, was not desegregated by the end of the decade.

The attempt to desegregate higher education returned to Athens for a showdown at the University of Georgia. In the summer of 1959 two black students, Hamilton Holmes and Charlayne Hunter, applied for admission and were denied. A year and several applications later Holmes and Hunter filed suit, with Horace Ward as one of their attorneys. On 6 January 1961, a federal judge, William Bootle, ordered the university to admit Holmes and Hunter for the winter term, which was set to begin the following week. Later that evening a crowd of 150 to 200 students gathered at a prominent location on campus, chanted, "Two, four, six, eight, we don't want to integrate," hanged a black-faced effigy, and sang "Dixie."

Over the next week there was considerable legal and political maneuvering. One obstacle to desegregation at the University of Georgia was the state's 1956 Appropriations Act authorizing the governor to cut off state funds to desegregated colleges and universities. By 9 January 1961, Governor Vandiver believed he had no alternative to cutting off state funds to the university, but he had to wait until Holmes and Hunter actually enrolled before doing so. Over the next couple of days the US Supreme Court ruled in favor of the students, and Judge Bootle permanently enjoined the governor from complying with the Appropriations Act. The path was clear for Holmes and Hunter to enroll at the University of Georgia and attend classes. However, on the evening of 11 January 1961 a crowd of a thousand to fifteen hundred students rioted outside of Charlayne Hunter's dormitory, shouting obscenities, breaking windows, and starting a fire. Despite the students' behavior, the University of Georgia was finally desegregated.

Other colleges and universities throughout the state followed suit and enrolled black students. During the summer of 1961 Georgia Tech announced that it would admit three black students in the fall term and did so without incident. The fall of 1963 saw the successful and peaceful desegregation of Emory University and Mercer University. By the mid-1960s the state had successfully desegregated higher education.

Voting Rights

Another important aspect of the Civil Rights Era in Georgia concerned voting rights. Since the ratification of the Fifteenth Amendment in 1870, African Americans had been prevented from voting. During Reconstruction, violence and intimidation were used to keep blacks from the polls. The state's 1877 constitution included a poll tax provision, which a short time later became comprehensive and was a rather effective measure to dissuade blacks from voting. Later, during the Jim Crow era, the Democratic Party adopted the white primary (in 1900) and the state legislature passed laws that disfranchised black voters (in 1907). These disfranchisement mechanisms included the grandfather clause, literacy tests, character assessments, and poll taxes. In 1939, in Bibb County, blacks attempting to register were asked to explain the Supreme Court jurisdiction clause in the US Constitution to fulfill the literacy test. This particular clause was chosen, according to county officials, because even God couldn't understand it. In 1910 only 4 percent of eligible black voters were registered; by 1940 roughly twenty thousand African Americans were registered in Georgia.

Beginning in the 1940s and continuing into the 1970s the number of African Americans in Georgia registered to vote increased and, in fact, many participated in the electoral process. The effort to break through voting barriers in Georgia started with the 1944 legal challenge to the state's white primary, as noted earlier. The following year, 1945, the General Assembly repealed the state's poll tax. Those two actions paved the way for increased

African American voter registration; by 1947 the number of black registered voters increased to 125,000, or 18.8 percent of those eligible. Georgia lawmakers quickly moved to stop that progress. In 1949 the state legislature enacted a registration and purge law, designed to eliminate registered voters from the registration lists. Under this law, if a voter did not vote at least once during a two-year period that voter was removed from the registration list and had to reregister. In order to successfully reregister, a voter had to take a test and correctly answer ten of thirty questions—a variant of a literacy test. The answers to these questions, however, could change from time to time, as there were no standard answers. The questions included "Who is the Solicitor General of your circuit?" and "Who is the Ordinary of your county?" Naturally, the registration and purge law succeeded in reducing the number of black voters in Georgia.

One of the ramifications of increased black voter registration and participation was the possibility of black voters deciding the outcome of elections. One example is the election of Helen Douglas Mankin to Congress following a special election in 1946 to fill the vacant US House seat of Robert Ramspeck, who resigned in 1945. Mankin, who had served several terms in the state legislature and allied with Governor Ellis Arnall, entered the special election. While in the General Assembly she had worked with Governor Arnall to abolish the state's poll tax, for which she earned the support of many black voters. Mankin won this special election largely because she won the black vote. Her margin of victory was 800 votes, and in a largely black district in Atlanta she collected 963 of the 1,039 votes cast. Her victory caused considerable consternation in politically conservative Georgia, and she was defeated for reelection later in 1946. Mankin symbolized the potential for black political power when African American voters united behind a candidate or cause.

During the 1950s registration drives were held in Georgia, an attempt to further increase the number of registered black voters. Following the passage of the Civil Rights Act of 1957, the Southern Christian Leadership Conference (SCLC), led by Martin Luther King, Jr., announced a registration drive in the South. As a result of this drive, by 1958 there were 158,000 African Americans registered to vote in Georgia, a significant increase from a decade before. Again the state legislature passed a voters' test law in 1958, similar to the 1949 registration and purge law. Despite the obstacles, more African Americans in Georgia were registering to vote: 180,000 in 1960 and 225,000 in 1963. A turning point in the registration of voters in Georgia, and the South generally, was the Voting Rights Act of 1965. Between 1964 and 1972, the number of new black registered voters increased by 282,000, according to the United States Commission on Civil Rights. It also reported that by 1972 there were 450,000 black registered voters in the state, which was 67 percent of those eligible (as compared to 70 percent for white voters).

The number of African Americans who held elective office also increased significantly, especially in federal, state, and mayoral offices. Few if any black politicians were elected to the state legislature, though, and none was elected to Congress or mayors of Georgia cities, but that soon changed. By 1968 there were only two African Americans in the Georgia Senate and nine in the House. Later in 1972, Andrew Young was elected to the US House of Representatives, the first black congressman from Georgia since Reconstruction. A year later, Maynard Jackson was elected the first black mayor of Atlanta; he was the first African American mayor of a major Southern city.

Georgia's record in race relations improved considerably between the 1940s and the 1970s as the state moved from a program of massive resistance to significant desegregation of schools and other public facilities and accommodations. The percentage of registered black voters increased from single digits to almost 70 percent by the early 1970s, and more African Americans were elected to public office. Progress was difficult, and many obstacles and prejudices had to be overcome before Georgia could become a modern state.

Chapter 10

Modern Georgia

Comparing snapshots of Georgia from 1970 and from the first decade of the twenty-first century, we can see the progress Georgia has made in becoming a truly modern state. In many aspects the state has moved closer to modernity and farther from its traditional provincialism. During those years, per capita personal income in Georgia increased from $3,332 ($18,423 when adjusted for inflation) in 1970 to $33,786 in 2009. The total civilian labor force increased, from 1,960,900 in 1970 to 4,311,700 in 2009. The state's economy also diversified, relying less on agriculture and more on industry and manufacturing. Total manufacturing establishments in Georgia increased from 6,967 in 1967 to 8,699 in 2007; the number of nonagricultural workers in the state also increased, from 1,557,500 in 1970 to 3,876,600 in 2009. A larger percentage of Georgians lived in urban settings rather than rural settings in the twenty-first century. In 1980 1,345,794 Georgians lived in rural settings while 4,117,188 lived in urban settings. Estimates for 2009 put 1,809,097 Georgians living in a rural setting and 8,020,114 in an urban setting. The number of students enrolled in University System of Georgia (USG) institutions more than tripled, from 84,149 during the 1969–70 school year to 292,879 during the 2008–09 school year.

Despite his racial prejudices, Governor Herman Talmadge can be considered an early leader in Georgia's economic development. During his second term from 1951 to 1955, school appropriations increased from $37 million to $99 million, and in

1954 $168 million was budgeted for school construction. Talmadge oversaw other improvements in the state's education system, including an expansion of the school year and the addition of a twelfth grade to public schools. By the time his administration ended, Georgia devoted 53 percent of its budget to public education. He also oversaw an extensive highway construction program that was financed through gasoline and automobile tag taxes—more than ten thousand miles of new roads were built. Talmadge expanded the state's Port Authority, hoping to attract industrial development. During his six years in office, Governor Talmadge laid the foundation for significant future economic development in Georgia.

Modernizing Georgia Politics

The groundwork for political progress and development in Georgia was laid in the early 1960s and made state politics more equal. Since 1917 the county unit system had been used to determine winners in statewide elections, leading to an uneven distribution of power between rural and urban areas, and by 1960 little had changed. In that year one unit vote in tiny, rural Echols County represented 938 residents while one unit vote in urban Fulton County represented 92,721 residents.

The unfairness of the county unit system was evident, and a legal challenge to it was launched. Fulton County voter James Sanders filed suit against, among others, James Gray, Chairman of the State Executive Committee of the Democratic Party, because the county unit system violated the Equal Protection Clause of the Fourteenth Amendment. The resulting case was styled *Gray v. Sanders*, and in 1962 a federal district court invalidated the county unit system, ruling that it led to "invidious discrimination." State elections later that year—including the gubernatorial election—

were determined by popular vote for the first time in several generations. The district court's ruling was appealed to the US Supreme Court, and in 1963 that court upheld the lower court's ruling. Georgia's county unit system was abolished, and the principle of "one person, one vote" reigned in state elections. This was a significant measure of progress, indicating that the state's political system was becoming more modern and less provincial.

After the Reconstruction period, when Georgia was "redeemed" in 1871, the Democratic Party had absolute control over the state government; the Republican Party was essentially nonexistent. For years the most important state election in Georgia was the Democratic primary, and since there were no Republican opponents, the candidates who won the Democratic primary won the general election. In national elections, Republican presidential candidates did not fare well in the state for many years. A measure of political development (and progress) in Georgia was the formation of the Republication Party in the state, which created a true two-party political system.

It was the presidential campaigns of Republican Dwight D. Eisenhower in 1952 and 1956 that established more than token support for Republican candidates in the state. Eisenhower received 30 percent of Georgia's vote in 1952 and 33 percent in 1956; while not enough to garner the state's electoral votes, it was more than prior Republican candidates had received. In 1960 Richard Nixon added to Eisenhower's total by winning 37 percent of Georgia's vote, but the real breakthrough came in 1964 when Barry Goldwater became the first Republican presidential candidate to receive Georgia's electoral vote. Goldwater received 616,000 Georgia votes and Democrat Lyndon Johnson got 522,000. One of the most important reasons for Goldwater's success can be attributed, in part, to his position on race relations.

The Civil Rights Act of 1964 had passed Congress earlier that year, and Goldwater vehemently opposed it and voted against it. This caused most white voters in Georgia to embrace Goldwater. Civil rights and race issues were among the important causes for the rise of the Republican Party in Georgia and the South. As Democratic activists and politicians encouraged the civil rights movement, more white Georgians found themselves aligned with the Republican Party.

The first serious Republican challenge to the Democratic power structure in Georgia came in the 1966 gubernatorial election. At that time state governors could not serve two consecutive terms, so the sitting governor Carl Sanders was ineligible to run. Building on their success in the 1964 presidential campaign, Republicans nominated Howard "Bo" Callaway as their gubernatorial standard bearer. Callaway, formerly a supporter of the Talmadge faction of the Democratic Party, became a Republican convert and Goldwater supporter in 1964. In that year he became the first Republican from Georgia elected to Congress since the Reconstruction era. His task was more difficult because the Republican Party had no primary election. This meant he had to get 5 percent of the registered voters in the state to sign a petition; he needed 87,000 signatures—and got more than 150,000. His expected Democratic opponent, former governor Ellis Arnall, looked forward to running against Callaway and signed his petition. Arnall, however, did not win the Democratic primary, and Callaway instead faced well-known segregationist Lester Maddox. Rumors circulated that Callaway supporters crossed over and voted for Maddox in the Democratic primary, thinking that the former owner of the Pickrick Cafeteria would be a lesser challenge for Callaway. Maddox had never held public office and had, in fact, lost elections for lieutenant governor (1962) and for mayor of Atlanta (1957 and 1961).

The scenario seemed perfect for a Republican victory—a successful Republican congressman against a man who had lost three straight elections. However, Arnall supporters threw a wrench into the election when they announced that a write-in campaign was being organized for the former governor. On the day of the election, Callaway won a plurality of votes, with a count of 453,000; Maddox was a close second with 450,000, but Arnall's 52,000 write-in votes prevented any candidate from receiving a majority. Since no candidate won a majority of votes, the General Assembly chose the new governor when it next convened. On 10 January 1967, the legislature elected Lester Maddox by the lopsided vote of 182–66, with more than thirty Democrats voting for Callaway. Though Callaway did not win the 1966 election, it can be considered the beginning of a true two-party political system in Georgia.

Establishing Georgia's Republican Party in Georgia was a slow and, for some, agonizing affair. The party had to establish a base in the state, raise money, and attract both potential candidates for office and voters to support those candidates. It took time to establish the Republican Party as a legitimate opponent, and an examination of gubernatorial elections from the 1960s to the twenty-first century bears this out. As noted earlier, in 1966 there was not even a Republican primary election, and Howard Callaway had to get signatures on a petition to even appear on the general election ballot. A dozen years later in 1978, the Republican candidate for governor Rodney Cook collected only 128,000 votes, compared with 534,000 that were cast for his Democratic opponent, George Busbee (616,000 Georgians had voted for Barry Goldwater in 1964). Throughout the 1980s, the

Republican Party made more progress in the state, but still was not close to claiming the governor's office, as the Democrats successfully elected Joe Frank Harris twice. In those elections, in 1982 and 1986, the Republican candidates polled 434,000 and 346,000 votes respectively (while the Democratic candidate received 734,000 and 828,000 votes), again not coming close to Goldwater's 1964 total. By the 1990s, however, the Republican Party was a much more formidable opponent, and gubernatorial elections were hotly contested. Despite the increasing popularity of the Republican Party, it still did not succeed in winning the governorship, losing out to Democrats Zell Miller in 1990 and 1994 and Roy Barnes in 1998. The breakthrough came in 2002, with the election of Sonny Perdue. Perdue was the first Republican governor in Georgia since Reconstruction and went on to win reelection in 2006. He was then followed by another Republican, Nathan Deal, who took the helm in 2011.

It is fair to say that a truly modern Georgia emerged in 1962 with the election of Carl Sanders as the state's chief executive. Besides the changes in the electoral process with the invalidation of the county unit system, Sanders himself represented progress and modernity. Sanders hailed from Augusta, and candidates from urban centers had not fared well since the county unit system was established; 1962 was the first real opportunity for an urban candidate to succeed. The Sanders campaign emphasized looking ahead to the future, not back to the past, calling his platform "a program of progress." He consistently referred to the "new politics" of the era throughout the campaign, and Sanders can truly be called Georgia's first "New South" governor. In his inaugural address Sanders suggested the state was on the threshold of greatness and that this was a new day, a new era, and a new

Georgia. The New South had arrived in Georgia's political structure.

In addition to symbolizing the emergence of the New South in Georgia, the Sanders administration improved the state's image. Sanders himself cooperated with the Kennedy and Johnson administrations in Washington, particularly on civil rights issues, and became recognized as a more "national" Democrat, not a provincial Southerner. His most important and lasting accomplishments were in education. Sanders recognized the importance of education (he called education in Georgia a "modern crisis") in an advanced society and made significant improvements. Tens of millions of dollars was appropriated for education, teacher salaries increased, new junior colleges and vocational schools were built, scholarships and loans were made available, and the Governor's Honors Program for advanced students was created. Education in Georgia received an emphasis like never before.

Though Carl Sanders set the state on a course of progressive reform, politics at times got bogged down in old, provincial issues, usually related to race. Race reared its ugly head in the campaigns that elected the state's next two governors, Lester Maddox in 1966 and Jimmy Carter in 1970. Prior to being elected Governor in 1966, Lester Maddox was a staunch segregationist and a symbol of Southern defiance, dating back to his ownership of the Pickrick Cafeteria in Atlanta. During his campaign Maddox suggested that he would kick Martin Luther King, Jr. out of the state and invite George Wallace into Georgia. Likewise, he implied that he would forego federal education funds that were tied to integration, and raise state taxes instead. In his 1970 campaign, Carter ran under similar auspices, though his campaign was more muted than Maddox's. Largely because of his opposition in the Democratic primary (Carl Sanders and C.B. King), Carter found himself appealing to the conservative, segregationist segment of the population—the Maddox supporters from 1966. Carter masked the nature of his campaign by calling it populism, and emphasized class rather than race distinctions, but there was no mistaking the sentiment, superficial though it was.

Fortunately for the state, the campaign rhetoric in 1966 and 1970 was just that—campaign rhetoric. Both Maddox and Carter ran administrations that were relatively free of segregationist sentiment; both men pursued progressive agendas. The Maddox administration was indeed a pleasant surprise considering his staunch segregationist background. Governor Maddox appointed mostly competent men to positions in the administration, including more African Americans than all previous governors combined. Though he was not a college graduate himself, Maddox provided substantial support for higher education. One of his most innovative ideas was "People's Day," during which he opened his office to anybody who wished to speak with the governor. The Maddox administration was not without controversy, though: In 1968 he refused to lower the flags at state institutions to half-mast during Martin Luther King's funeral procession. Even so, the controversies do not overshadow his administration's accomplishments.

The Carter administration, likewise, did not follow in the same vein as the 1970 campaign rhetoric, something Governor Carter made clear in his inaugural address when he announced, "I say to you quite frankly that the time for racial discrimination is over." Carter appointed the first African American to serve on the Board of Regents and was the first governor to have portraits of black Georgians hang in the Capitol. One of the highlights of Carter's term was the reorganization of the state government, as numerous agencies and bureaus were consolidated. The governor also wished to preserve the state's natural resources and helped establish the Georgia Heritage Trust program to accomplish that goal. Despite his disagreements with Lieutenant Governor Lester Maddox, Carter was identified as a New South governor, as Carl Sanders had been ten years earlier. Carter even appeared on the cover of *Time* magazine in May 1971.

Carter went on to assume the presidency, the only Georgian to be elected President of the United States. In the years following, Carter has become something of a symbol for the state and people of Georgia. He has established a reputation as a powerful and influential international diplomat, often traveling to troubled areas of the world to help resolve conflicts. These activities are frequently carried out under the auspices of the Carter Center, located in Atlanta. For his work in this field, Carter was awarded the Nobel Peace Prize in 2002. In addition to his international diplomacy, Carter works with Habitat for Humanity, a philanthropic organization that assists needy Americans in building new homes. The former governor has also become a prolific writer, having authored numerous volumes on a wide range of topics, including his own memoirs, a memoir of his mother, a novel about the American Revolution, and other books on politics and diplomacy. Carter has also opened up his religious life to all people, as anybody can worship with the former governor and president at his church in Plains, Georgia. Jimmy Carter is without doubt one of Georgia's most recognized and accomplished citizens.

Economic Growth and the Rise of Atlanta

By the mid- to late 1970s the issue of race had, to a large extent, disappeared from state politics; race was an ever-present concern for the remainder of the century, but it was not the focus of political campaigns as it had been for several decades. Race relations continued to be problematic for Georgia at times over the next two decades, such as the controversy over the state flag in the 1990s and early 2000s, but other concerns tended to take precedence. One of the most important issues in the state by the late 1970s, and continuing into the twenty-first century, was that of economic development. Attracting new industries to Georgia was far more important than rehashing old provincial and discriminatory attitudes and beliefs.

Among the first to pursue significant economic development in Georgia was Governor George Busbee, who served 1975–1983; he was the first governor to serve two consecutive four-year terms (the law permitting governors to serve two consecutive terms passed the legislature in 1976). Georgia was beginning to change during the late 1970s and early 1980s. The state's population, in addition to considerable growth (Georgia was the fifth-fastest-growing state in this era, with an increase of 700,000 residents), was becoming less rural and more urban. Though more than one-third of the state's population was considered rural, more and more Georgians were moving to urban areas, and more Georgians were working in non-agricultural jobs than ever before. These developments necessitated changes and adaptations, most notably in economic policy.

One factor in economic development was attracting new business concerns to the state, and Governor Busbee was active and aggressive in pursuit of them. The governor attempted to attract foreign businesses and traveled extensively to make these business connections. As a result, the number of international companies in Georgia increased from 150 in 1975 to 680 in 1982. Part of Busbee's legislative agenda was a bill that permitted international banks to operate in the state, which the General

Assembly passed in 1976. By the end of Busbee's administration, sixteen international banks were doing business in Georgia. The state also established offices in various foreign cities, such as Athens, Bonn, Brussels, Hong Kong, and Tokyo, to attract additional foreign business and encourage trade partnerships with Georgia industries.

To attract and keep these new businesses, the state's transportation and support systems had to be upgraded. Through state expenditures the port facilities in Savannah and Brunswick were improved and expanded. The highway system was also improved through considerable effort on the part of Governor Busbee and the Department of Transportation. Another institution that assisted in attracting and promoting economic benefits for the state was the Georgia World Congress Center. The GWCC, which currently hails its mission as "promoting and facilitating events and activities that generate economic benefits to the citizens of the State of Georgia," was created by the General Assembly in 1971 and opened for business in 1976 (near the beginning of Busbee's administration). The authority that operates the center has operational control of the almost four million square feet of convention space and the more modern Georgia Dome and Centennial Olympic Park. These facilities can host any number of convention, entertainment, and sporting events, all of which add to the economic development of Georgia.

As Georgia developed economically it became clear that the city of Atlanta led this development. From its humble beginnings in the 1830s, Atlanta grew to become the most spectacular city in the South and one of the most important in the nation. In 1837 the end of the Western & Atlantic line was located at a place called Terminus. Several other railroads ran through Terminus, making it an important railroad junction. In 1843 the name

Marthasville was used for the town, and two years later its name became Atlanta. Because Atlanta's early history and character were largely determined by the railroads, it was destined to be dominated by commercial interests rather than agricultural.

During the Civil War Atlanta became a manufacturing center for the Confederacy, producing a considerable amount of supplies for the war effort. The city's factories made muskets, pistols, swords, ammunition, cartridge boxes, percussion caps, shoes, and various other items. The industries also caused a dramatic increase in Atlanta's population as thousands of people descended upon the city for employment. It was, however, Atlanta's status as a railroad junction that made it a target for the Union Army, and in 1864 a hundred thousand blue-clad soldiers headed for Atlanta under the command of General William T. Sherman. On the first day of September, Confederate forces abandoned Atlanta, and on the second day Union troops occupied the city. The capture of Atlanta was one of the significant turning points in the war, as it ensured Abraham Lincoln's reelection in November and the continued prosecution of the conflict. One ramification of the war on Atlanta was the destruction of the city, with all of the rail lines taken out of service.

In the postwar period Atlanta built upon its prewar commercial foundation and became a regional leader in commerce and manufacturing. By the turn of the century, Atlanta was the South's undisputed leader in commercial development, though it never became a true industrial city. Its significance was further accentuated when it became the state's capital in 1868. Between the Civil War and the turn of the century the city's population grew from 9,554 (1860) to 89,872 (1900); Atlanta had become one of the largest cities in the South. By 1900 Atlanta had embraced the New South economic gospel that Henry Grady had been preaching for some time, that of diversity.

The city's emphasis on commerce and manufacturing, and its railroad network, made it the ideal location for large-scale economic summits. The first significant event held in Atlanta was the International Cotton Exposition of 1881. A two-and-a-half month event, the exposition included 1,113 exhibits related to cotton technology. This was exactly the kind of New South economic boosterism that Henry Grady was promoting, and demonstrated to a worldwide audience that the South could indeed become an industrial and manufacturing center. The exposition also helped define Atlanta's place in the New South economics—the city would play a central role in transforming the South's economy. Fourteen years later, the 1895 Cotton States and International Exposition highlighted Atlanta's economic significance and helped attract investments into the city. This exposition may be best known, however, for Booker T. Washington's speech that became known as the "Atlanta Compromise Speech." Both the 1881 and 1895 expositions enhanced Atlanta's economic stature in the region and nation.

In the first few decades of the twentieth century Atlanta was trending in several directions. First, the population of the city more than tripled between 1900 and 1930, going from 89,000 to 270,000 people. As the twentieth century progressed, the city limits also increased. By the turn of the twenty-first century Atlanta encompassed a twenty-eight-county metropolitan area, called Atlanta Metropolitan Statistical Area. In the 2010 census, the population of this area was 5.7 million, with the city of Atlanta at 420,000.

A second trend in Atlanta involved the separation of the races throughout the city. The 1906 race riot was one of the worst examples of race violence in the state (see chapter seven). As a result of Jim Crowism, African Americans in Atlanta could not live downtown near Peachtree Street, but created a separate community a few miles outside of the city center. Their focal point was Auburn Avenue, also referred to as "Sweet Auburn." Auburn Avenue was home to a thriving black middle class and was renowned as the center of African American society and culture. Auburn Avenue included many prominent black churches, such as Ebenezer Baptist Church where Martin Luther King, Jr. and his father preached. Atlanta University Center, the largest collection of African American private colleges and universities, was also located near Auburn Avenue. Formed in 1929, the Atlanta University Center includes Clark Atlanta University, Morehouse College, Spelman College, and the Woodruff Library, which possesses one of the richest collections of African American research material in the country.

Like most places in America, Atlanta was not prepared for the economic decline in the 1920s and 1930s. Atlantans embraced President Roosevelt's New Deal relief programs and welcomed the millions of dollars that were pumped into the city's economy. Real recovery, however, had to wait until 1941 when World War II came to America. Once the conflict started, Atlanta played a central role in bringing the war to a successful conclusion. Thousands of soldiers trained at instillations throughout the Atlanta area, and wartime industries employed thousands more. Bell Bomber, located in Marietta, was the largest of the military industries in the Atlanta region. One industry that benefited from the war was Coca-Cola, which offered its product to military personnel overseas at a greatly discounted price. This was a turning point of sorts for the company, as it became a truly international product.

In the postwar years, the city of Atlanta and the metropolitan area continued to grow physically and economically. Several annexations added dozens of square miles and brought hundreds of new businesses and industries within the city limits. Atlanta also benefited from President Eisenhower's interstate highway program, connecting the city to the rest of the southeast and beyond.

The postwar years were also marked by the civil rights movement of the 1950s and 1960s, and Atlanta did not escape unscathed. Luckily for the city, the violence that the movement engendered in other cities did not erupt in Atlanta. Though the movement's progress was terribly slow at times, there was little violence; in fact Atlanta's Mayor Hartsfield was credited with saying that Atlanta was "the City too Busy to Hate." By the fall of 1961 the city's school system had been successfully, and peacefully, desegregated, as had the downtown public facilities. In 1973 the city of Atlanta elected its first African American mayor, Maynard Jackson, who eventually served three terms in office.

By the 1970s Atlanta had come to dominate the state; it had come to represent and symbolize Georgia. Many products that came to be identified with Georgia originated in Atlanta, perhaps the most important and well known of these being Coca-Cola. Created by John S. Pemberton in 1886, Coca-Cola was a non-alcoholic beverage made from extracts from the coca leaf and kola nut. Initially made to be served as a fountain drink, the formula has remained a well-kept secret; it is known publicly only as "7x." The first advertisement for the drink appeared in the *Atlanta Journal* in May 1886. A few years later Pemberton sold the rights to his concoction to Asa Griggs Candler, who advertised and emphasized the non-alcoholic nature of the beverage (the city of Atlanta had passed a Prohibition ordinance in 1885). By the end of the nineteenth century, Coca-Cola had expanded beyond the fountain drink of the local drug store, and deals were negotiated with several individuals to bottle the beverage for wider distribution. In 1916 the iconic Coca-Cola bottle was designed.

Today, though the carbonated drink is the mainstay of the company, it has expanded to include a sports drink (Powerade), fruit juice (Minute Maid orange juice and lemonade), flavored and vitamin-enhance water (Glaceau), along with numerous variations on the original Coca-Cola. Coke enthusiasts can also visit the World of Coca-Cola in Atlanta and pay homage to the beverage.

Another aspect of Georgia that embodies the state's culture is the international airport in Atlanta. Formally called Hartsfield-Jackson Atlanta International Airport, the airport is one of the busiest in the world. Founded in 1925, it was first called Candler Field, after Coca-Cola's Asa Griggs Candler, and two years after it's opening, famed aviator Charles Lindbergh made an appearance at the airfield in his *Spirit of St. Louis*. A significant development occured when Delta Air Service (later Delta Air Lines) moved its headquarters to Atlanta in 1941. The first international flights took off from the airport in 1971, and its name was changed to include international flights. By the end of the twentieth century, Atlanta's airport was designated as the busiest in the world after accommodating 73.5 million travelers in 1998. This distinction was repeated several times over the next few years, most recently in 2004 after serving 83.6 million passengers. With Delta firmly established in Atlanta, virtually any airline traveler flying in or out of the South has to go through Hartsfield-Jackson airport.

Georgia Culture in the Modern Era

In the last decade of the twentieth century, Georgia voters elected a reform-minded governor, Zell Miller. Graduating with a master's degree in History from the University of Georgia, Miller began his political career by serving as mayor of his hometown Young Harris. In the 1970s and 1980s, Miller served four consecutive terms, sixteen years, as Georgia's lieutenant governor and by 1990 was poised to win election to the state's highest office. After being elected governor in 1990 one of Miller's first priorities was to increase funding for higher education. To do that the governor proposed a state lottery. The proceeds from the sale of lottery tickets would go to fund scholarships for Georgia students attending in-state institutions. In January 1991, Miller's first month in office, the legislature passed the appropriate legislation to create the lottery, and in November 1992 Georgia voters approved of the measure, but barely. The scholarship program was called HOPE—Helping Outstanding Pupils Educationally. The first lottery tickets were sold in June 1993, and three months later the first HOPE scholarship was awarded. According to the Georgia Student Finance Commission, between September 1993 and June 2011 the program awarded 1,472,608 scholarships totaling $6 billion. Every year between 1993 and 2011 the amount of HOPE awards has increased, demonstrating the popularity of the program. Without doubt this is one of Governor Miller's most popular and successful measures.

Another proposal put forth by Governor Miller, one that was far more emotional and controversial than the lottery, was changing the state flag. In 1956 the General Assembly included the Confederate battle emblem on Georgia's flag, a distinct and definite message of defiance against the US Supreme Court's 1954 *Brown* decision. Miller abandoned the idea because of resistance throughout the state, but Miller's successors, Roy Barnes and Sonny Perdue, both tangled with the public over the flag issue. Elected in 1998, Governor Barnes successfully pushed a bill through the legislature that removed the Confederate battle emblem from the state flag in 2001. This change angered many Georgians, who vowed to vote against Barnes in the 2002 gubernatorial election. Republican Sonny Perdue defeated Barnes, in part after promising that the public would have the opportunity to vote on the state flag. Many Georgians believed Perdue deceived them, for when the vote was held in 2003 the 1956 flag design was not an option. The current state flag resembles the Confederacy's Stars and Bars national flag. The Georgia flag still has a Confederate symbol on it, but not the more controversial battle emblem.

An important part of Georgia's culture is associated with athletics, and the state has a significant history of amateur and professional sports. The state has produced some awe-inspiring performers, including golf's Bobby Jones, baseball's Hank Aaron, and football's Herschel Walker. Jones is the only golfer, professional or amateur, to successfully complete the Grand Slam, which he accomplished in 1930. Winning the US Open, US Amateur, British Open, and British Amateur in the same calendar year constituted the Grand Slam. It was a prodigious accomplishment that has not been duplicated. After winning the Grand Slam Jones retired from competitive golf and focused on his legal career and golf course design. One of those courses was the Augusta National Golf Course, home to The Masters, arguably the most famous and prestigious tournament in the world. Hank Aaron, who is considered one of the greatest baseball players of all time, broke Babe Ruth's record for home runs in a career. In April 1974 Aaron hit his 715th home run to break the record; he eventually finished his career with 755 home runs. Aaron played all but two seasons with the Milwaukee/Atlanta Braves. Herschel Walker, a running back who played at the University of Georgia, is considered one of the greatest players in college football history. In his three years at UGA, Walker was a three-time All-American, led the Bulldogs to the 1980 national championship, and won the Heisman Trophy in 1982.

The pinnacle of amateur sports in Georgia was, without doubt, the 1996 Olympic Games held in Atlanta. For three weeks in 1996, Atlanta was the center of the sports world as ten thousand athletes from 197 nations converged on Georgia's capital. In 1990 Atlanta was chosen to host the games ahead of several other cities, including Athens, Belgrade, Manchester, Melbourne, and Toronto. Between 1990 and 1996 the city of Atlanta and state of Georgia embarked on a construction program to provide adequate facilities for the events. The economic impact of the Olympic Games on Georgia and Atlanta was estimated at $5 billion, and the facilities that were constructed became a permanent part of Atlanta's infrastructure. Overall, the 1996 Olympics had a lasting impact on Atlanta and the state of Georgia.

The city of Atlanta has also been the home to several major professional sports franchises. The longest-tenured organization is the National Football League's Atlanta Falcons, a new franchise granted in 1965. The Falcons have experienced mild success, having reached the Super Bowl only once, during the 1998 season. The next longest-tenured professional franchise is Major League Baseball's Atlanta Braves, who moved from Milwaukee in 1966. The Braves became a dominant team in the 1990s and won the World Series in 1995. Two years after the Braves moved to Atlanta, the National Basketball Association's St. Louis Hawks also moved to Atlanta. The Atlanta Hawks experienced only mild success, reaching the playoffs numerous times but failing to win a championship. The National Hockey League has had a love-hate relationship with Atlanta over the years, with the first NHL franchise, the Atlanta Flames, lasting only from 1972 to 1980 before moving to Calgary and becoming the Calgary Flames. In 1997 Atlanta was awarded another NHL franchise, the Thrashers. The Thrashers franchise followed the same course as the Flames— little success and a move to Canada; they moved to Winnipeg in 2011. Lastly (and most recently), the Women's National Basketball Association awarded a franchise to Atlanta in 2008, the Atlanta Dream. The Dream has made the playoffs in two of its first three years of existence and reached the championship series once, in 2010.

Georgia's 20th century culture is marked by writers, performers, and artists of all kinds. Among writers Margaret Mitchell is perhaps the most well-known. She is the author of the novel *Gone with the Wind*, which was awarded a Pulitzer Prize in 1937 and was made into an award-winning film in 1939. In 1999 Mitchell was voted one of the most influential Georgians of the 20th century, behind only Martin L. King, Jr. Another Pulitzer Prize winner was Caroline Miller, the first Georgian to win the prestigious award. Miller won in 1934 for her novel *Lamb in His Bosom*. Poet Conrad Aiken also won the Pulitzer for his 1930 *Selected Poems*. Alice Walker, daughter of Georgia sharecroppers, was awarded the Pulitzer in 1983 for her novel *The Color Purple*. Erskine Caldwell focused his writing on poor rural Georgians and one book, *Tobacco Road*, was named one of the 100 most influential novels in English in the 20th century. One of America's greatest fiction writers was Flannery O'Connor, whose short stories and novels were set in Georgia. These six are just a small sampling of Georgia's authors, and all are enshrined in the Georgia's Writers Hall of Fame.

Georgia has a rich musical history with artists whose works cut across all genres. A pioneer in what was called soul music was

Ray Charles who will forever be associated with the state with his rendition of "Georgia on My Mind," which was designated the state song in 1979. Other performers who fall into this category are Augusta's James Brown, Atlanta's Gladys Knight, who reached #1 on the pop charts in 1973 with "Midnight Train to Georgia," Dawson's Otis Redding, and Isaac Hayes, who moved to Atlanta in the 1970s. The artist credited with the transition from rhythm and blues to rock and roll was Macon's Richard Wayne Penniman, better known as Little Richard. The Allman Brothers Band out of Macon is credited with creating the southern rock genre, paving the way for many others. R.E.M., out of Athens, is most identified with the college rock movement of the 1980s. Also hailing from Athens is the B-52's. The Indigo Girls were playing in Atlanta nightclubs when they were discovered in 1988. Several well-known country and western (also called rockabilly) singers got their start in Georgia, such as Newnan's Alan Jackson, Monticello's Trisha Yearwood, Atlanta's Usher Raymond, and Jerry Reed, also from Atlanta. A 21st century rhythm and blues musician is Atlanta's Usher Raymond, who is known simply as Usher. Atlanta's Christopher Bridges, better known as Ludacris, performs southern hip-hop, the "Dirty South" style of rap. All of these artists are members of the Georgia Music Hall of Fame, located in Macon until it closed in June 2011.

Another integral part of Georgia's history and culture, especially in the years following World War II, is its numerous military instillations. Some of the largest include Fort Benning in Columbus (Army), Fort Gordon in Augusta (Army), Fort Stewart in Hinesville (Army), Robins Air Force Base in Warner Robins, Moody Air Force Base in Valdosta, and King's Bay Naval Submarine Base north of St. Mary's. Many of these bases make significant contributions to the local economies, including the hiring of civilian employees. With so many of military installations in the state, the periodic Base Realignment and Closure (BRAC) reviews conducted by the Department of Defense make for tense times in Georgia. The state has fared well in these reviews, but in 2005 the Department of Defense recommended that several installations be closed. The Atlanta metropolitan area took the biggest hit as Fort McPherson, Fort Gillem, and Naval Air Station Atlanta were earmarked for closure. The loss for the Atlanta area was more than 4,000 military and more than 2,600 civilian employees. Other Georgia installations were enlarged or had their missions realigned, actions that had a positive impact on the local communities. The Armor Center and School was relocated to Fort Benning in Columbus, which added more than 9,000 military and more than 600 civilian employees to the community. Moody Air Force Base in Valdosta was realigned, adding 1,200 military personnel to the community. In the end, Georgia came out of the 2005 review with mixed results: 5,890 military employees added and 2,254 civilian employees lost. Those communities with military installations continue to hold their collective breath with every Department of Defense Base Realignment and Closure review.

Georgia is also noted for the distribution of news and information. Established in Atlanta in 1980, Cable News Network (CNN) is arguably the most well known television news channel in the country. Though many were skeptical that a 24-hour, all-news network would succeed (or was necessary), CNN became a daily staple for many Americans shortly after its creation. With CNN's success, another 'round the clock' information network was created devoted entirely to weather. The Weather Channel, founded in 1982, has its corporate offices in Atlanta and provides worldwide forecasts, including severe weather alerts. Also headquartered in

Atlanta, the Centers for Disease Control and Prevention (CDC) is the country's most significant public health agency. Originally founded as the Communicable Disease Center in 1946, the agency found survival anything but certain. Its role in the campaign to eradicate smallpox from the early 1960s until eradication was accomplished in the 1970s helped establish the CDC's credibility. Currently the CDC contains numerous centers, each with a specific health and medical expertise. Collectively these centers make the CDC the most important public health agency in the nation.

By the first decade of the twenty-first century, Georgia has made great strides in becoming a more modern state. A one-party political system has returned, albeit with Republicans the dominant party of white Georgians. Georgians do not seem to be obsessed with race, but rather economic development issues. The growth and development of Atlanta has made Georgia a destination for many Americans. Even with progress toward modernity already made, the state of Georgia looks forward to a bright and promising future.

APPENDIX A

Population of Georgia

YEAR	TOTAL	WHITE	BLACK	HISPANIC
1790	82,548	52,886	29,662	Unknown
1800	162,686	102,261	60,425	Unknown
1810	252,433	145,414	107,019	Unknown
1820	340,989	189,570	151,419	Unknown
1830	516,823	296,806	220,017	Unknown
1840	691,392	407,695	283,697	Unknown
1850	906,185	521,572	384,613	Unknown
1860	1,057,286	591,550	465,698	Unknown
1870	1,184,109	638,926	545,142	Unknown
1880	1,542,180	816,906	725,133	Unknown
1890	1,837,353	978,357	858,815	Unknown
1900	2,216,331	1,181,294	1,034,813	Unknown
1910	2,609,121	1,431,802	1,176,987	Unknown
1920	2,895,832	1,689,114	1,206,365	Unknown

Georgia

1930	2,908,506	1,837,021	1,071,125	Unknown
1940	3,123,723	2,038,278	1,084,927	Unknown
1950	3,444,578	2,380,577	1,062,762	Unknown
1960	3,943,116	2,817,223	1,122,596	Unknown
1970	4,590,000	3,391,242	1,187,149	Unknown
1980	5,464,265	3,948,007	1,465,457	Unknown
1990	6,478,216	4,600,148	1,746,565	108,922
2000	8,186,453	5,327,281	2,349,542	435,227
2010	9,687,653	5,787,440	2,950,435	835,689

Appendix B

Governors of Georgia

NAME	YEARS OF SERVICE
James Oglethorpe	1733–43 (Trustee)
William Stephens	1743–51 (President of the Colony of Georgia)
Henry Parker	1751–52 (President of the Colony of Georgia)
Patrick Graham	1752–54 (President of the Colony of Georgia)
John Reynolds	1754–57
Henry Ellis	1757–60
James Wright	1760–76
George Walton	1775–76 (President of the Council of Safety)
Archibald Bulloch	1776–77 (President of the Council of Safety)
Button Gwinnett	1777 (President of the Council of Safety)
John Treutlen	1777–78
John Houstoun	1778–79
John Wereat	1779–80 (President of Executive Council)
George Walton	1779–80
James Prevost	1779 (British military governor)

Georgia

James Wright	1779–82 (Restored colonial governor)
Richard Howley	1780
Stephen Heard	1780 (President of Executive Council)
Myrick Davies	1780–81 (President of Executive Council)
Nathan Brownson	1781–82
John Martin	1782–83
Lyman Hall	1783–84
John Houstoun	1784–85
Samuel Elbert	1785–86
Edward Telfair	1786–87
George Mathews	1787–88
George Handley	1788–89
George Walton	1789
Edward Telfair	1789–93
George Mathews	1793–96
Jared Irwin	1796–98
James Jackson	1798–1801
David Emanuel	1801 (President of the Senate)
Josiah Tattnall, Jr.	1801–02
John Milledge	1802–06

Jared Irwin   1806–09 (President of the Senate)

David Mitchell   1809–13

Peter Early   1813–15

David Mitchell   1815–17

William Rabun   1817-1819

Matthew Talbot   1819 (President of the Senate)

John Clark   1819–23

George Troup   1823–27

John Forsyth   1827–29

George Gilmer   1829–31

Wilson Lumpkin   1831–35

William Schley   1835–37

George Gilmer   1837–39

Charles McDonald   1839–43

George Crawford   1843–47

George Towns   1847–51

Howell Cobb   1851–53

Herschel Johnson   1853–57

Joseph E. Brown   1857–65

James Johnson   1865 (Provisional Governor)

Georgia

Charles Jenkins   1865–68

Gen. Thomas Ruger   1868 (Provisional Governor)

Rufus Bullock   1868–71

Benjamin Conley   1871–72 (President of the Senate)

James Smith   1872–77

Alfred Colquitt   1877–82

Alexander Stephens   1882–83

James Boynton   1883 (President of the Senate)

Henry McDaniel   1883–86

John Gordon   1886–90

William Northen   1890–94

William Atkinson   1894–98

Allen Candler   1898–1902

Joseph Terrell   1902–07

Hoke Smith   1907–09

Joseph M. Brown   1909–11

Hoke Smith   1911

John Slaton   1911–12 (President of the Senate)

Joseph M. Brown   1912–13

John Slaton   1913–15

Nathaniel Harris   1915–17

Hugh Dorsey   1917–21

Thomas Hardwick   1921–23

Clifford Walker   1923–27

Lamartine Hardman   1927–31

Richard Russell, Jr.   1931–33

Eugene Talmadge   1933–37

Eurith Rivers   1937–41

Eugene Talmadge   1941–43

Ellis Arnall   1943–47

Melvin Thompson   1947–48

Herman Talmadge   1948–55

Marvin Griffin   1955–59

Ernest Vandiver   1959–63

Carl Sanders   1963–67

Lester Maddox   1967–71

James Carter   1971–75

George Busbee   1975–83

Joe Frank Harris   1983–91

Zell Miller   1991–99

Georgia

Roy Barnes   1999–2003

Sonny Perdue   2003–11

Nathan Deal   2011–

APPENDIX C

Counties in Order of Creation

1. Wilkes (5 February 1777)

2. Richmond (5 February 1777)

3. Burke (5 February 1777)

4. Effingham (5 February 1777)

5. Chatham (5 February 1777)

6. Liberty (5 February 1777)

7. Glynn (5 February 1777)

8. Camden (5 February 1777)

9. Franklin (25 February 1784)

10. Washington (25 February 1784)

11. Greene (3 February 1786)

12. Columbia (10 December 1790)

13. Elbert (10 December 1790)

14. Screven (14 December 1793)

15. Hancock (17 December 1793)

16. Warren (19 December 1793)

17. Oglethorpe (19 December 1793)

18. McIntosh (19 December 1793)

19. Bryan (19 December 1793)

20. Montgomery (19 December 1793)

21. Bulloch (8 February 1796)

22. Jackson (11 February 1796)

23. Jefferson (20 February 1796)

24. Lincoln (20 February 1796)

25. Tattnall (5 December 1801)

26. Clarke (5 December 1801)

27. Wayne (11 May 1803)

28. Wilkinson (11 May 1803)

29. Baldwin (11 May 1803)

30. Morgan (10 December 1807)

31. Jasper (10 December 1807)

32. Jones (10 December 1807)

33. Putnam (10 December 1807)

34. Laurens (10 December 1807)

35. Telfair (10 December 1807)

36. Pulaski (13 December 1808)

37. Twiggs (14 December 1809)

38. Madison (5 December 1811)

39. Emanuel (10 December 1812)

40. Early (15 December 1818)

41. Irwin (15 December 1818)

42. Appling (15 December 1818)

43. Walton (15 December 1818)

44. Gwinnett (15 December 1818)

45. Hall (15 December 1818)

46. Habersham (15 December 1818)

47. Rabun (21 December 1819)

48. Dooly (15 May 1821)

49. Houston (15 May 1821)

50. Monroe (15 May 1821)

51. Fayette (15 May 1821)

52. Henry (15 May 1821)

53. Newton (24 December 1821)

54. DeKalb (9 December 1822)

55. Bibb (9 December 1822)

56. Pike (9 December 1822)

57. Crawford (9 December 1822)

58. Decatur (8 December 1823)

59. Upson (15 December 1824)

60. Ware (15 December 1824)

61. Lee (9 June 1825)

62. Muscogee (9 June 1825)

63. Troup (9 June 1825)

64. Coweta (9 June 1825)

65. Carroll (9 June 1825)

66. Baker (12 December 1825)

67. Thomas (23 December 1825)

68. Lowndes (23 December 1825)

69. Taliaferro (24 December 1825)

70. Butts (24 December 1825)

71. Meriwether (14 December 1827)

72. Harris (14 December 1827)

73. Talbot (14 December 1827)

74. Marion (14 December 1827)

75. Randolph (20 December 1828)

76. Campbell (20 December 1828)*

77. Heard (22 December 1830)

78. Stewart (23 December 1830)

79. Cherokee (26 December 1831)

80. Sumter (16 December 1831)

81. Forsyth (3 December 1832)

82. Lumpkin (3 December 1832)

83. Union (3 December 1832)

84. Cobb (3 December 1832)

85. Gilmer (3 December 1832)

86. Murray (3 December 1832)

87. Bartow (3 December 1832)

88. Floyd (3 December 1832)

89. Paulding (3 December 1832)

90. Walker (18 December 1833)

91. Macon (14 December 1837)

92. Dade (25 December 1837)

93. Chattooga (28 December 1838)

94. Gordon (13 February 1850)

95. Clinch (14 February 1850)

96. Polk (20 December 1851)

97. Spalding (20 December 1851)

98. Whitfield (30 December 1851)

99. Taylor (15 January 1852)

100. Catoosa (5 December 1853)

101. Pickens (5 December 1853)

102. Hart (7 December 1853)

103. Dougherty (15 December 1853)

104. Webster (16 December 1853)

105. Fulton (20 December 1853)

106. Worth (20 December 1853)

107. Fannin (21 January 1854)

108. Coffee (9 February 1854)

109. Chattahoochee (13 February 1854)

110. Clay (16 February 1854)

111. Charlton (18 February 1854)

112. Calhoun (20 February 1854)

113. Haralson (26 January 1856)

114. Terrell (16 February 1856)

115. Colquitt (25 February 1856)

116. Berrien (25 February 1856)

117. Miller (26 February 1856)

118. Towns (6 March 1856)

119. Dawson (3 December 1857)

120. Pierce (18 December 1857)

121. Milton (18 December 1857)*

122. Glascock (19 December 1857)

123. Mitchell (21 December 1857)

124. Schley (22 December 1857)

125. White (22 December 1857)

126. Wilcox (22 December 1857)

127. Clayton (30 November 1858)

128. Quitman (10 December 1858)

129. Banks (11 December 1858)

130. Johnson (11 December 1858)

131. Brooks (11 December 1858)

132. Echols (13 December 1858)

133. Douglas (17 October 1870)

134. McDuffie (18 October 1870)

135. Rockdale (18 October 1870)

136. Dodge (26 October 1870)

137. Oconee (25 February 1875)

138. Crisp (17 August 1905)

139. Grady (17 August 1905)

140. Jenkins (17 August 1905)

141. Tift (17 August 1905)

142. Jeff Davis (18 August 1905)

143. Stephens (18 August 1905)

144. Toombs (18 August 1905)

145. Turner (18 August 1905)

146. Ben Hill (6 November 1906)

147. Bleckley (5 November 1912)

148. Wheeler (5 November 1912)

149. Barrow (3 November 1914)

150. Candler (3 November 1914)

151. Bacon (3 November 1914)

152. Evans (3 November 1914)

153. Atkinson (5 November 1914))

154. Treutlen (5 November 1918)

155. Cook (5 November 1918)

156. Seminole (2 November 1920)

157. Lanier (2 November 1920)

158. Brantley (2 November 1920)

159. Long (2 November 1920)

160. Lamar (2 November 1920)

161. Peach (4 November 1924)

*Milton and Campbell counties merged with Fulton County on January 1, 1932.

APPENDIX D

State Symbols

Amphibian	Green Tree Frog
Bird	Brown Thrasher
Butterfly	Tiger Swallowtail
Crop	Peanut
Fish	Largemouth Bass
Flower	Cherokee Rose
Fossil	Shark Tooth
Fruit	Peach
Gem	Quartz
Insect	Honeybee
Marine Mammal	Right Whale
Mineral	Staurolite
Motto	"Wisdom, Justice, and Moderation"
Prepared Food	Grits
Reptile	Gopher Tortoise
Song	"Georgia on my Mind"

A Brief History

Tree	Live Oak
Vegetable	Vidalia Sweet Onion
Wildflower	Azalea

265

Further Readings

General Works

Bartley, Numan V. *The Creation of Modern Georgia.* 2nd ed. Athens: University of Georgia Press, 1990.

Cobb, James C. *Georgia Odyssey.* 2nd ed. Athens: University of Georgia Press, 2008.

Coleman, Kenneth, ed. *A History of Georgia.* 2nd ed. Athens: University of Georgia Press, 1991.

Coleman, Kenneth, and Charles Stephen Gurr, eds. *Dictionary of Georgia Biography.* 2 vols. Athens: University of Georgia Press, 1983.

Cook, James F. *The Governors of Georgia.* 3rd ed. Macon: Mercer University Press, 2010.

Hodler, Thomas W., and Howard A. Schretter. *The Atlas of Georgia.* Athens: Institute of Community and Area Development, 1986.

The New Georgia Encyclopedia. www.georgiaencyclopedia.org.

Meyers, Christopher C., ed. *The Empire State of the South: Georgia History in Documents and Essays.* Macon: Mercer University Press, 2008.

Scott, Thomas A., ed. *Cornerstones of Georgia History: Documents that Formed the State.* Athens: University of Georgia Press, 1995.

Williams, David S. *From Mounds to Megachurches: Georgia's Religious Heritage.* Athens: University of Georgia Press, 2008.

Chapter One: Natives, Europeans, and the Founding of Georgia

Braund, Catherine Holland. *Deerskins and Duffels: The Creek Indian Trade with Anglo-America, 1685–1815.* Lincoln: University of Nebraska Press, 1996.

Coleman, Kenneth. *Colonial Georgia: A History.* New York: Charles Scribner's Sons, 1976.

Davis, Harold E. *The Fledgling Province: Social and Cultural Life in Colonial Georgia, 1733–1776.* Chapel Hill: University of North Carolina Press, 1976.

Gallay, Alan. *The Indian Slave Trade: The Rise of the English Empire in the American South, 1670–1717.* New Haven, Connecticut: Yale University Press, 2002.

Hahn, Steven C. *The Invention of the Creek Nation, 1670–1763.* Lincoln: University of Nebraska Press, 2004.

Hudson, Charles. *Knights of Spain, Warriors of the Sun: Hernando de Soto and the South's Ancient Chiefdoms.* Athens: University of Georgia Press, 1998.
_____. *The Southeastern Indians.* Knoxville: University of Tennessee Press, 1976.
Juricek, John T. *Colonial Georgia and the Creeks: Anglo-Indian Diplomacy on the Southern Frontier, 1733–1763.* Gainesville: University Press of Florida, 2010.
Parker, Anthony W. *Scottish Highlanders in Colonial Georgia: The Recruitment, Emigration, and Settlement at Darien, 1735–1748.* Athens: University of Georgia Press, 1997.
Ramsey, William L. *The Yamasee War: A Study of Culture, Economy, and Conflict in the Colonial South.* Lincoln: University of Nebraska Press, 2008.
Smith, Marvin T. *Coosa: The Rise and Fall of a Southeastern Mississippian Chiefdom.* Gainesville: University Press of Florida, 2000.
Spalding, Phinizy. *Oglethorpe in America.* Chicago: University of Chicago Press, 1977.
Sweet, Julie Anne. *Negotiating for Georgia: British-Creek Relations in the Trustee Era, 1733–1752.* Athens: University of Georgia Press, 2005.
_____. *William Stephens: Georgia's Forgotten Founder.* Baton Rouge: Louisiana State University Press, 2010.
White, Max E. *The Archaeology and History of the Native Georgia Tribes.* Gainesville: University Press of Florida, 2002.

Chapter Two: Royal Colony and Revolution

Cashin, Edward J. *Governor Henry Ellis and the Transformation of British North America.* Athens: University of Georgia Press, 1994.
_____. *The King's Ranger: Thomas Brown and the American Revolution on the Southern Frontier.* Athens: University of Georgia Press, 1989.
_____. *Lachlan McGillivray, Indian Trader: The Shaping of the Southern Colonial Frontier.* Athens: University of Georgia Press, 1992.
Coleman, Kenneth. *The American Revolution in Georgia, 1763–1789.* Athens: University of Georgia Press, 1958.
Jackson, Harvey H. *Lachlan McIntosh and the Politics of Revolutionary Georgia.* Athens: University of Georgia Press, 1979.
Johnson, James M. *Militiamen, Rangers, and Redcoats: The Military in Georgia, 1754–1776.* Macon: Mercer University Press, 1993.
Johnston, Elizabeth Lichtenstein. *Recollections of a Georgia Loyalist.* Spartanburg, South Carolina: Reprint Co., 1972.
Hall, Leslie. *Land and Allegiance in Revolutionary Georgia.* Athens: University of Georgia Press, 2001.

Lockley, Timothy James. *Lines in the Sand: Race and Class in Lowcountry Georgia, 1750–1860*. Athens: University of Georgia Press, 2001.

Searcy, Martha Condray. *The Georgia-Florida Contest in the American Revolution, 1776–1778*. Tuscaloosa: University of Alabama Press, 1985.

Smith, Julia Floyd. *Slavery and Rice Culture in Low Country Georgia, 1750–1860*. Knoxville: University of Tennessee Press, 1985.

Wood, Betty. *Slavery in Colonial Georgia, 1730–1775*. Athens: University of Georgia Press, 1984.

Chapter Three: Land Frauds, Lotteries, and Indian Removal

Caughey, John Walton. *McGillivray of the Creeks*. Columbia: University of South Carolina Press, 2007.

Green, Michael D. *The Politics of Indian Removal: Creek Government and Society in Crisis*. Lincoln: University of Nebraska Press, 1982.

Hudson, Angela Pulley. *Creek Paths and Federal Roads: Indians, Settlers, and Slaves and the Making of the American South*. Chapel Hill: University of North Carolina Press, 2010.

King, Duane H., ed. *The Cherokee Indian Nation: A Troubled History*. Knoxville: University of Tennessee Press, 1979.

Lamplugh, George R. *Politics on the Periphery: Factions and Parties in Georgia, 1783–1806*. Newark: University of Delaware Press, 1986.

McGrath, C. Peter. *Yazoo: Law and Politics in the New Republic*. Providence, Rhode Island: Brown University Press, 1966.

Moulton, Gary E. *John Ross: Cherokee Chief*. Athens: University of Georgia Press, 1978.

Owsley, Frank Lawrence, Jr. *Struggle for the Gulf Borderlands: The Creek War and the Battle of New Orleans, 1812–1815*. Gainesville: University Press of Florida, 1981.

Perdue, Theda, ed. *Cherokee Editor: The Writings of Elias Boudinot*. Knoxville: University of Tennessee Press, 1983.

Saunt, Claudio. *A New Order of Things: Property, Power, and the Transformation of the Creek Indians, 1733–1816*. Cambridge, England: Cambridge University Press, 1999.

Wilkins, Thurman. *Cherokee Tragedy: The Ridge Family and the Decimation of a People*. Norman: University of Oklahoma Press, 1986.

Williams, David. *The Georgia Gold Rush: Twenty-Niners, Cherokees, and Gold Fever*. Columbia: University of South Carolina Press, 1993.

Woodward, Grace Steele. *The Cherokees*. Norman: University of Oklahoma Press, 1963.

Chapter Four: Planters, Plain Folk, and the Enslaved

Alexander, Adele L. *Ambiguous Lives: Free Women of Color in Rural Georgia, 1789–1879*. Fayetteville: University of Arkansas Press, 1991.

Bode, Frederick A., and Donald E. Ginter. *Farm Tenancy and the Census in Antebellum Georgia*. Athens: University of Georgia Press, 1986.

Bonner, J.C. *A History of Georgia Agriculture, 1732–1860*. Athens: University of Georgia Press, 1964.

Brown, John. *Slave Life in Georgia: A Narrative of the Life, Sufferings, and Escape of John Brown, a Fugitive Slave*. 1855. Edited with introduction by F.N. Boney, Savannah, Georgia: Beehive Press, 1972.

Carey, Anthony Gene. *Parties, Slavery, and the Union in Antebellum Georgia*. Athens: University of Georgia Press, 1997.

Craft, William. *Running a Thousand Miles for Freedom: The Escape of William and Ellen Craft from Slavery*. 1860. Reprint, with new forward and biographical essay by R.J.M. Blackett. Baton Rouge: Louisiana State University Press, 1999.

DeBats, Donald A. *Elites and Masses: Political Structure, Communication, and Behavior in Ante-Bellum Georgia*. New York: Garland Publishing, 1990.

Dusinberre, William. *Them Dark Days: Slavery in the American Rice Swamps*. New York: Oxford University Press, 1996.

Gilespie, Michele. *Free Labor in an Unfree World: White Artisans in Slaveholding Georgia, 1789–1860*. Athens: University of Georgia Press, 2000.

Harris, J. William. *Plain Folk and Gentry in a Slave Society: White Liberty and Black Slavery in Augusta's Hinterlands*. Middletown, Connecticut: Wesleyan University Press, 1985.

Kemble, Frances Anne. *Journal of a Residence on a Georgian Plantation in 1838–1839*. 1863. Edited with introduction by John A. Scott, Athens: University of Georgia Press, 1984.

Reidy, Joseph P. *From Slavery to Agrarian Capitalism in the Cotton South: Central Georgia, 1800–1880*. Chapel Hill: University of North Carolina Press, 1992.

Thurmond, Micheal. *Freedom: Georgia's Antislavery Heritage*. Atlanta: Longstreet Press, 2002.

Wallenstein, Peter. *From Slave South to New South: Public Policy in Nineteenth-Century Georgia*. Chapel Hill: University of North Carolina Press, 1987.

Chapter Five: Secession and Civil War

Andrews, William H. *Footprints of a Regiment: A Recollection of the First Georgia Regulars, 1861–1865*. Introduction by Richard M. McMurry. Atlanta: Longstreet Press, 1992.

Bailey, Anne J. *War and Ruin: William T. Sherman and the Savannah Campaign.* Wilmington, Delaware: Scholarly Resources, 2002.

Bryan, T. Conn. *Confederate Georgia.* 1953. Reprint, Athens: University of Georgia Press, 2009.

DeCredico, Mary A. *Patriotism for Profit: Georgia's Urban Entrepreneurs and the Confederate War Effort.* Chapel Hill: University of North Carolina Press, 1990.

Dyer, Thomas G. *Secret Yankees: The Union Circle in Confederate Atlanta.* Baltimore: Johns Hopkins University Press, 1999.

Fowler, John D., and David B. Parker, eds. *Breaking the Heartland: The Civil War in Georgia.* Macon: Mercer University Press, 2011.

Freehling, William W., and Craig M. Simpson, eds. *Secession Debated: Georgia's Showdown in 1860.* New York: Oxford University Press, 1992.

Inscoe, John C., ed. *The Civil War in Georgia: A New Georgia Encyclopedia Companion.* Athens: University of Georgia Press, 2011.

Johnson, Michael P. *Toward a Patriarchal Republic: The Secession of Georgia.* Baton Rouge: Louisiana State University Press, 1977.

Jones, James P. *Yankee Blitzkrieg: Wilson's Raid through Alabama and Georgia.* Athens: University of Georgia Press, 1976.

Marvel, William. *Andersonville: The Last Depot.* Chapel Hill: University of North Carolina Press, 1994.

Mohr, Clarence L. *On the Threshold of Freedom: Masters and Slaves in Civil War Georgia.* Athens: University of Georgia Press, 1986.

Parks, Joseph H. *Joseph E. Brown of Georgia.* Baton Rouge: Louisiana State University Press, 1977.

Schott, Thomas E. *Alexander H. Stephens of Georgia: A Biography.* Baton Rouge: Louisiana State University Press, 1988.

O'Donovan, Susan E. *Becoming Free in the Cotton South.* Cambridge, Massachusetts: Harvard University Press, 2007.

Sarris, Jonathan Dean. *A Separate Civil War: Communities in Conflict in the Mountain South.* Charlottesville: University of Virginia Press, 2006.

Taylor, Susie King. *Reminiscences of My Life in Camp.* 1902. Reprint, with introduction by Catherine Clinton, Athens: University of Georgia Press, 2006.

Weitz, Mark A. *A Higher Duty: Desertion Among Georgia Troops during the Civil War.* Lincoln: University of Nebraska Press, 2000.

Williams, David, Teresa Crisp Williams, and David Carlson. *Plain Folk in a Rich Man's War: Class and Dissent in Confederate Georgia.* Gainesville: University Press of Florida, 2002.

Chapter Six: Post Civil War Georgia

Cimbala, Paul A. *Under the Guardianship of the Nation: The Freedmen's Bureau and the Reconstruction of Georgia, 1865–1870.* Athens: University of Georgia Press, 1997.

Conway, Alan. *The Reconstruction of Georgia.* Minneapolis: University of Minnesota Press, 1966.

Davis, Harold E. *Henry Grady's New South.* Tuscaloosa: University of Alabama Press, 1990.

Drago, Edmund L. *Black Politicians and Reconstruction in Georgia: A Splendid Failure.* Athens: University of Georgia Press, 1992.

Duncan, Russell. *Freedom's Shore: Tunis Campbell and the Georgia Freedmen.* Athens: University of Georgia Press, 1986.

————. *Entrepreneur for Equality: Governor Rufus Bullock, Commerce, and Race in Post-Civil War Georgia.* Athens: University of Georgia Press, 1994.

Eckert, Ralph L. *John Brown Gordon, Soldier, Southerner, American.* Baton Rouge: Louisiana State University Press, 1989.

Ferald, J. Bryan, *Henry Grady or Tom Watson? The Rhetorical Struggle for the New South, 1880–1890.* Macon: Mercer University Press, 1994.

Hahn, Steven. *The Roots of Southern Populism: Yeoman Farmers and the Transformation of the Georgia Upcountry, 1850–1890.* Updated edition. New York: Oxford University Press, 2006.

Jones, Jacqueline. *Soldiers of Light and Love: Northern Teachers and Georgia Blacks, 1865–1873.* Chapel Hill: University of North Carolina Press, 1980.

Nathans, Elizabeth Studley. *Losing the Peace: Georgia Republicans and Reconstruction, 1865–1871.* Baton Rouge: Louisiana State University Press, 1968.

Outland, Robert B. *Tapping the Pines: The Naval Stores Industry in the American South.* Baton Rouge: Louisiana State University Press, 2004.

Parks, Joseph. *Joseph E. Brown of Georgia.* Baton Rouge: Louisiana State University Press, 1977.

Range, Willard. *A Century of Georgia Agriculture, 1850–1950.* Athens: University of Georgia Press, 1954.

Reidy, Joseph P. *From Slavery to Agrarian Capitalism in the Cotton Plantation South: Central Georgia, 1800–1880.* Chapel Hill: University of North Carolina Press, 1992.

Shaw, Barton. *The Wool Hat Boys.* Baton Rouge: Louisiana State University Press, 1984.

Wallenstein, Peter. *From Slave South to New South: Public Policy in Nineteenth-Century Georgia.* Chapel Hill: University of North Carolina Press, 1987.

Woodward, C. Vann. *Tom Watson, Agrarian Rebel.* New York: Oxford University Press, 1938.

Chapter Seven: The Progressive Era and Jim Crow

Brundage, W. Fitzhugh. *Lynching in the New South: Georgia and Virginia, 1880–1930.* Urbana: University of Illinois Press, 1993.

Brundage, W. Fitzhugh. *A Socialist Utopia in the New South: The Ruskin Colonies in Tennessee and Georgia, 1894–1901.* Urbana: University of Illinois Press, 1996.

Dinnerstein, Leonard. *The Leo Frank Case.* Athens: University of Georgia Press, 1966.

Dittmer, John. *Black Georgia in the Progressive Era, 1900–1920.* Urbana: University of Illinois Press, 1977.

Godshalk, David F. *Veiled Visions: The 1906 Atlanta Race Riot and the Reshaping of American Race Relations.* Chapel Hill: The University of North Carolina Press, 2005.

Grantham, Dewey. *Hoke Smith and the Politics of the New South.* Baton Rouge: Louisiana State University Press, 1958.

Green, Elna C. *Southern Strategies: Southern Women and the Woman Suffrage Question.* Chapel Hill: University of North Carolina Press, 1997.

Inscoe, John, ed. *Georgia in Black and White: Explorations in the Race Relations of a Southern State, 1865–1950.* Athens: University of Georgia Press, 1994.

Kemp, Kathryn W. *God's Capitalist: Asa Candler of Coca-Cola.* Macon: Mercer University Press, 2002.

Mixon, Gregory. *The Atlanta Riot: Race, Class, and Violence in a New South City.* Gainesville: University Press of Florida, 2005.

Oney, Steve. *And the Dead Shall Rise: The Murder of Mary Phagan and the Lynching of Leo Frank.* New York: Random House, 2003.

Wheeler, Marjorie Spruill. *New Women of the New South: The Leaders of the Woman Suffrage Movement in the Southern States.* New York: Oxford University Press, 1993.

Woodward, C. Vann. *Tom Watson, Agrarian Rebel.* New York: Oxford University Press, 1938.

Chapter Eight: The Depression, New Deal, and World War II

Anderson, William. *The Wild Man From Sugar Creek: The Political Career of Eugene Talmadge.* Baton Rouge: Louisiana State University Press, 1975.

Ball, Lamar Q. *Georgia in World War II: A Study of the Military and Civilian Effort.* Atlanta: Department of Archives and History, 1946.

Biles, Roger. *The South and the New Deal*. Lexington: University of Kentucky Press, 1994.

Ferguson, Karen. *Black Politics in New Deal Atlanta*. Chapel Hill: The University of North Carolina Press, 2002.

Fite, Gilbert. *Richard B. Russell, Jr., Senator from Georgia*. Chapel Hill: The University of North Carolina Press, 1991.

Henderson, Harold P. *The Politics of Change in Georgia: A Political Biography of Ellis Arnall*. Athens: University of Georgia Press, 1991.

Henderson, Harold P. and Gary L. Roberts, ed. *Georgia Governors in an Age of Change: From Ellis Arnall to George Busbee*. Athens: University of Georgia Press, 1988.

Holmes, Michael S. *The New Deal in Georgia: An Administrative History*. Westport, Connecticut: Greenwood Press, 1974.

Lee, Dallas. *The Cotton Patch Evidence: The Story of Clarence Jordan and the Koinonia Farm Experiment*. New York: Harper and Row, 1971.

Talmadge, John E. *Rebecca Latimer Felton: Nine Stormy Decades*. Athens: University of Georgia Press, 1960.

Chapter Nine: The Civil Rights Era

Bayor, Ronald H. *Race and the Shaping of Twentieth-Century Atlanta*. Chapel Hill: University of North Carolina Press, 2000.

Carson, Clayborne. *In Struggle: SNCC and the Black Awakening of the 1960s*. Cambridge: Harvard University Press, 1981.

Grady-Willis, Winston A. *Challenging U.S. Apartheid: Atlanta and Black Struggles for Human Rights, 1960–1977*. Durham: Duke University Press, 2006.

Henderson, Harold P. *Ernest Vandiver, Governor of Georgia*. Athens: University of Georgia Press, 2000.

McDonald, Laughlin. *A Voting Rights Odyssey: Black Enfranchisement in Georgia*. New York: Cambridge University Press, 2003.

Pratt, Robert. *We Shall Not Be Moved: The Desegregation of the University of Georgia*. Athens: University of Georgia Press, 2002.

Roche, Jeff. *Restructured Resistance: The Sibley Commission and the Politics of Desegregation in Georgia*. Athens: University of Georgia Press, 1998.

Short, Bob. *Everything is Pickrick: The Life of Lester Maddox*. Macon: Mercer University Press, 1999.

Spritzer, Lorraine Nelson. *The Belle of Ashby Street: Helen Douglas Mankin and Georgia Politics*. Athens: University of Georgia Press, 1982.

Tuck, Stephen. *Beyond Atlanta: The Struggle for Racial Equality in Georgia, 1940–1980*. Athens: University of Georgia Press, 2001.

Zinn, Howard. *Albany: A Study in National Responsibility*. Atlanta: Southern Regional Council, 1962.

Chapter Ten: Modern Georgia

Bayor, Ronald. *Race and the Shaping of Twentieth-Century Atlanta*. Chapel Hill: University of North Carolina Press, 2000.

Cook, James F. *Carl Sanders: Spokesman of the New South*. Macon: Mercer University Press, 1993.

Etheridge, Elizabeth. *Sentinel for Health: A History of the Centers for Disease Control*. Berkeley: University of California Press, 1982.

Fink, Gary M. *Prelude to the Presidency: The Political Character and Legislative Leadership Style of Governor Jimmy Carter*. Westport, Connecticut: Greenwood Press, 1980.

Fleischmann, Arnold and Carol Pierannunzi. *Politics in Georgia*. Athens: University of Georgia Press, 1997.

Harris, Joe Frank. *Joe Frank Harris: Personal Reflections on a Public Life*. Macon: Mercer University Press, 1998.

Henderson, Harold P. and Gary L. Roberts, ed. *Georgia Governors in an Age of Change: From Ellis Arnall to George Busbee*. Athens: University of Georgia Press, 1988.

Hyatt, Richard. *Zell: The Governor Who Gave Georgia HOPE*. Macon: Mercer University Press, 1997.

Keating, Larry. *Atlanta: Race, Class, and Urban Expansion*. Philadelphia: Temple University Press, 2001.

Kruse, Kevin. *White Flight: Atlanta and the Making of Modern Conservatism*. Princeton: Princeton University Press, 2005.

Martin, Harold. *Atlanta and the Environs: A Chronicle of Its People and Events*. Athens: University of Georgia Press, 1987.

Perdue, Theda. *Race and the Atlanta Cotton States Exposition of 1895*. Athens: University of Georgia Press, 2010.

Short, Bob. *Everything is Pickrick: The Life of Lester Maddox*. Macon: Mercer University Press, 1999.

Yarbrough, C. Richard. *And They Call Them Games: An Inside View of the 1996 Olympics*. Macon: Mercer University Press, 2000.

Index